NEW YORK

NEW

FRANCISCO HIDALGO

YORK
PUBLISHED BY PROTEUS

I HAVE NEVER BEEN TO NEW YORK. I KNOW THE GREAT METROPOLIS THROUGH PICTURES AND THROUGH FILMS, AND I LOVE IT THROUGH THE PHOTOGRAPHS OF FRANCISCO HIDALGO. I MARVEL AT ITS GRANDEUR, ITS GLITTER, THE INCOMPARABLE BEAUTY OF ITS COLORS, ITS FORMS AND RHYTHMS. ITS SKYSCRAPERS GRAZING THE CLOUDS AND REFLECTED IN THE WATER FORM A MONOLITHIC SILHOUETTE MORE COMPARABLE TO A ROCK FORMATION THAN TO ARCHITECTURE CONCEIVED BY MAN. BETWEEN THE SHEER ROCK WALLS RUN CHASMS OF STREETS, FULL OF MOVEMENT AND COLOR AND PULSATING LIFE. PAST ENDLESS COLUMNS OF AUTOMOBILES THE CROWD SURGES MADE UP OF PEOPLE OF ALL COLORS, MOVING, ADVANCING, THREADING ITS WAY BETWEEN LIGHT AND SHADOW, CATCHING CARS, TRAINS, BOATS. AND OVER IT ALL MOVES THE SUN, CHANGING THE GRAY TO GOLD AND THE SILVER TO GLOWING BRONZE. THOUSANDS OF LIGHTS CHANGE NIGHT TO DAY, TRANSMITTING A NEW PLAY OF COLOR, UNEXPECTED SHAPES, EXCITING PERSPEC-

TIVES. IT IS TRUE THAT THESE DREAMS TAKE US FAR FROM THE REALITY OF DAY-TO-DAY NEW YORK. THEY INDUCE CONTEMPLATION, WORSHIP AND WONDERMENT. LIKE ALL DREAMS, THEY DEPART FROM REALITY BUT AT THE SAME TIME THEY EVOKE A GLIMMER OF WHAT THAT REALITY MIGHT BE. FRANCISCO HIDALGO GRASPS THAT PARADOX AND MAKES IT THE MASTER IDEA OF HIS ART. WHEREVER A WINDOW OPENS ON THE LAND OF DREAMS, HE GIVES US AN IMAGE OF THOSE REVERIES. WHEREVER DAILY REALITY PERMITS A TOUCH OF THE FANTASTIC, HE GIVES FREE REIN TO FANTASY. THE DIVERSE IMPRESSIONS COME TOGETHER LIKE MOSAICS TO FORM A NEW YORK THAT NEVER WAS BUT THAT LIVES IN FEELINGS AND IN DREAMS. WITH A FLOOD OF IMPRESSIONS HIDALGO HAS TRANSFORMED SYMBOLS INTO IMAGES AND CREATED A PERSONAL PORTRAIT OF THIS CITY OF DREAMS THAT IS NEW YORK. IN EACH DETAIL, IN THE PANORAMAS AS IN THE PORTRAITS, IS CONTAINED A HINT OF THE MASTER VIEW. THE FIRE HYDRANT, THE FRONT OF A LETTER BOX, A COUPLE IN

CENTRAL PARK, THE OCEAN OF LIGHTS THE CITY BECOMES AT NIGHT, ALL THESE REPRESENT NEW YORK. THE RHYTHMIC SUCCESSION INCREASES THE OVERALL FEELING, LIKE THE MEMORY OF A TAXI RIDE OR OF A FLIGHT IN A HELICOPTER. HIDALGO LIBERATES HIS MOTIFS, EXPLORES THEM, CONDENSES THEM IN A UNIQUE AND INTENSIVE VISUAL EXPERIENCE. WHERE STRUCTURE PERMITS HE FAR EXCEEDS THE USUAL LIMITS OF PICTORIAL REPRODUCTION. WITH FAR-REACHING VISION HE DETACHES OBJECTS FROM THEIR REAL VOLUME, ABANDONS HIMSELF TO THE EFFECTS OF THEIR FORMS AND COLORS AND CONVERTS THEM INTO PURE LIGHT. HIDALGO IS A MAGICIAN OF LIGHT, THAT STUFF THAT DREAMS ARE MADE OF. HE IS NOT A PHOTOGRAPHER OF THE MOMENT, RECORDING AN INSTANT IN TIME LIKE THE HUNDREDS OR THOUSANDS OF PEOPLE WHO SHARE THAT INSTANT WITH HIM. HE STILL IS, AS HE HAS ALWAYS BEEN, A PAINTER. FOR HIS GRAPHICS OF LIGHT HE HAS REPLACED PALETTE AND BRUSHES WITH A CAMERA, A MEDIUM FOR OUR AGE. BUT HIS ART IS BASED ON TRADITION

AND GOES FAR BEYOND THE IDEAS WE USUALLY HAVE OF PHOTOGRAPHY. THINK BACK FOR EXAMPLE TO THE PANORAMIC PORTRAITS OF CITIES OF THE 17TH CENTURY; THEIR BIRDS-EYE PERSPECTIVES SUGGEST ANALOGIES WITH MODERN TECHNIQUES, LIKE SHOTS TAKEN WITH A FISH-EYE LENS... THE OVERALL VIEW, THE TOTALITY OF A CITY EMBRACED BY A PERSPECTIVE IMPOSSIBLE TO CAPTURE WITH THE HUMAN EYE. THE LENS, WITH THE ARTIST BEHIND IT, ENCOMPASSES IT ALL, GATHERS IT UP IN ONE VAST SWEEP AND PLACES IT BEFORE US. WE STAND AWESTRUCK: THERE IS NEW YORK. OTHER PICTURES RECALL THE OLD DIORAMAS OF THE LAST CENTURY, THOSE MAGIC BOXES THAT WERE AN ATTRACTION OF EVERY TRAVELLING FAIR AND CARNIVAL. THROUGH THE PEEP-HOLE ONE COULD SEE A SIMULATED IMAGE OF A PLACE, WITH ALL ITS WONDERS FLASHING BY IN RAPID SUCCESSION, CREATING NOT AN ORDERLY VIEWING OF THE SIGHTS, BUT A VISUAL EXPERIENCE FASHIONED BY FANTASY AND DREAMS. BUT THESE ARE METAPHORS FROM THE PAST, NO LONGER NEEDED IN OUR

AGE WHEN MODERN MEDIA BRING US IMAGES FROM FAR AWAY WITH ALL THE REALISM WE COULD WANT. HIDALGO'S ART SPEAKS TO A MODERN AUDIENCE IN A MODERN WORLD. YET IT IS BASED ON AN INTERPRETATION THAT CANNOT BE UNDERSTOOD WITHOUT A BRIEF INCURSION INTO ART HISTORY. THE SIMPLEST AND MOST SUPERFICIAL APPROACH WOULD BE THROUGH IMPRESSIONISM. HIS WAY OF SEEING, HIS CONCEPTION OF REALITY, THE RELATION HE FEELS BETWEEN FORM AND COLOR ARE CLEARLY ROOTED IN IMPRESSIONISM. BUT ANOTHER NAME IS INESCAPABLE, THAT OF TURNER, THE ENGLISH LANDSCAPIST WHO FIRST SUCCEEDED IN GIVING EXPRESSION IN COLOR TO RAIN AND MIST AND MOVEMENT. IF THE IMPRESSIONISTS WERE ABLE TO CAPTURE CALM, STILLNESS, CONTEMPLATION, THE HARMONY OF NATURE, TURNER OPENED THE WAY TO AN ANTI-ROMANTICISM AND TRIED TO BUILD A BRIDGE TO THE FUTURE, IN ONE GREAT THRUST THAT STILL APPEARS VERTIGINOUS EVEN TO OUR 20TH CENTURY EYES. TURNER WAS THE FIRST TO DEPICT THE BEAUTY

OF TECHNOLOGY AND OF MACHINES FASHIONED BY MAN. BUT THERE WAS A CONTRADICTION BETWEEN HIS AIM AND HIS MEANS, FOR HIS MEDIUM WAS SOON DISPLACED, AND REPLACED BY PHOTOGRAPHY, FASTER AND MORE EFFICIENT, BETTER-EQUIPPED THAN PAINTING TO INTERPRET OUR ERA. IT WOULD BE FUTILE, HOWEVER, TO CATALOG HIDALGO'S ART IN THE SYSTEM OF ART HISTORY SIMPLY AS IMPRESSIONISM REALIZED BY MEANS OF PHOTOGRAPHY. IT WOULD BE MISUNDERSTANDING THE AIMS OF PHOTOGRAPHY TO THINK IT MERELY RETRACES THE HISTORY OF ART, FILLING IN GAPS IN THE PAST. IT WOULD BE IGNORING ALL THE TRENDS AND STYLES THAT HAVE TRIED TO BUILD THAT SOARING BRIDGE BETWEEN TECHNOLOGY AND AESTHETICS, BETWEEN PAINTING AND PHOTOGRAPHY. PERHAPS IN THE FUTURE, HISTORIANS WILL DISCOVER THE ROOTS OF HIDALGO'S ART IN TACHISME AND COMPARE HIS PICTURES TO CERTAIN INTELLECTUAL CURRENTS IN ABSTRACT PAINTING. PERHAPS THEY WILL GO EVEN FURTHER AND SEEK THEIR ORIGIN AT THAT POINT WHERE MODERN

RATIONAL TECHNOLOGY BECOMES ITSELF A WORK OF ART. THE FUTURIST MANIFESTO, THE WORK OF MARINETTI, THE PICTURES OF CARRÀ AND BOCCINI AND THE DREAMS OF MEGALOPOLIS OF ANTONIO SANT-ELIA CERTAINLY HAVE MORE THAN A FLEETING RELATIONSHIP WITH THIS BOOK. YET ALL ATTEMPTS TO CATALOG HIDALGO ARE ACADEMIC EXERCISES. HOW MUCH BETTER SIMPLY TO MARVEL AT HIS WAY OF SEEING AND INTERPRETING WITH A CAMERA. THESE EXPLANATIONS DO NOTHING TO LEGITIMIZE HIS WORK, WHICH IS NEW AND MARVELOUS IN ITSELF. IMAGE BY IMAGE, EXPRESSION BY EXPRESSION, HIDALGO REFUTES THE THESIS OF THEORETICIANS WHO SAY THAT PHOTOGRAPHY IS NOTHING MORE THAN SIGNS, THAT IT IS ONLY THE PRODUCT OF SOCIETY AND NOT THE CREATION OF THE ARTIST. WITH HIS ART OF LIGHT, HE BECOMES A BEARER OF IMAGES, A WORLD OF IMAGES THAT ARE HIS, THAT HE HAS DREAMED. THUS HIS PICTURES CANNOT BE EXPLAINED BY SEMANTICS. THEIR EXPRESSION, THEIR VALUE ARE IMMANENT AND CAN ONLY BE FELT. PHOTOGRAPHY

MAY BE A SCIENCE BUT PHOTOGRAPHS ARE WORKS OF ART, CREATIONS IN THEIR OWN RIGHT. THIS CONCEPT IS FUNDAMENTAL TO HIDALGO'S ENTIRE WORK. HE IS NOT CONTENT TO PRESENT HIS PHOTOS SIMPLY IN A FINE BOOK. HE ASSEMBLES THEM WITH HIS OWN HANDS, FOLLOWING HIS OWN IMAGINATION, SO THAT THE WHOLE BECOMES A WORK OF ART, A BOOK SURPASSING ORDINARY BOOKS, WITH EACH PICTURE AN INTEGRAL PART OF THE TOTAL CREATION. REJECTING ALL COMPROMISES, HIDALGO SUPERVISES THE PHOTOENGRAVING, THE PRINTING, THE SMALLEST DETAILS OF LAYOUT AND TYPEFACE. AND THE FINAL WORK IS BORN OUT OF THIS STRIVING FOR PERFECTION, THE REFUSAL TO BE SATISFIED WITH ANYTHING LESS THAN A PERFECT RESULT. THE ULTIMATE CITY HAS FOUND ITS INTERPRETATION IN A UNIQUE BOOK. AND A RADIANT AND EXALTED NEW YORK OPENS ITS WINDOW ON UTOPIA.

DAVID MEILI

SOMETIME TOO HOT THE EYE OF HEAVEN SHINES.
SHAKESPEARE

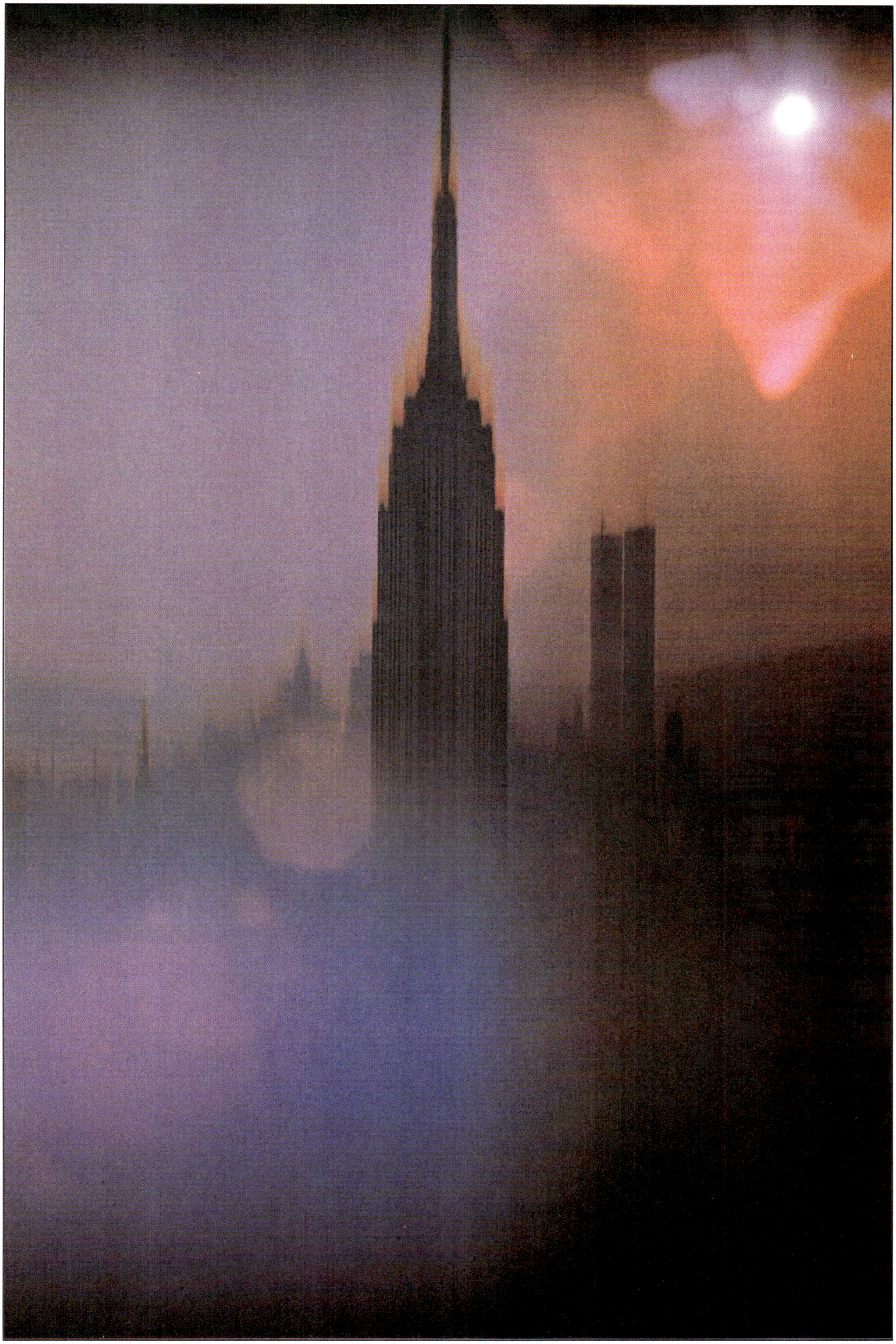

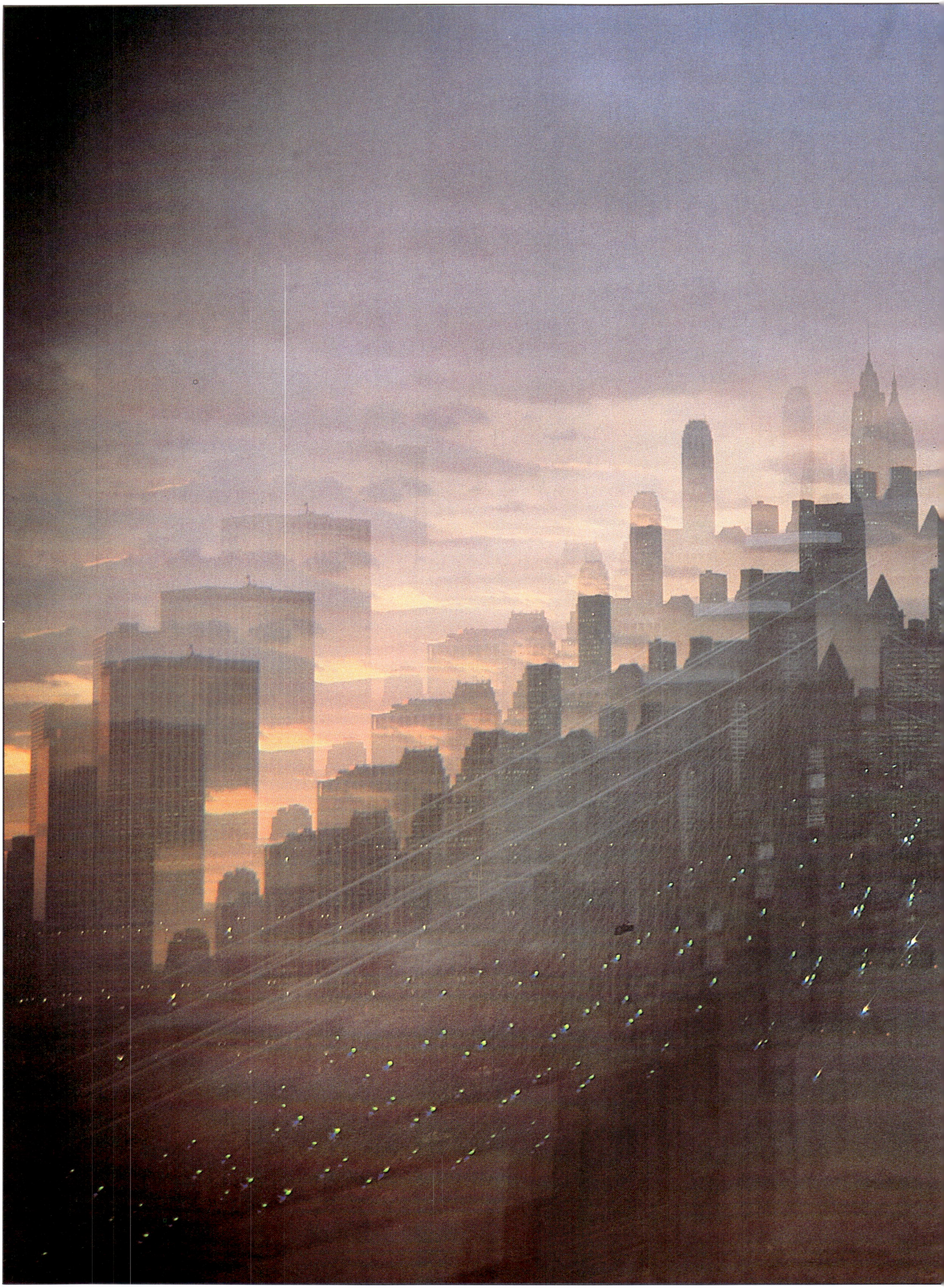

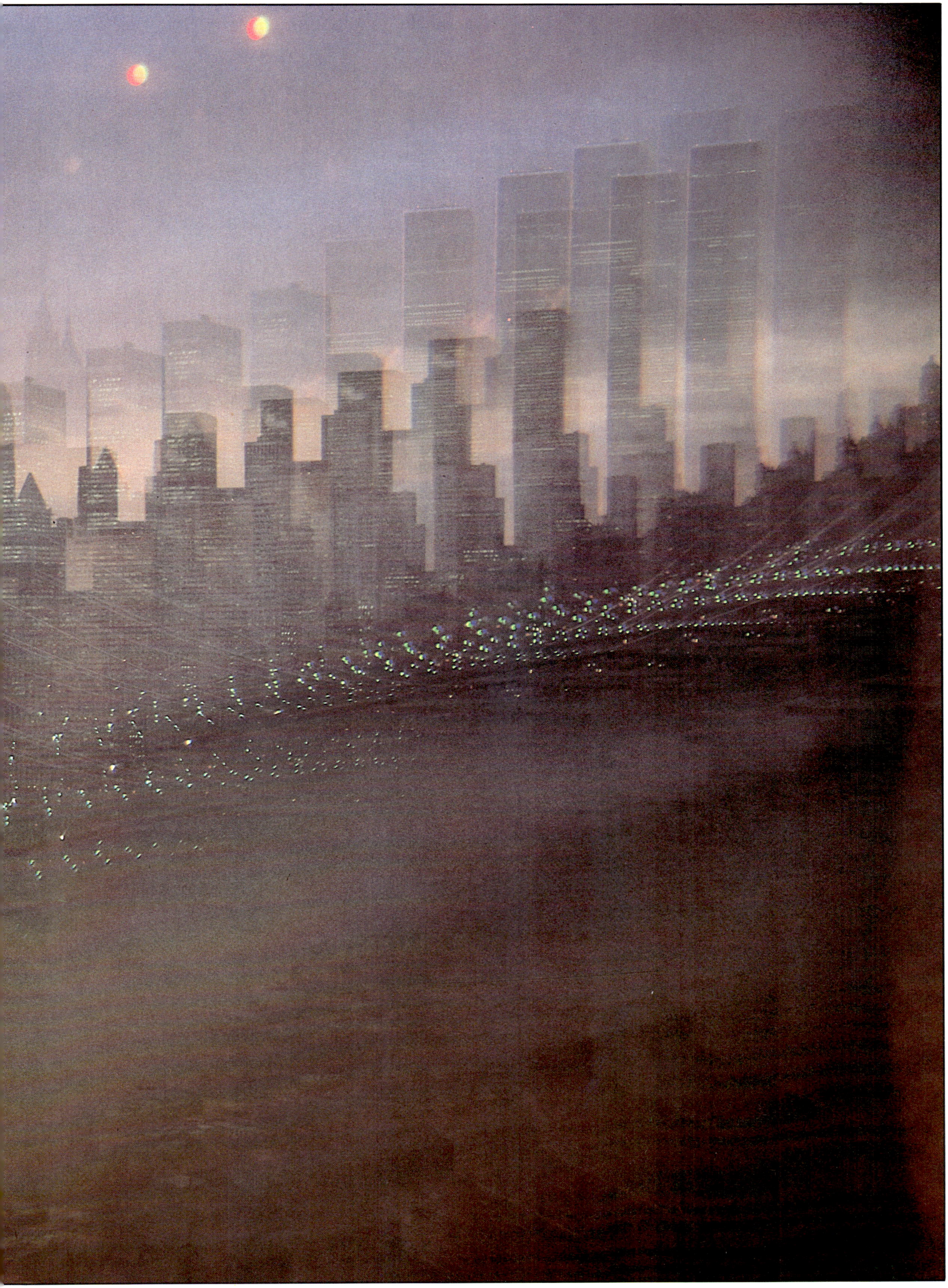

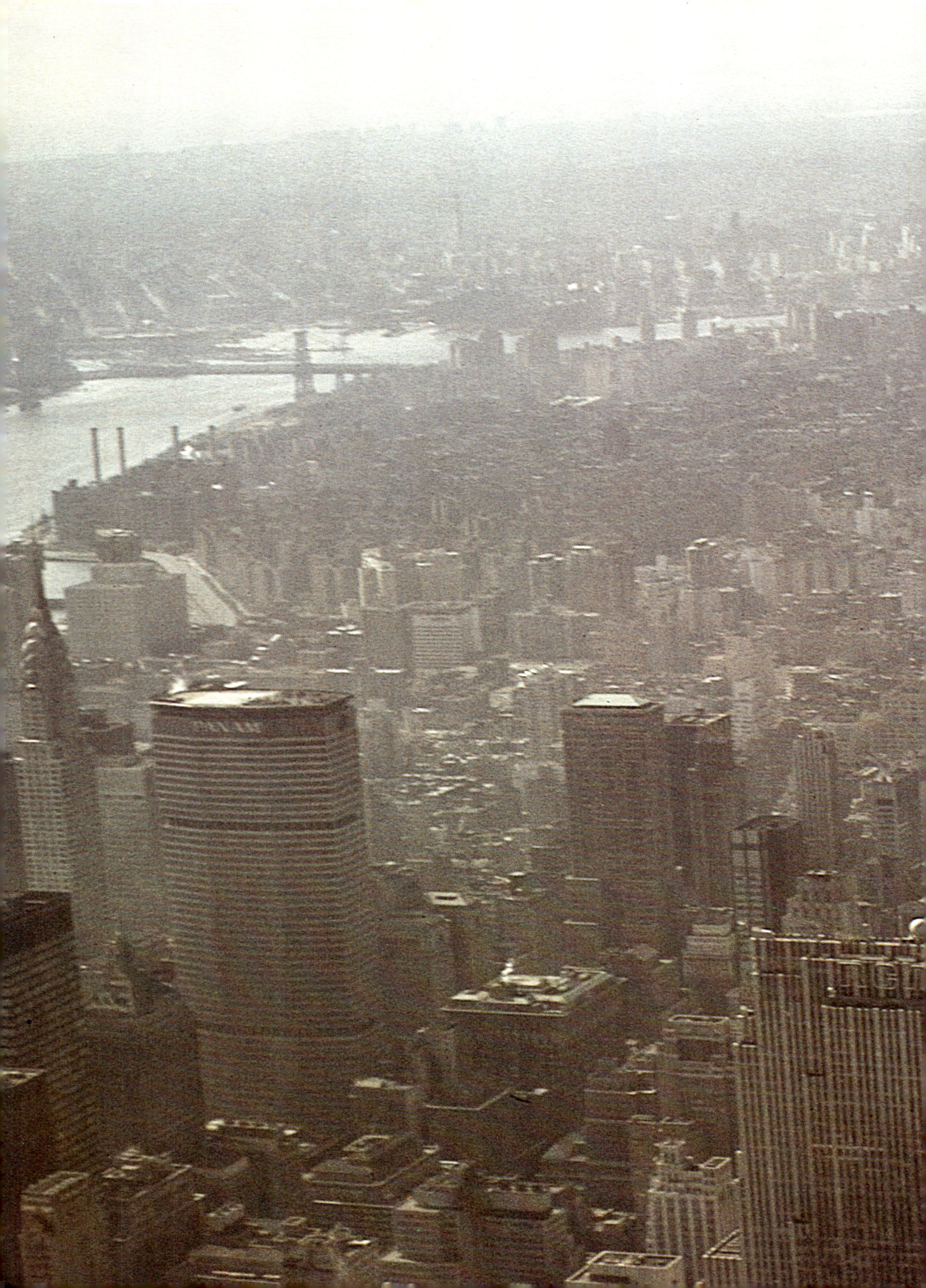

THE SKY IS LACED WITH FITFUL COLOURS
THE CIRCLING MISTS AND SHADOWS FLEE.
OSCAR WILDE

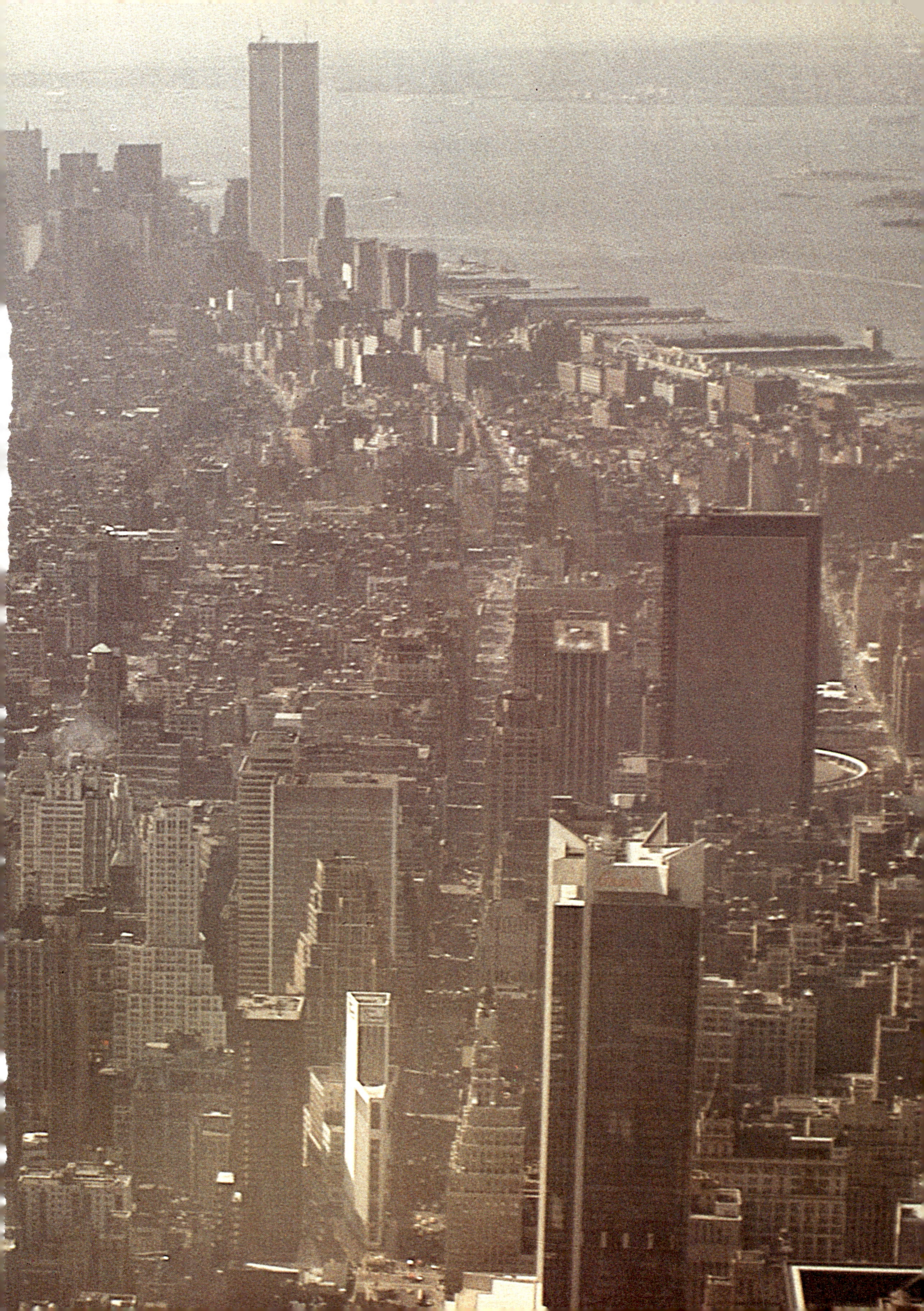

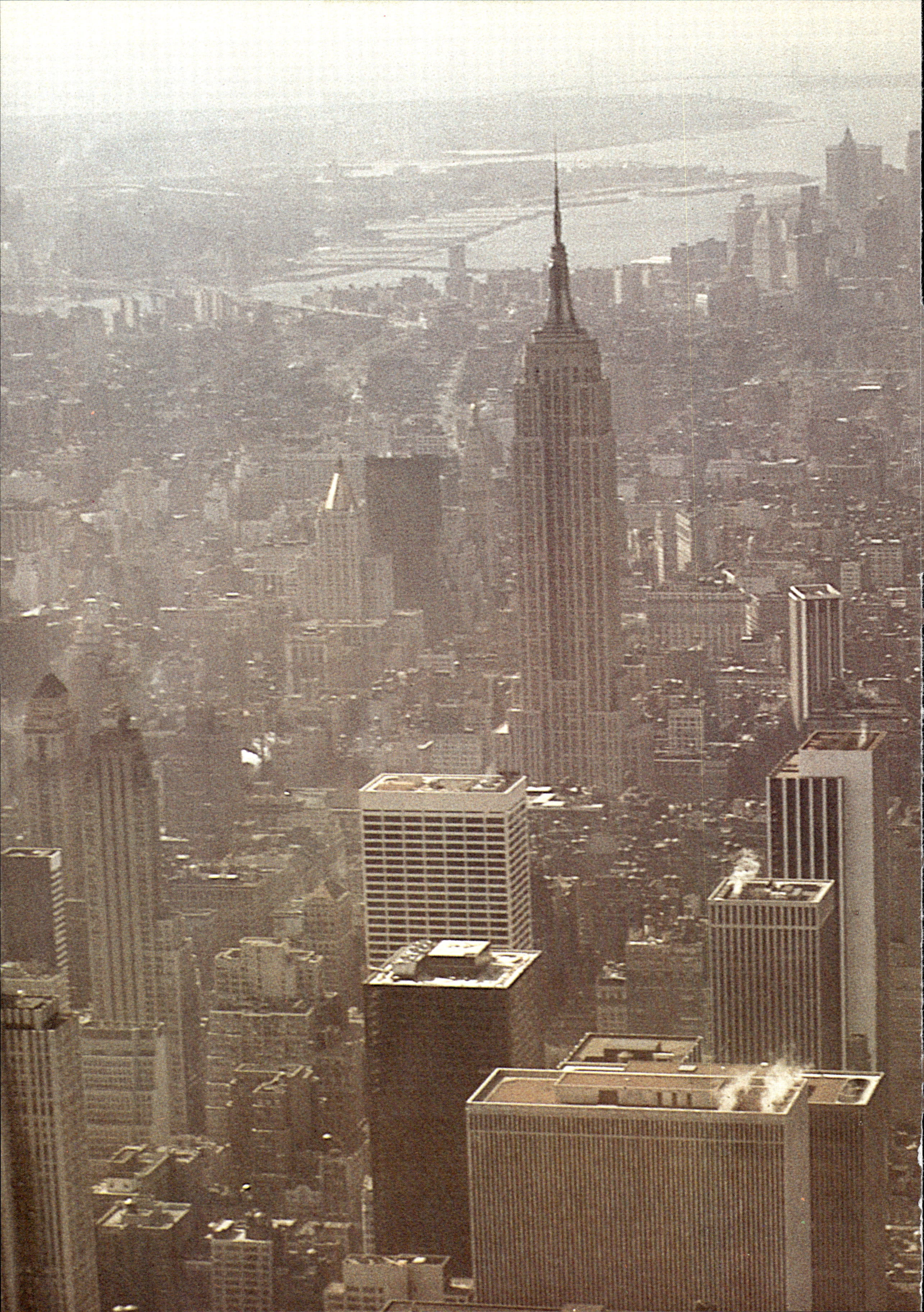

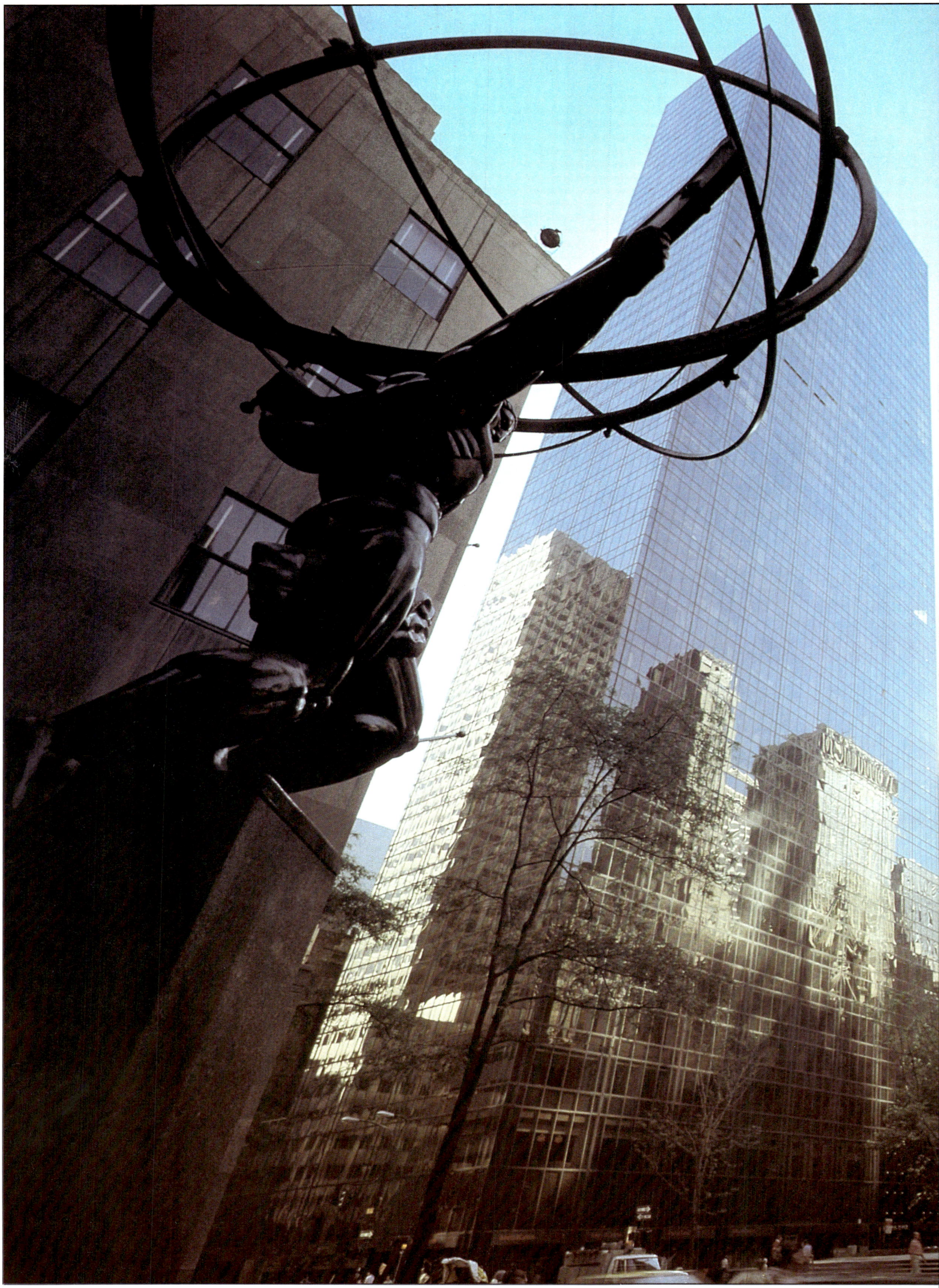

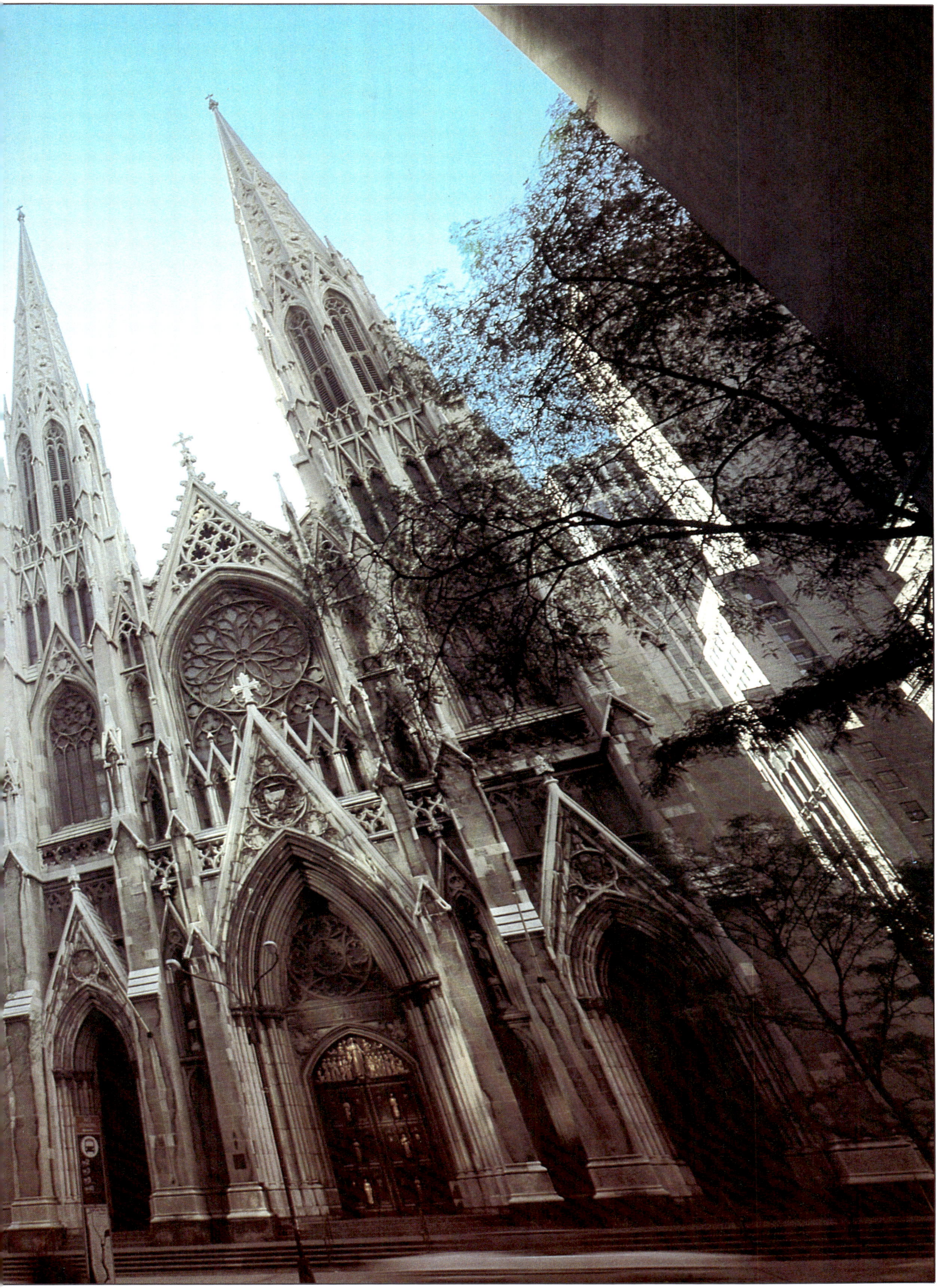

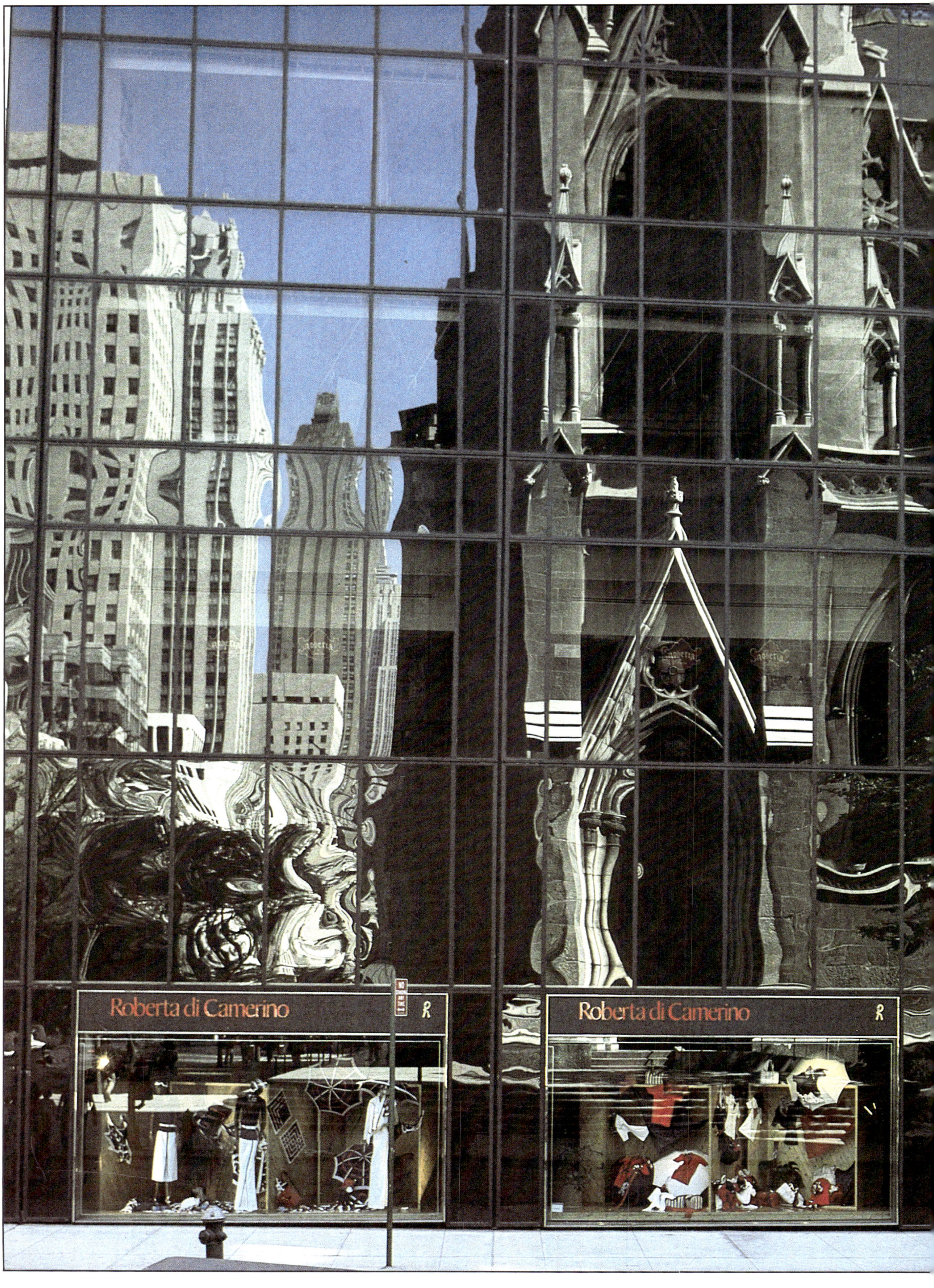
Roberta di Camerino
Roberta di Camerino

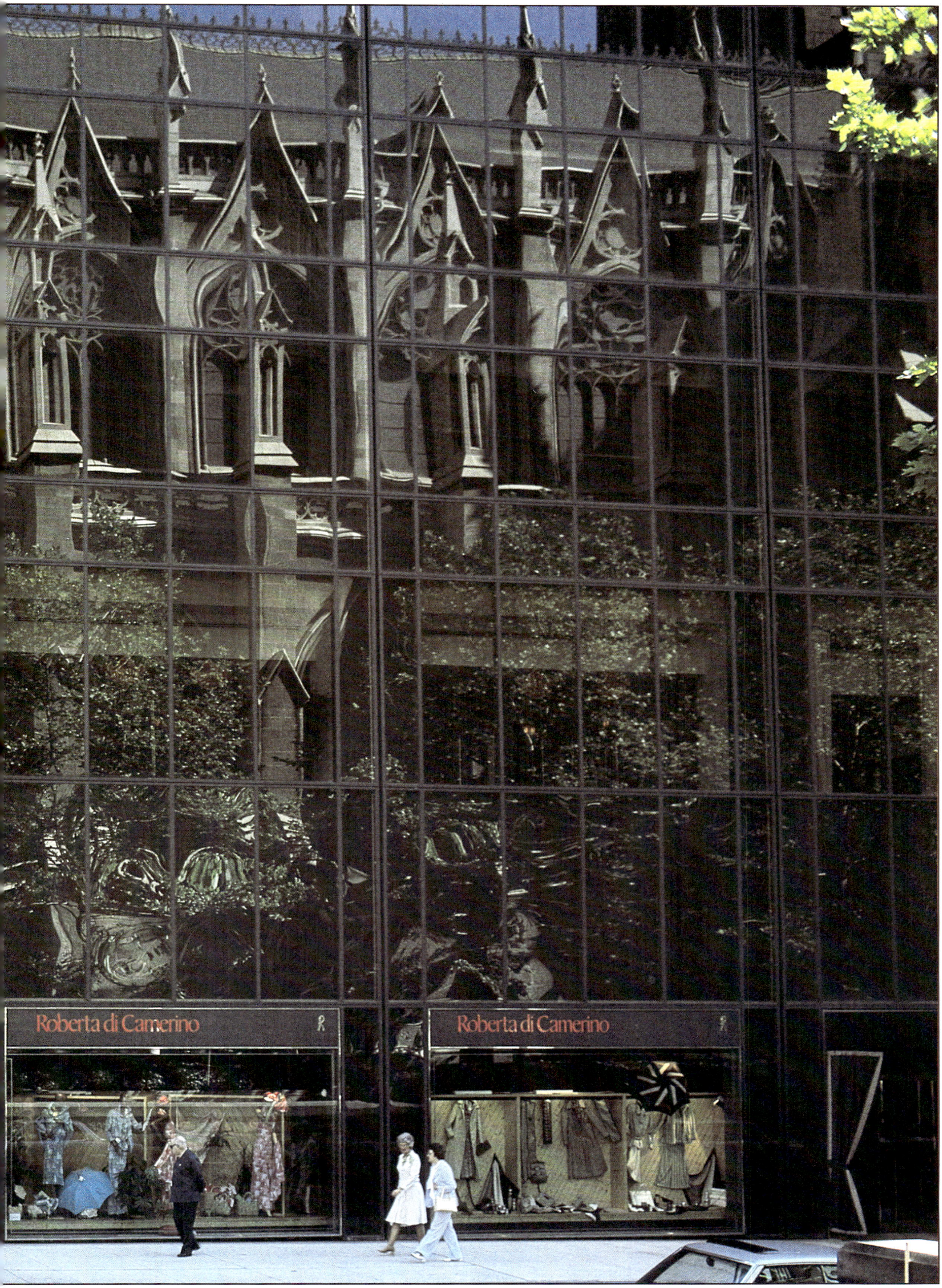
Roberta di Camerino
Roberta di Camerino

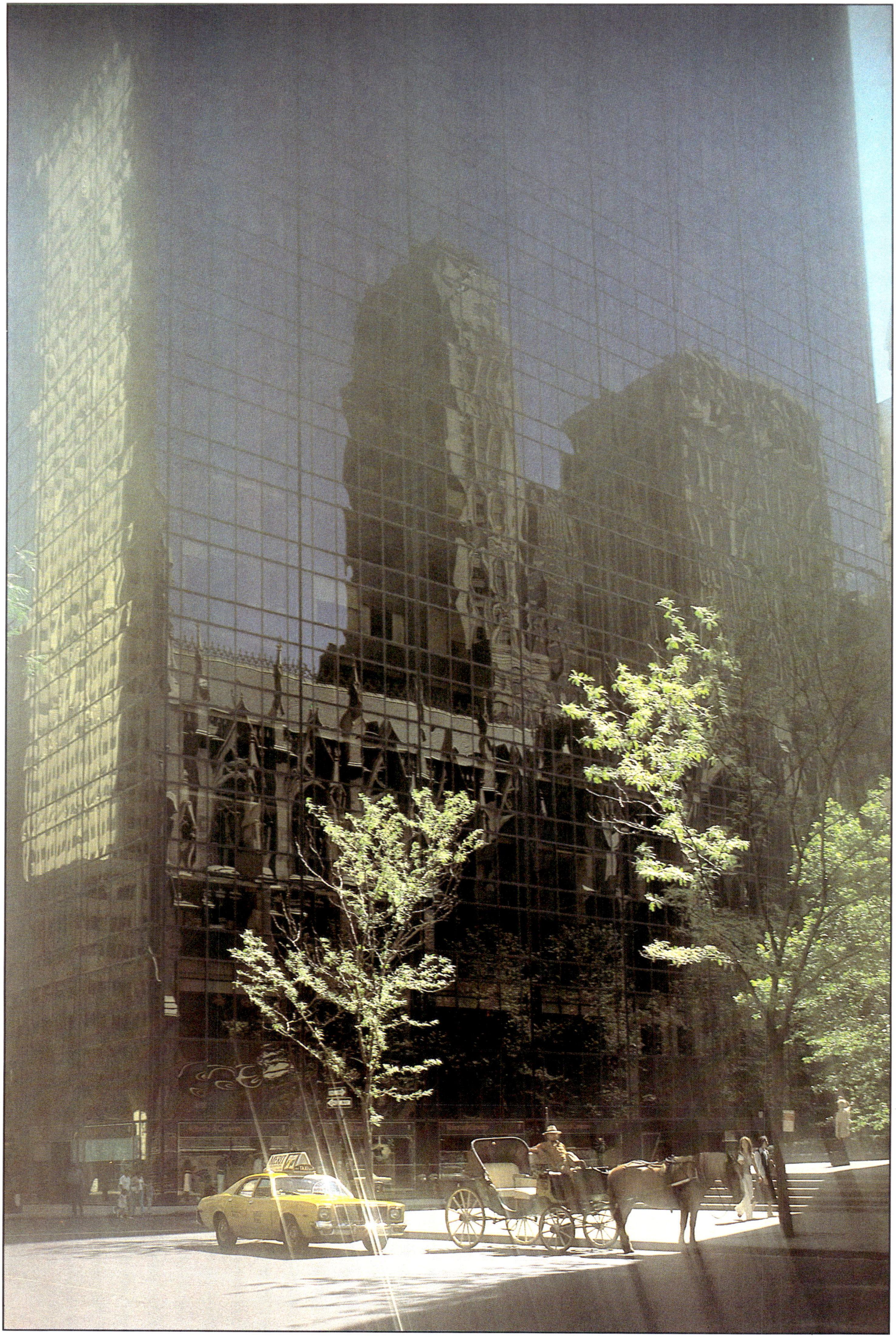

AND A LONG WAVE OF YELLOW LIGHT
BREAKS SILENTLY ON TOWER AND HALL.
OSCAR WILDE

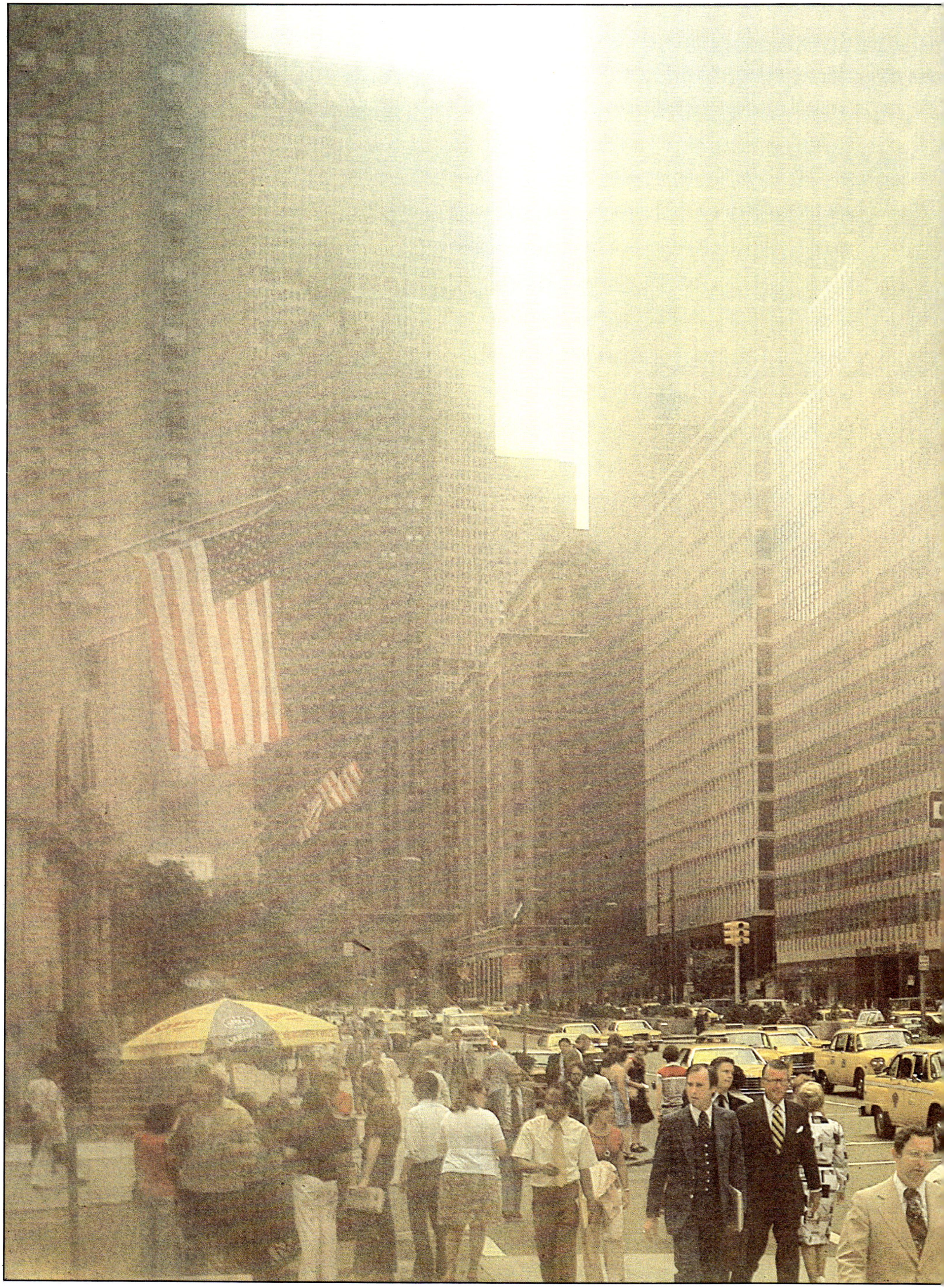

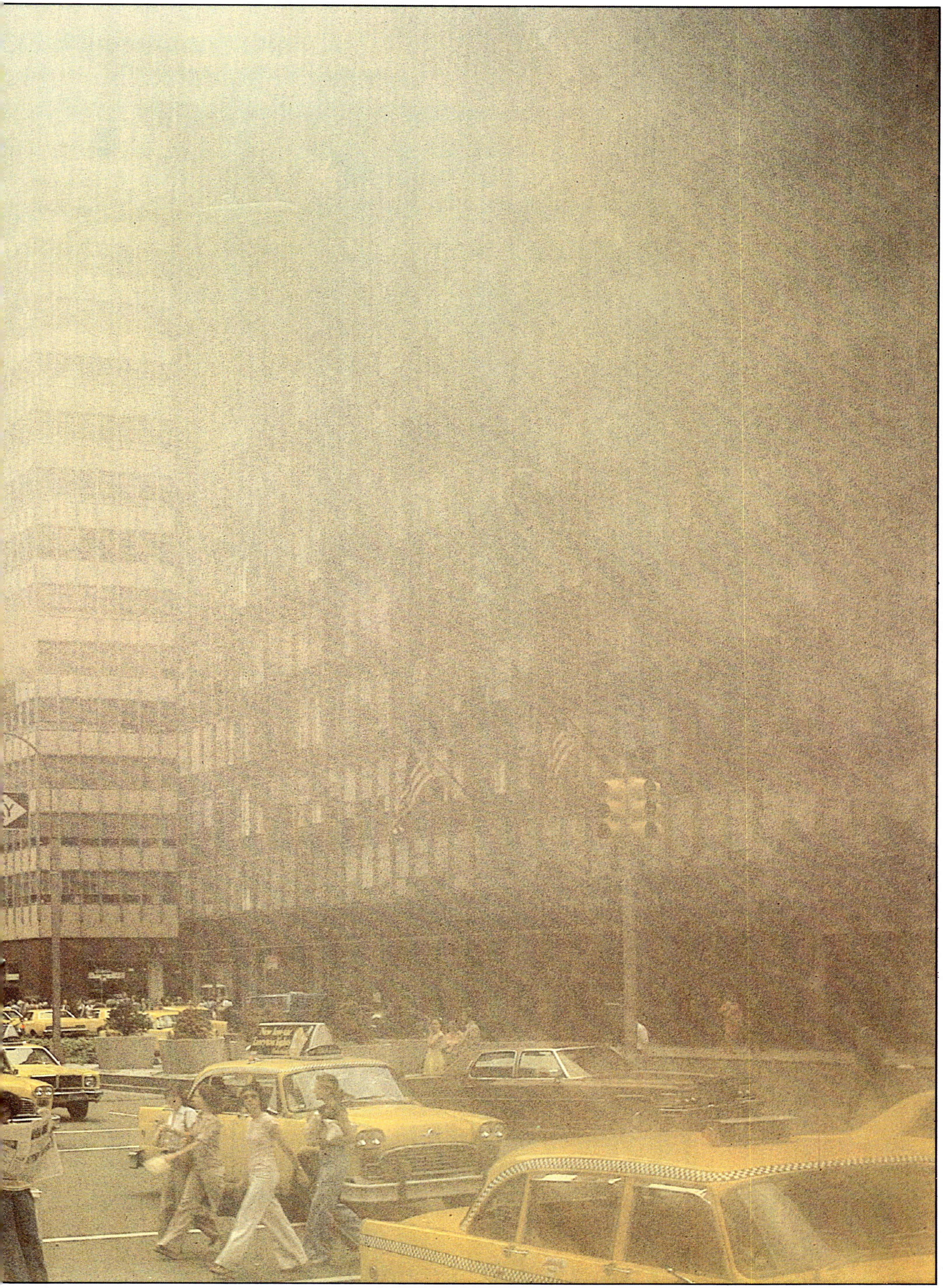

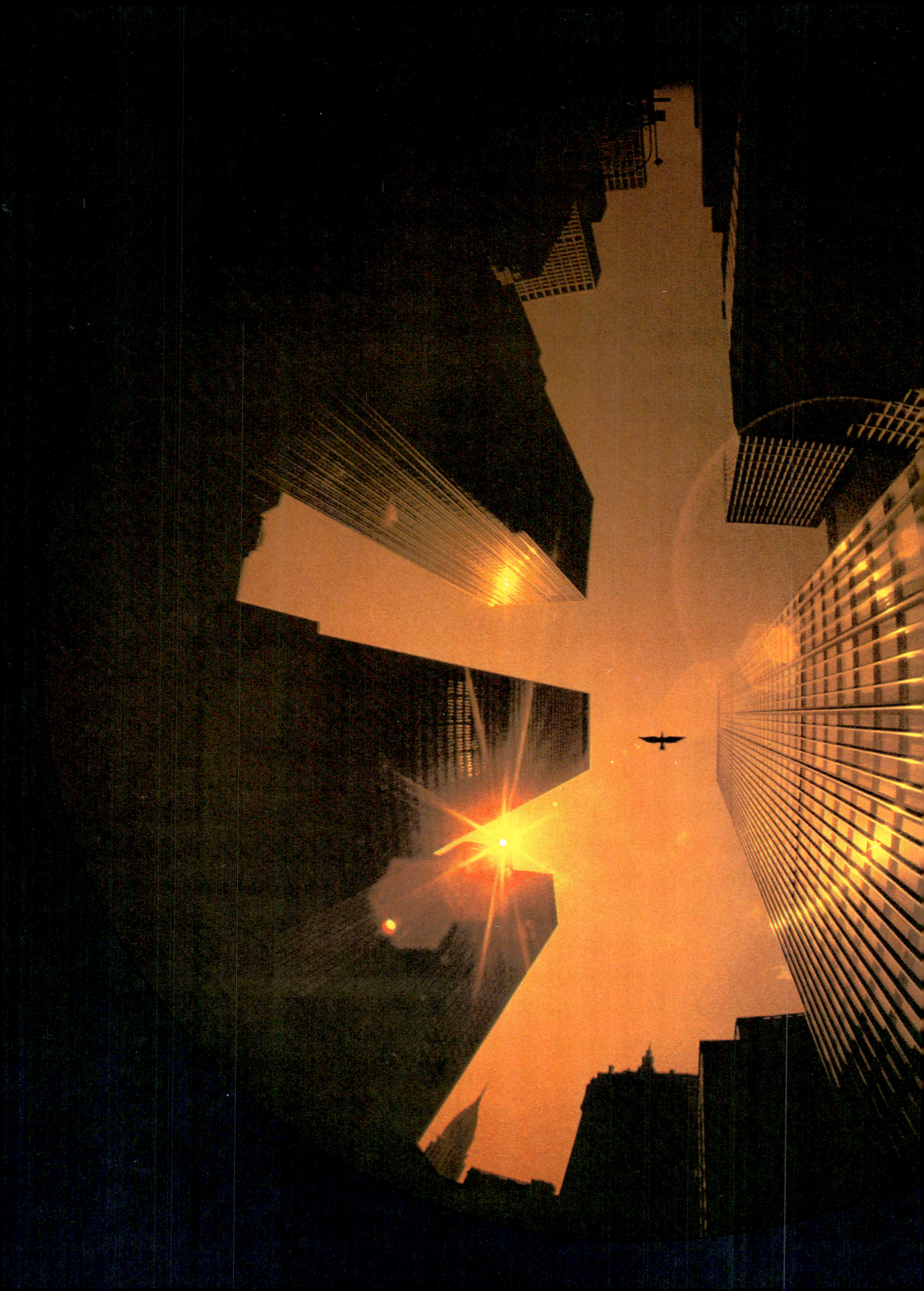

THEN SUDDENLY THE STREETS WERE STIRRED
WITH COUNTRY WAGGONS AND A BIRD
FLEW TO THE GLISTENING ROOFS AND SANG.
OSCAR WILDE

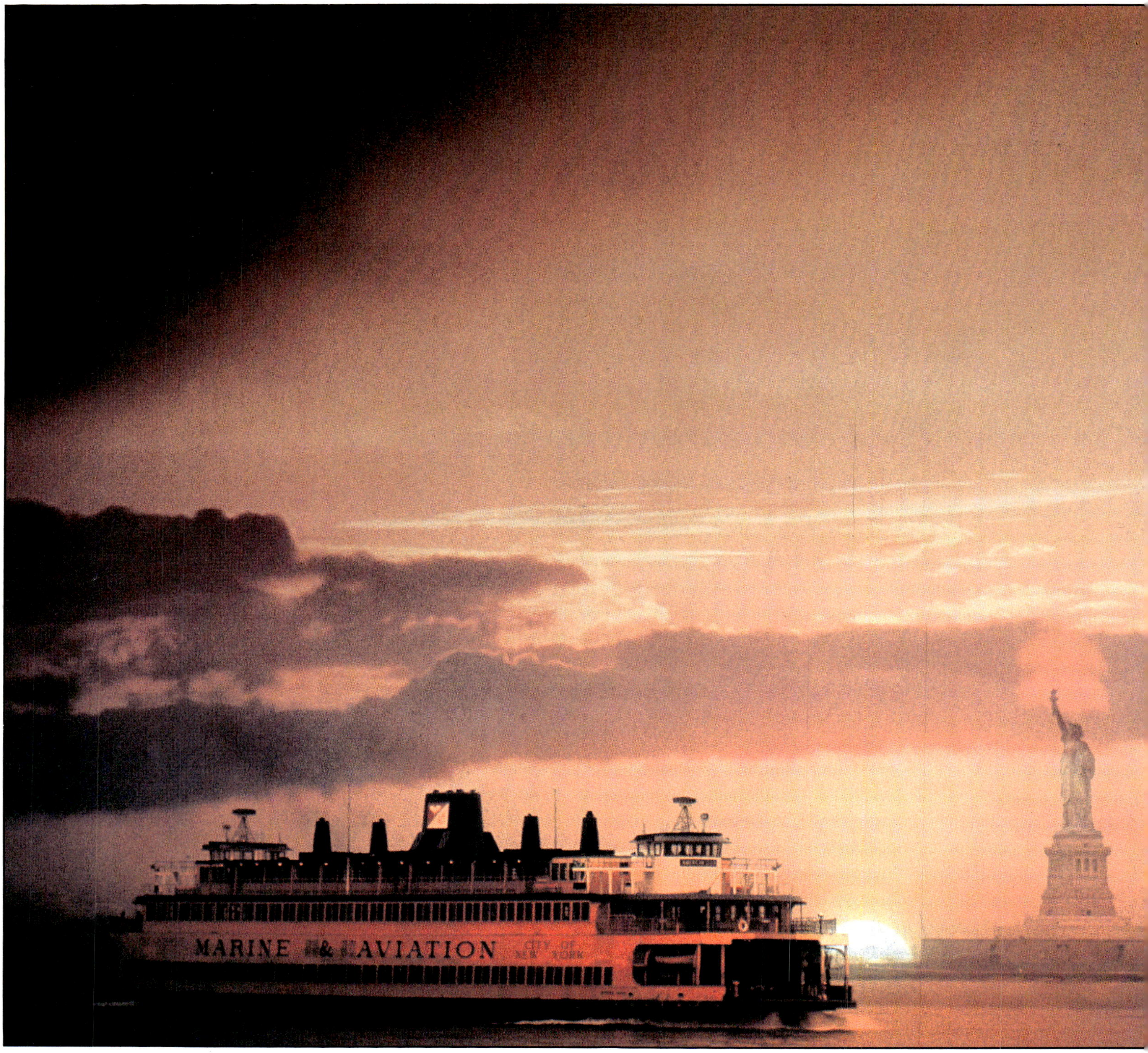
MARINE & AVIATION

THE VERY LAST MOMENTS OF THE DAY
HOLD SINGULAR POWER OVER ME
MINGLING SADNESS, ENCHANTMENT, EMOTION
AND A SORT OF PAINFUL LUCIDITY.
PAUL VALÉRY

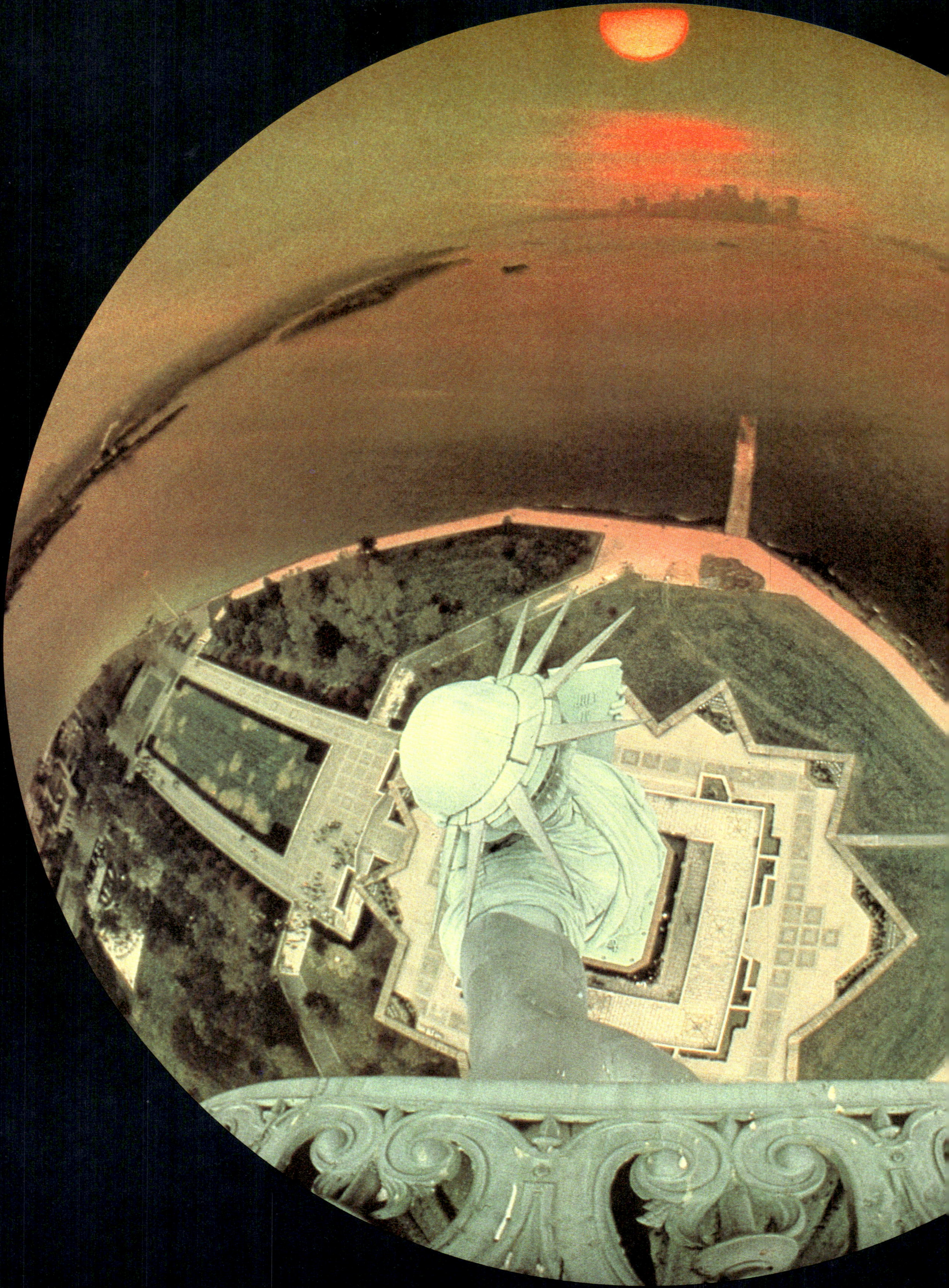

BE MISTRESS, SISTER, SWEETNESS TRANSITORY
OF SPLENDID AUTUMN OR OF SETTING SUN.
BAUDELAIRE

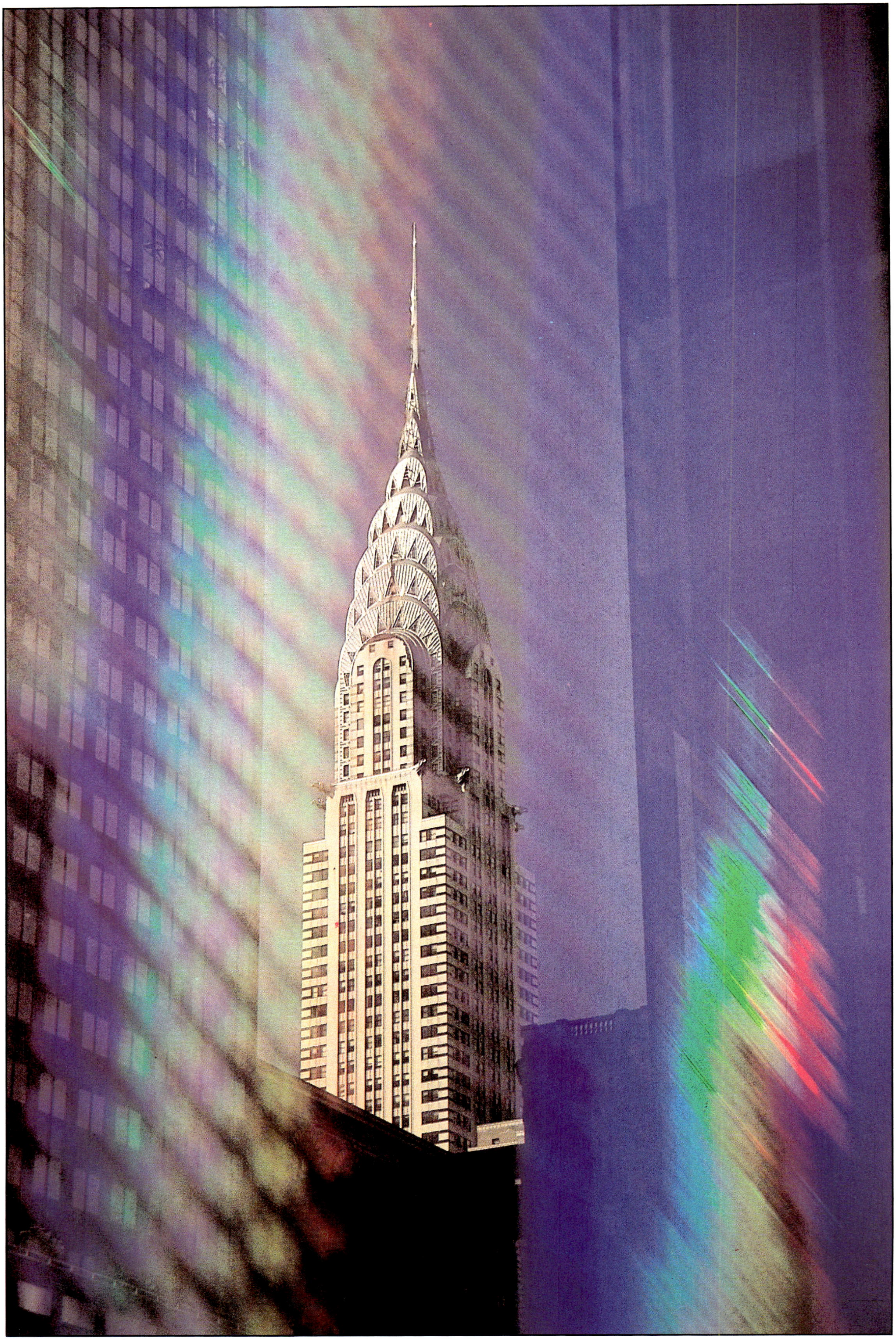

NO STAR, NO VESTIGES OF SUN
TO LIGHT THESE PRODIGIES GLOWING
WITH THEIR OWN FIRE.
BAUDELAIRE

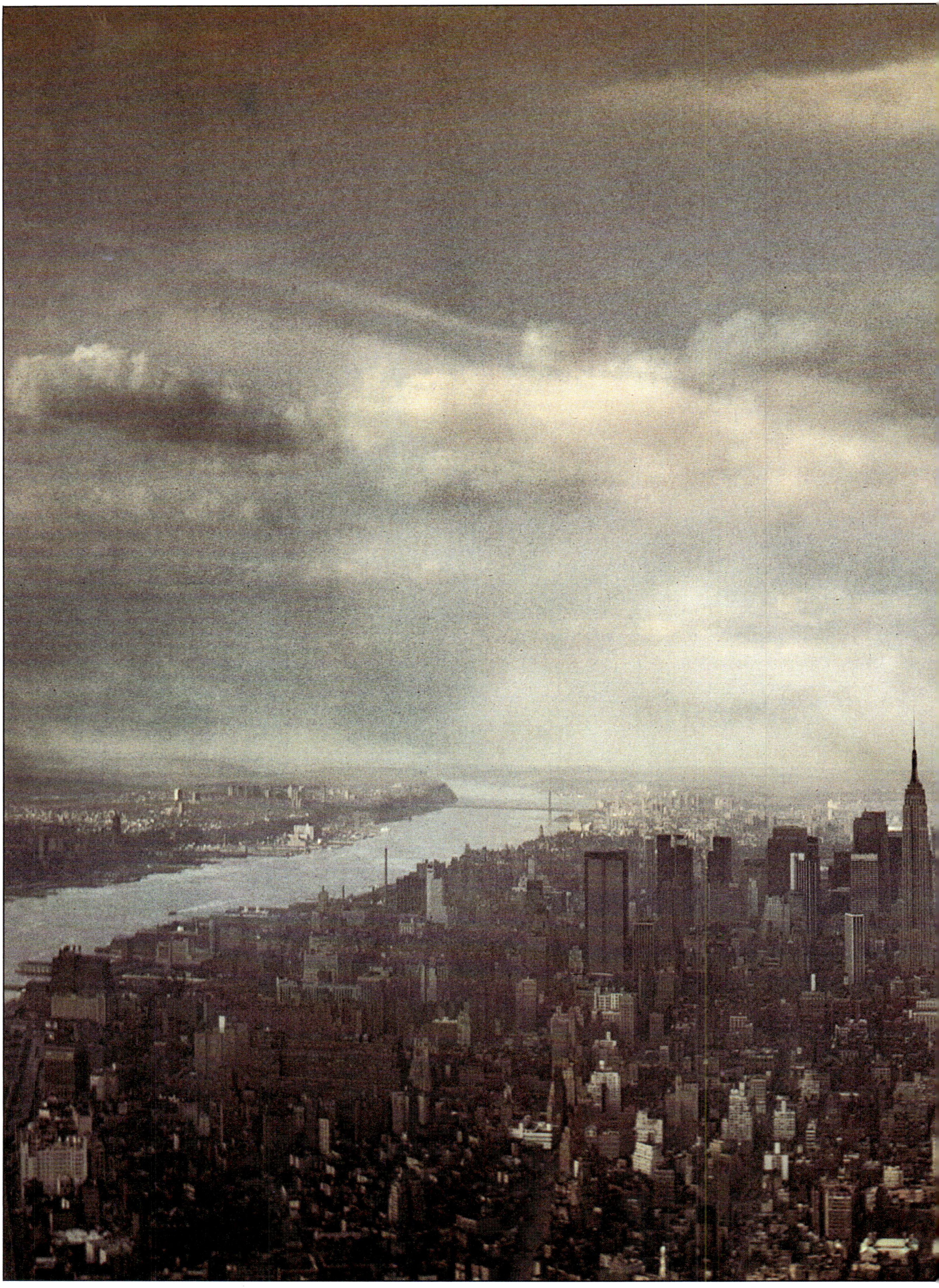

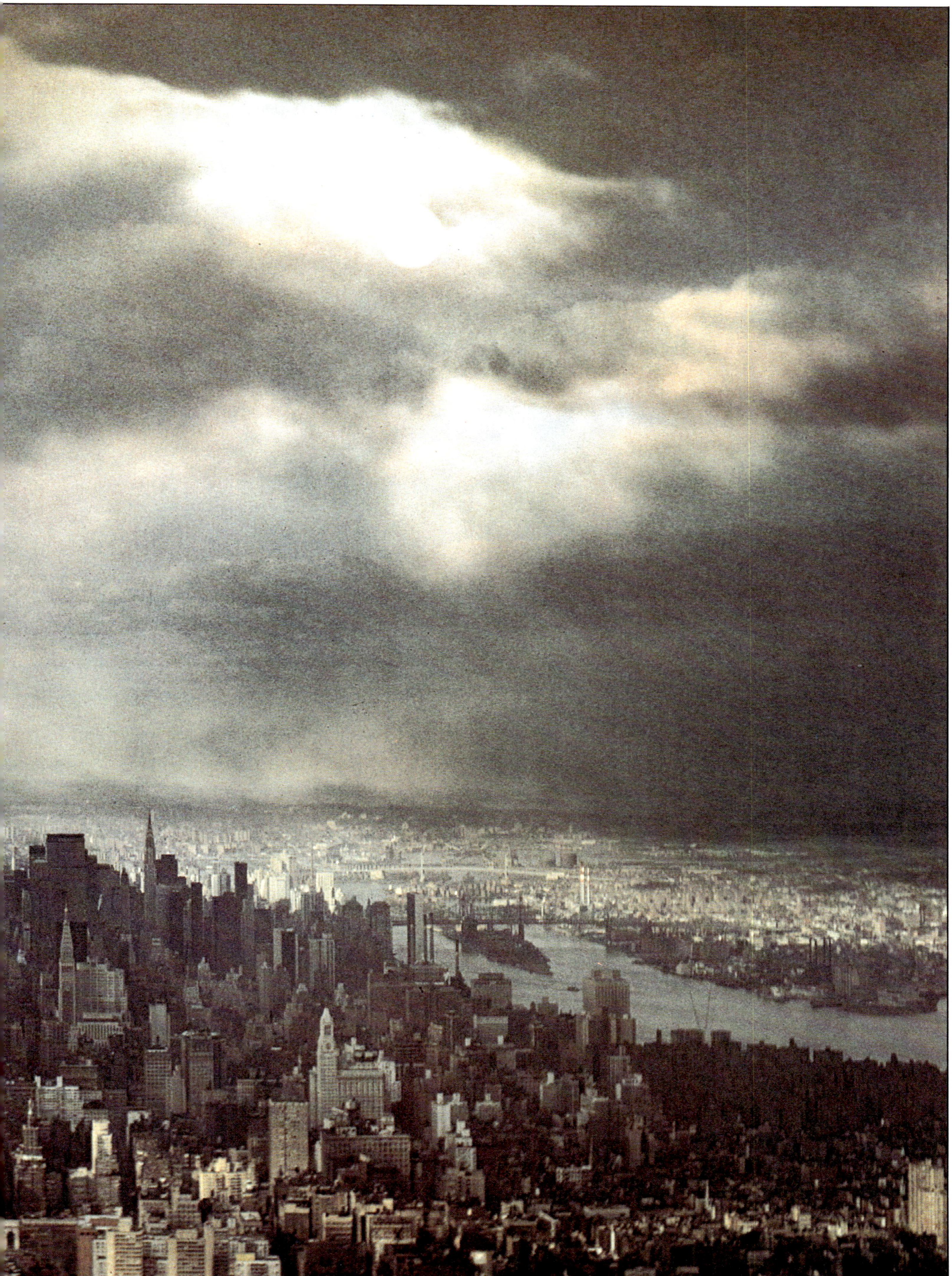

OUR HEARTS' DREAMS, THE HORIZON'S FOLDS,
THE DAWN AND ITS TEARS, THE SOUNDS OF THE TOWN

AFLOAT IN A NETWORK OF VAGUE MELODIES.
THERE IS MUSIC IN ALL. A HYMN FROM THE EARTH.
VICTOR HUGO

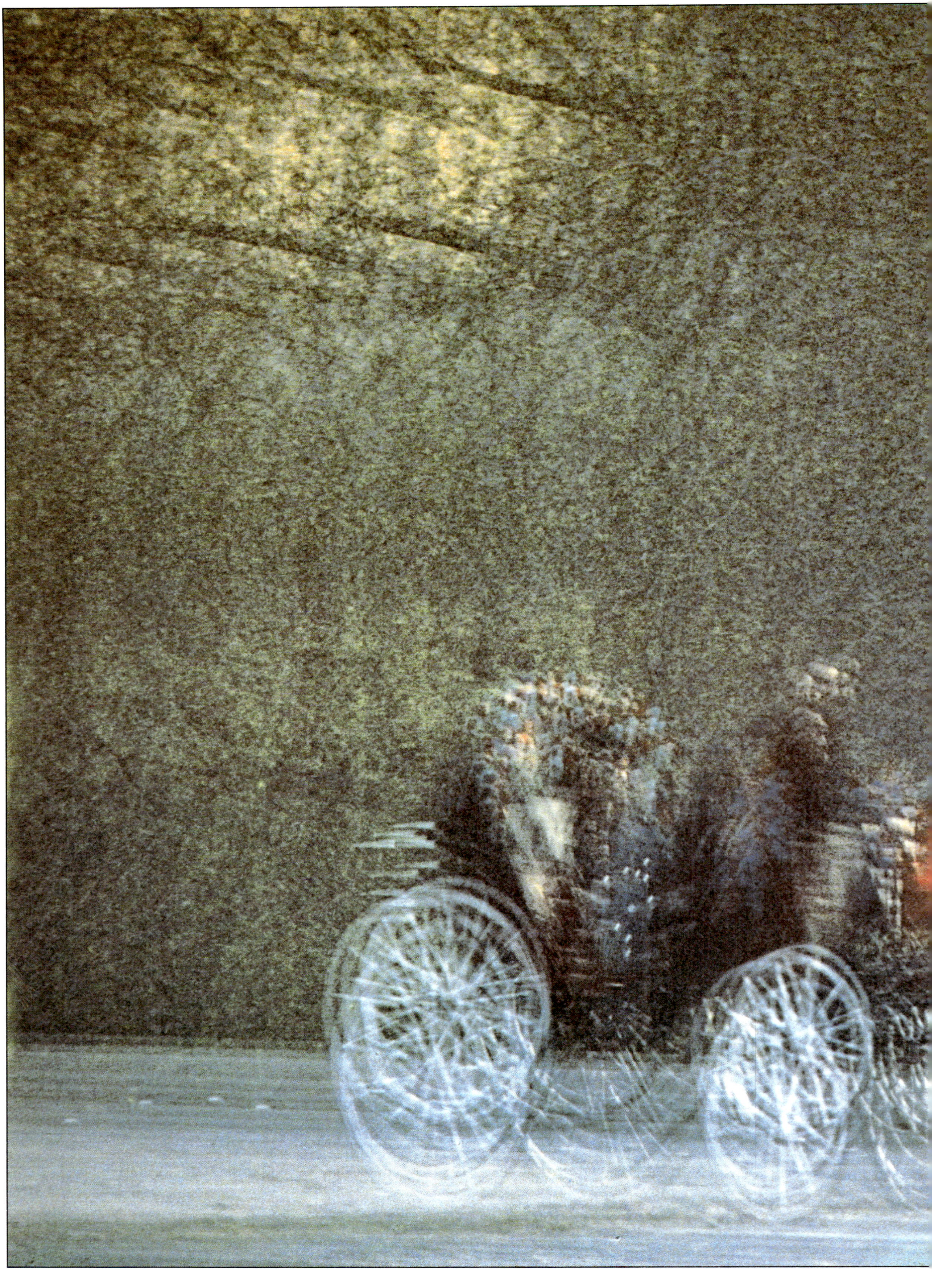

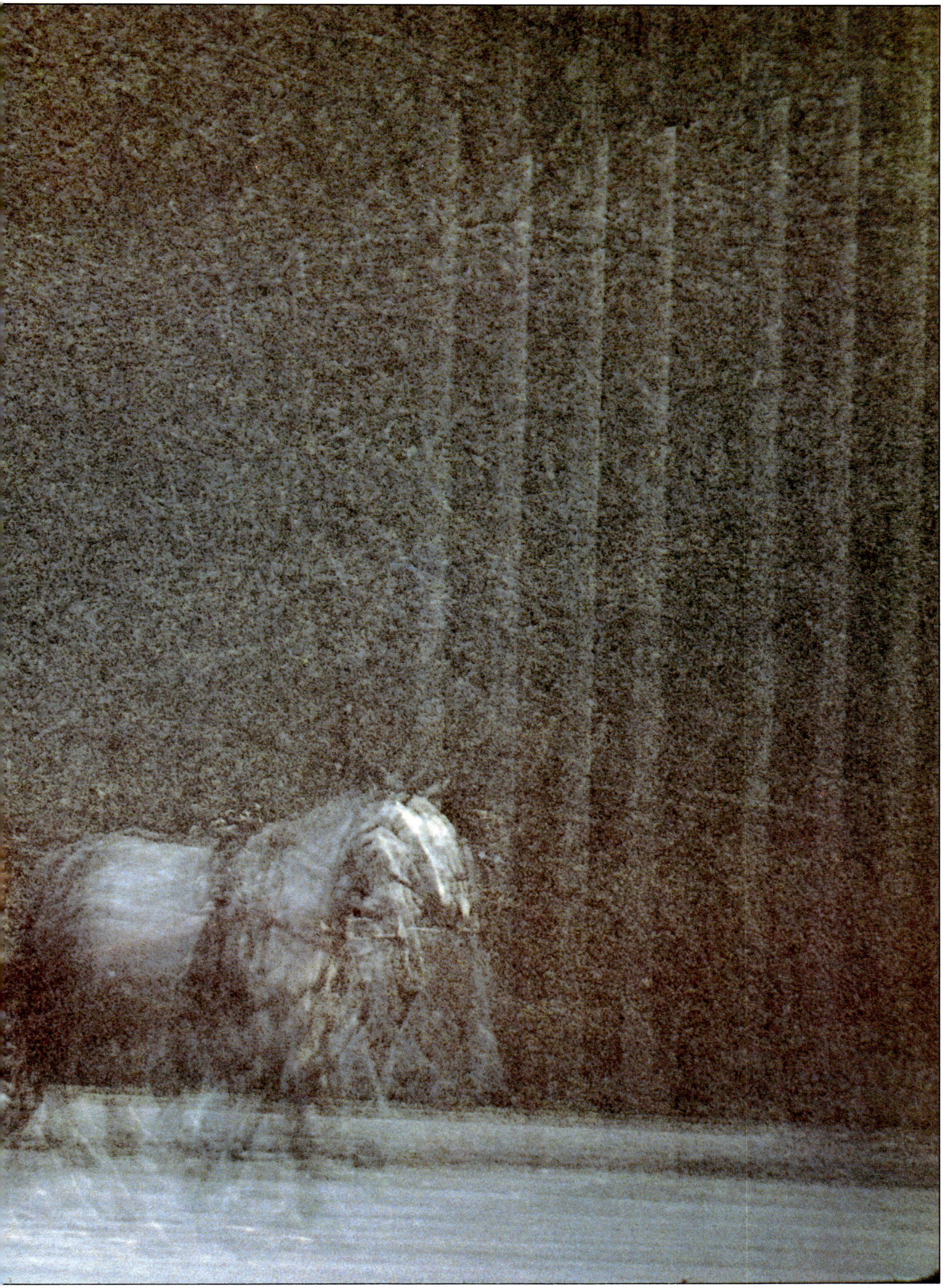

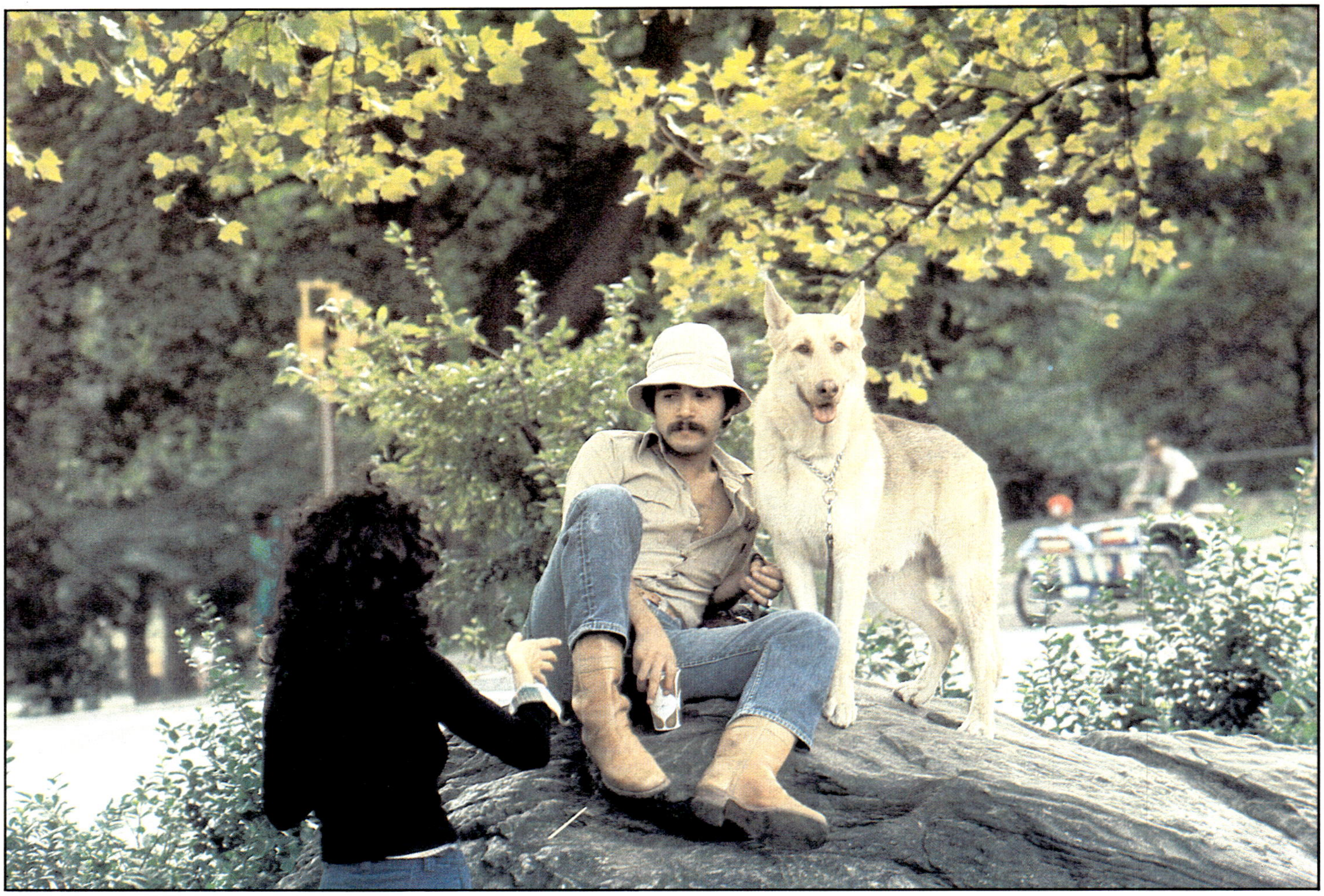

DRUNKEN APOLLO, POSSESSED OF A THOUSAND FRENZIES
WITH BEAMING EYES
AND WITHIN HIS BROW THE GOD'S UNENDED DREAM!
VERLAINE

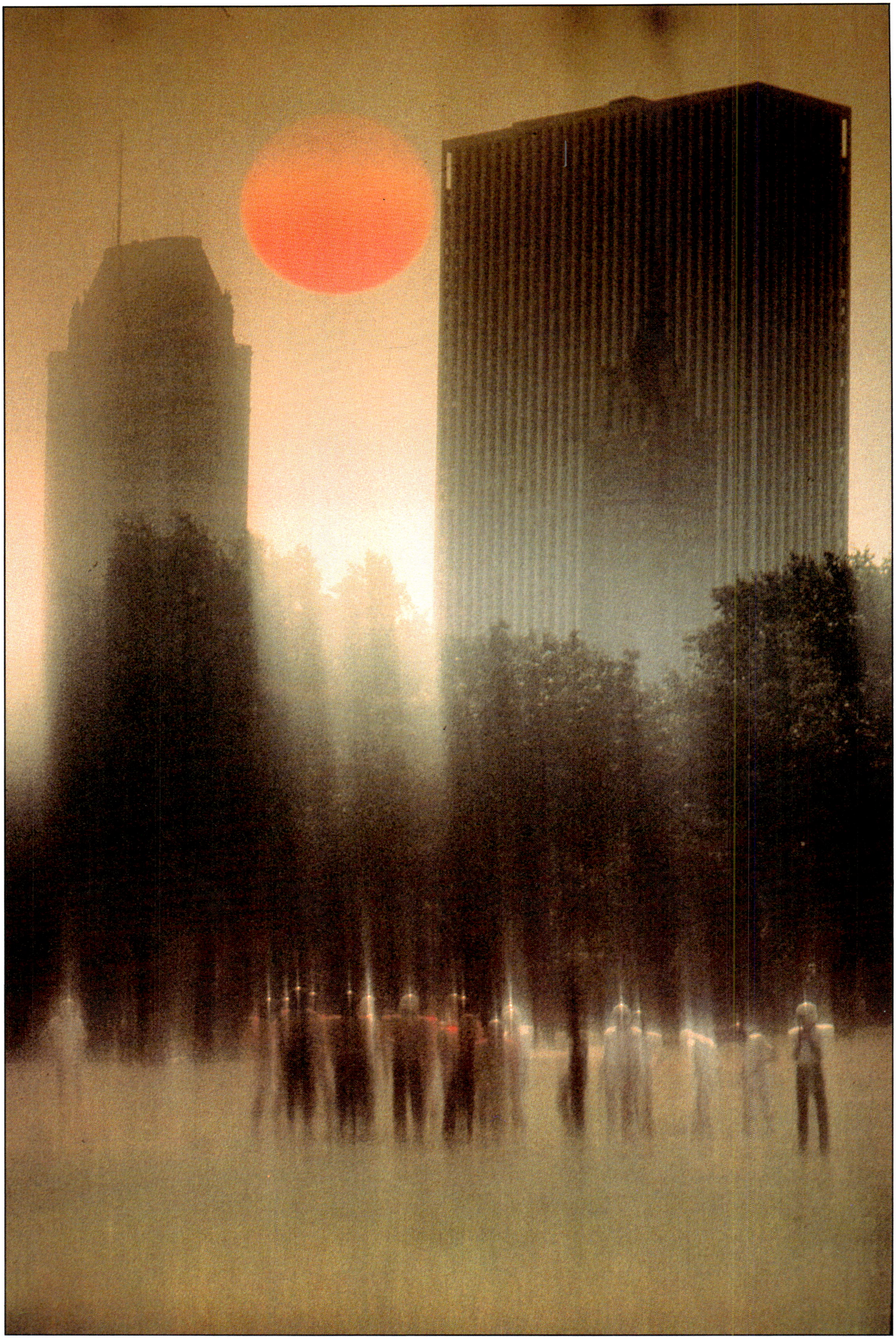

O, THOU MY LOVELY BOY, WHO IN THY POWER
DOST HOLD TIME'S FICKLE GLASS AND HOUR.
SHAKESPEARE

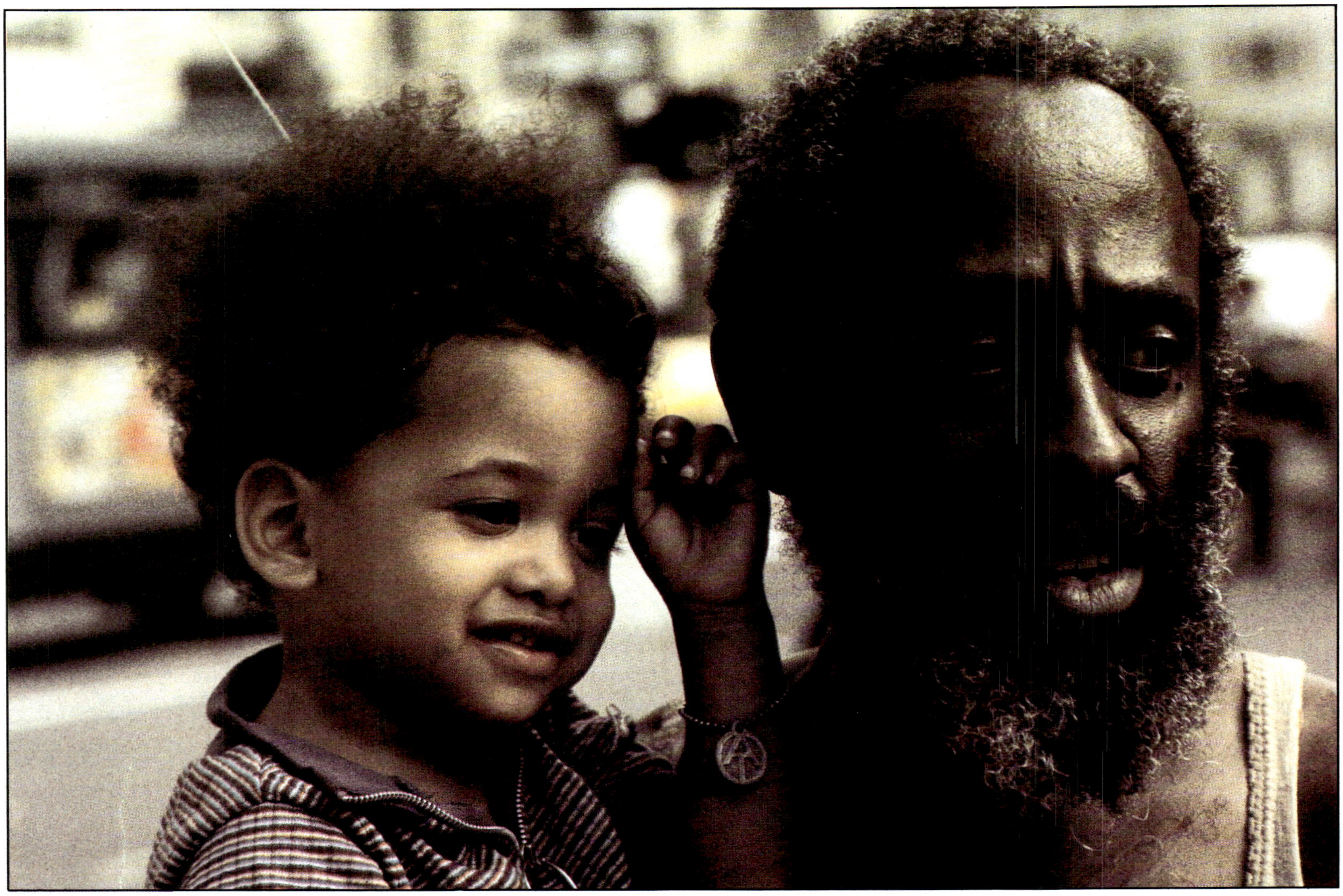

TIME DOTH TRANSFIX THE FLOURISH SET ON YOUTH
AND DELVES THE PARALLELS IN BEAUTY'S BROW.
SHAKESPEARE

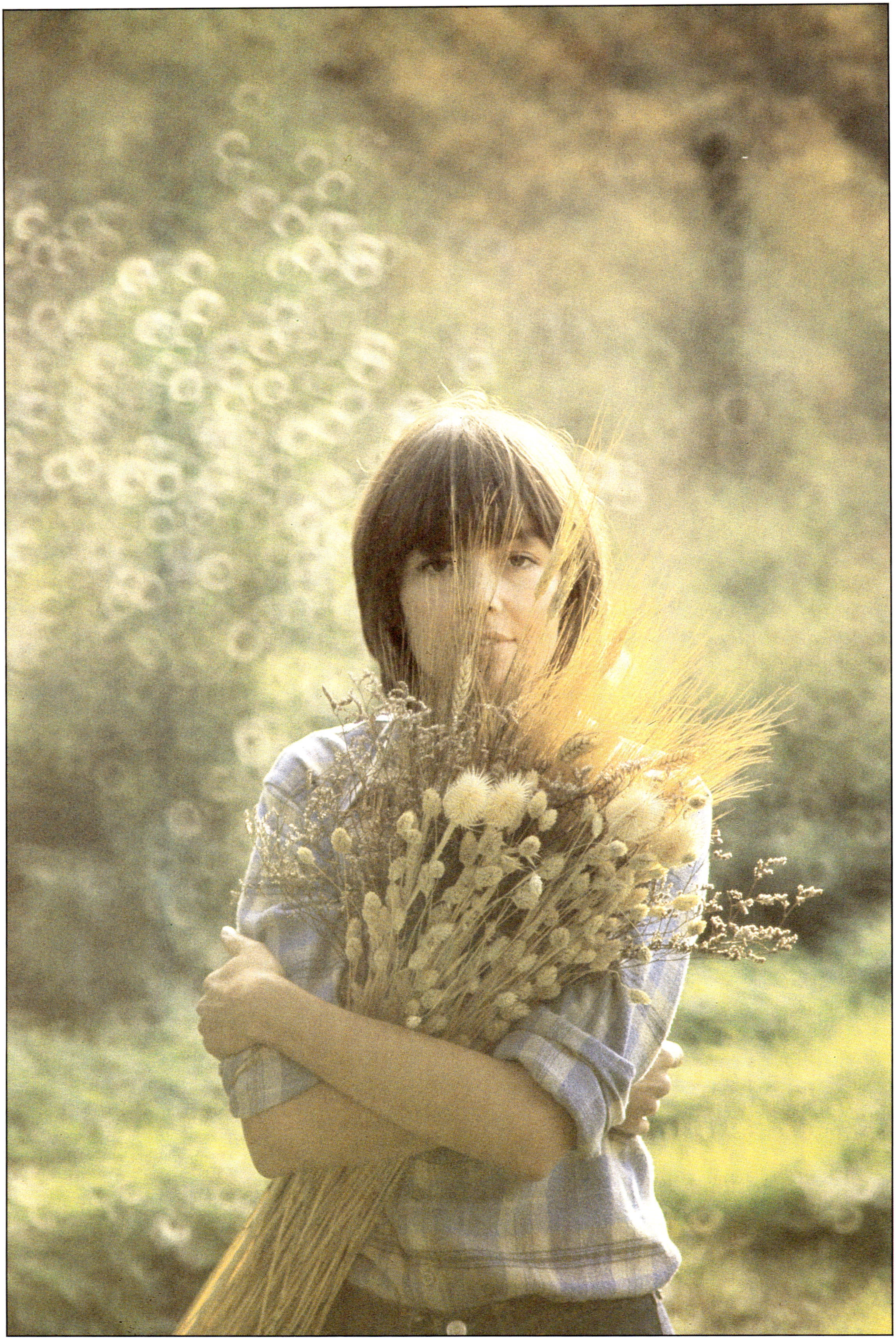

BUT THOU, CONTRACTED TO THINE OWN BRIGHT EYES,
FEED'ST THY LIGHT'S FLAME.
SHAKESPEARE

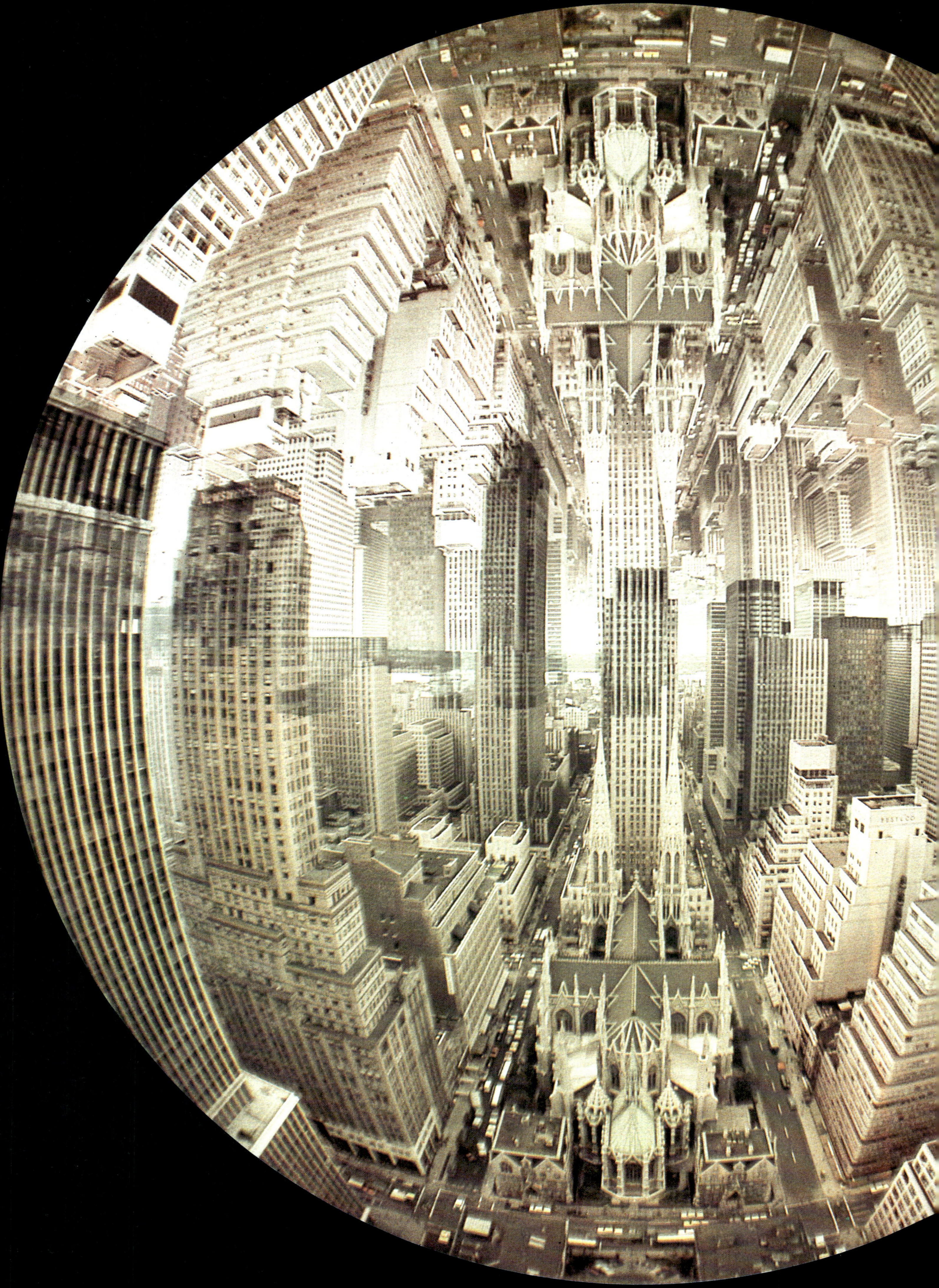

A SUN, WITH WORLDS AROUND
CENTRES THEMSELVES, BY MOONS SURROUNDED;
THERE, TWIN GLOBES, TURNING IN PAIRS;
THAT STAR AT THE HEART, BEAMING, SUBLIME…
VICTOR HUGO

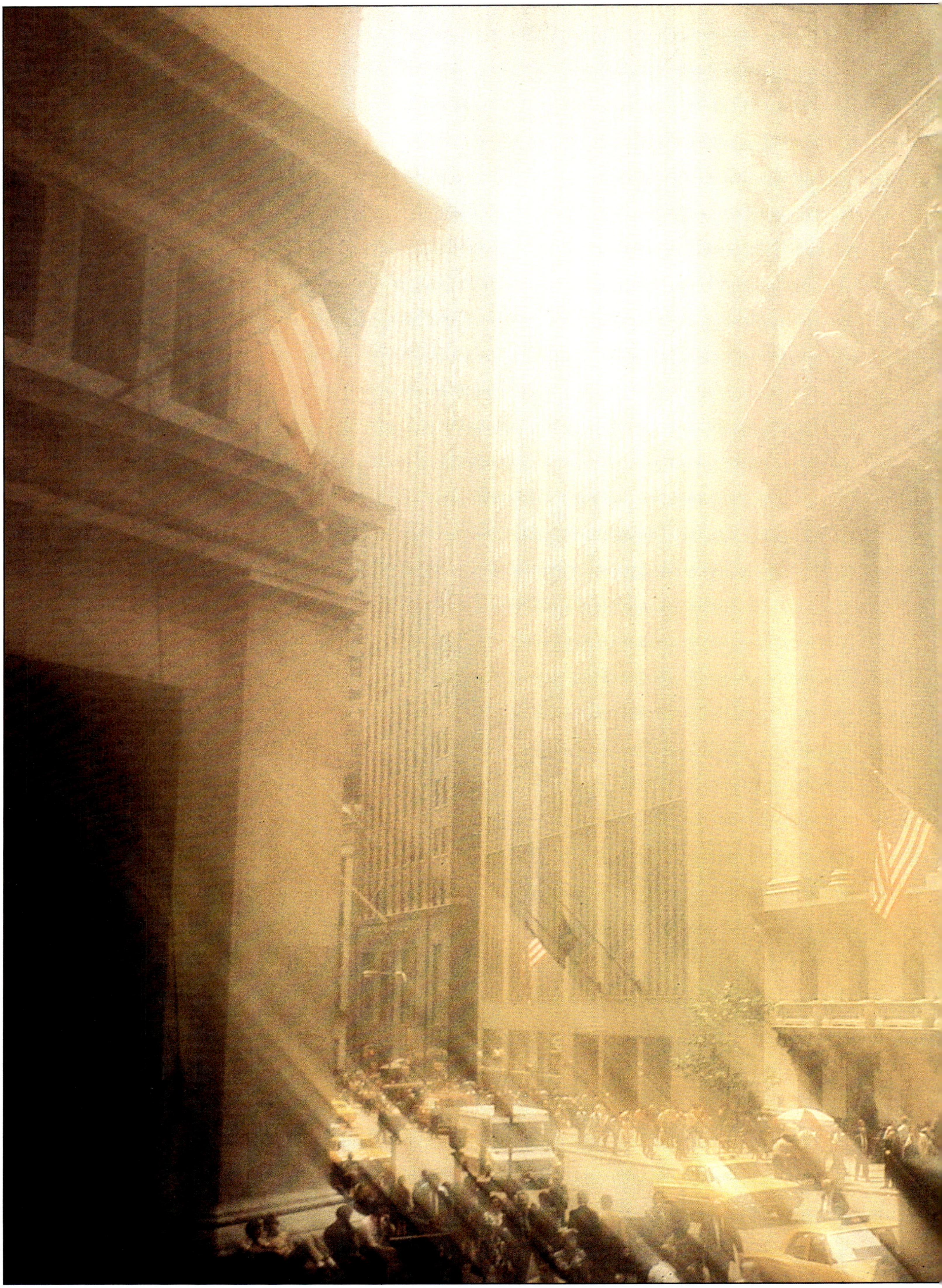

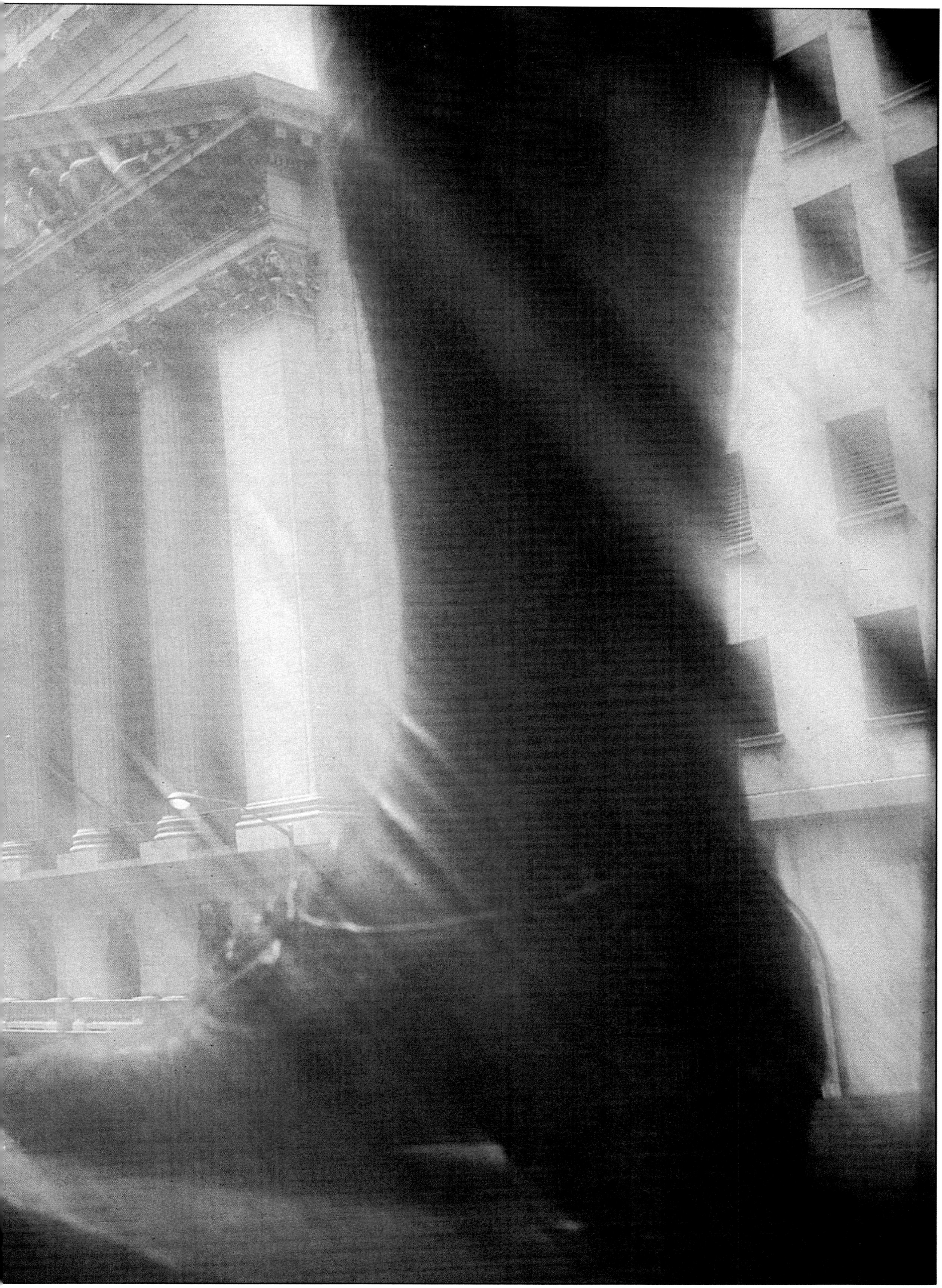

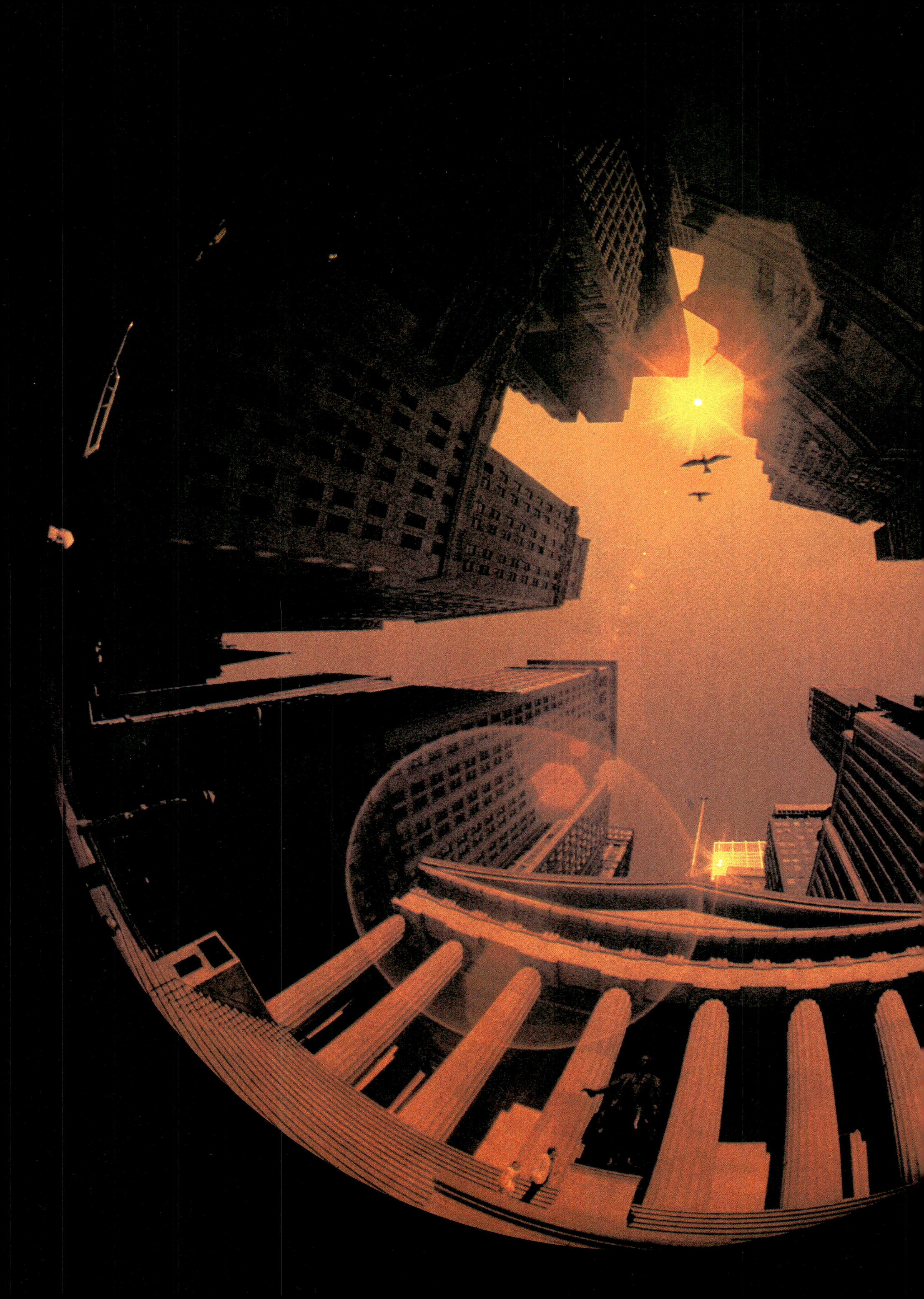

THE CLIMBING LARK AT BREAK OF DAY,
SINGING A HYMN AT HEAVEN'S GATE.
SHAKESPEARE

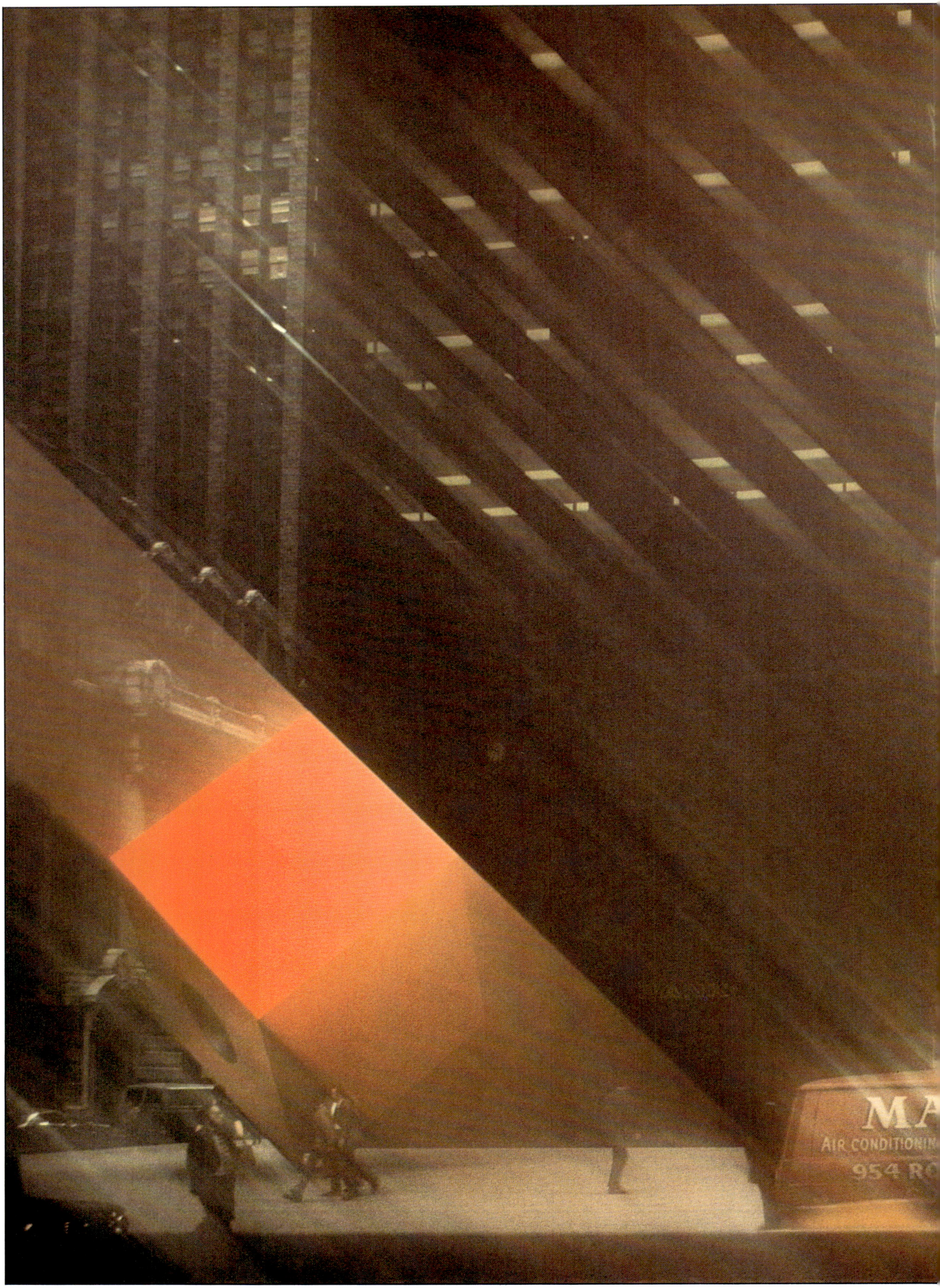
MA
AIR CONDITIONIN
954 RO

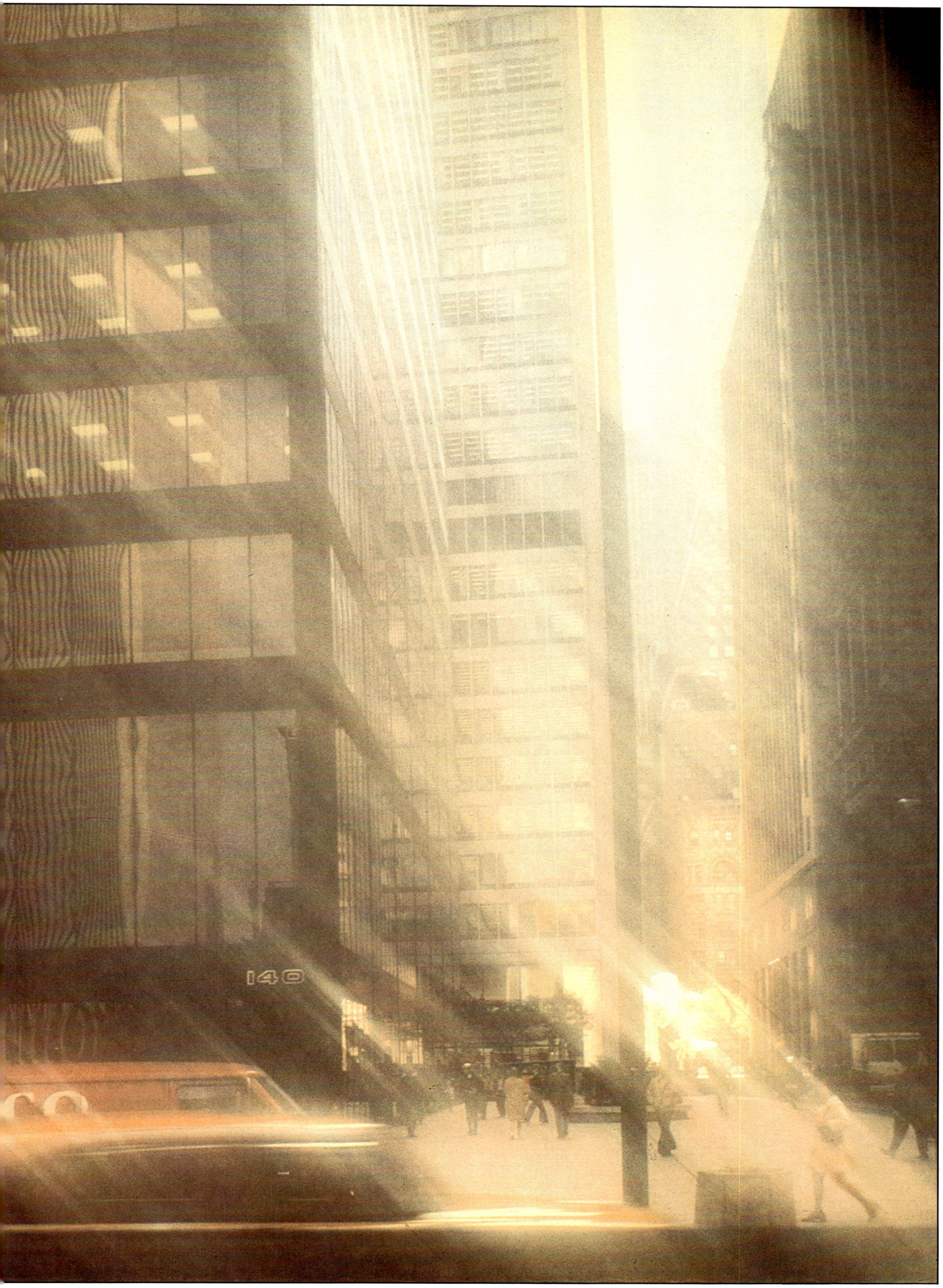
140

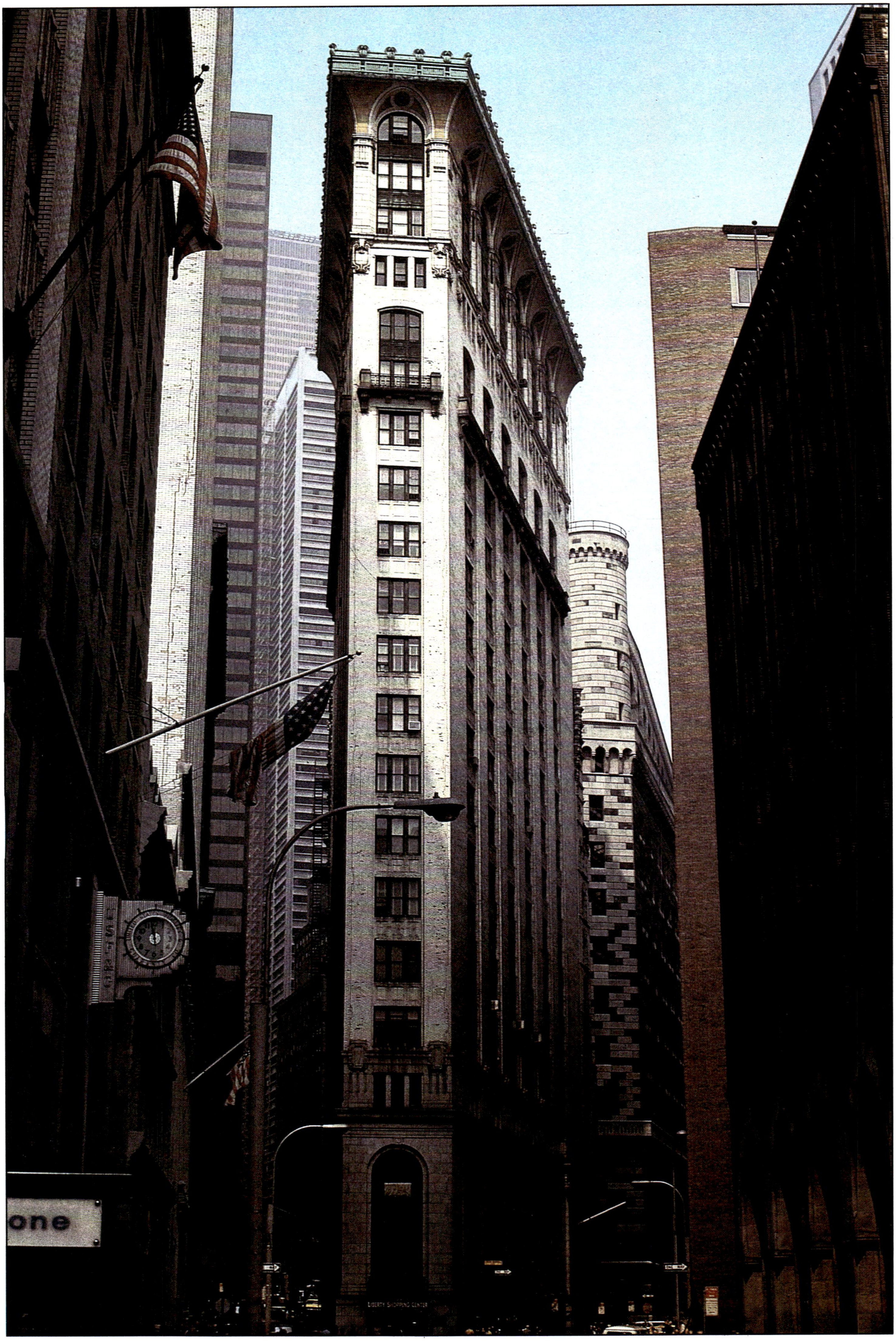
one

TONIGHT, THE RAINBOW RAY
OF THE SINKING SUN
A SOFTER FAREWELL LEAVES.
ALFRED DE MUSSET

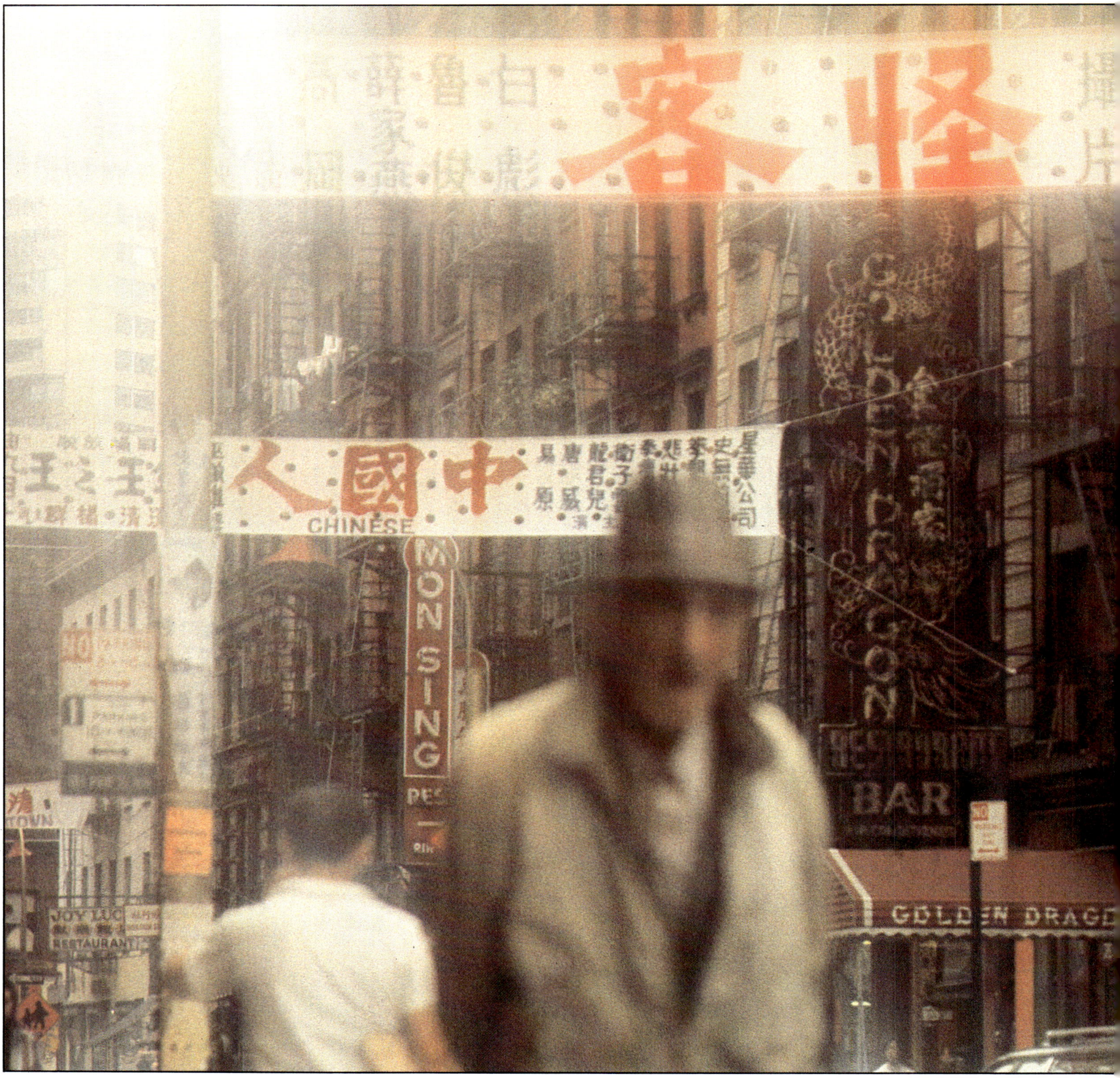
怪客
中國人
CHINESE
MON SING
BAR
JOY LUC
RESTAURANT

IN WINDING FOLDS OF ANCIENT CAPITALS
WHERE ALL THINGS HAVE ENCHANTMENT, EVEN FEAR,
I WAIT, OBEYING HUMOURS WHIMSICAL,
TO SEE FRAIL CREATURES SWEET AND SINGULAR.
BAUDELAIRE

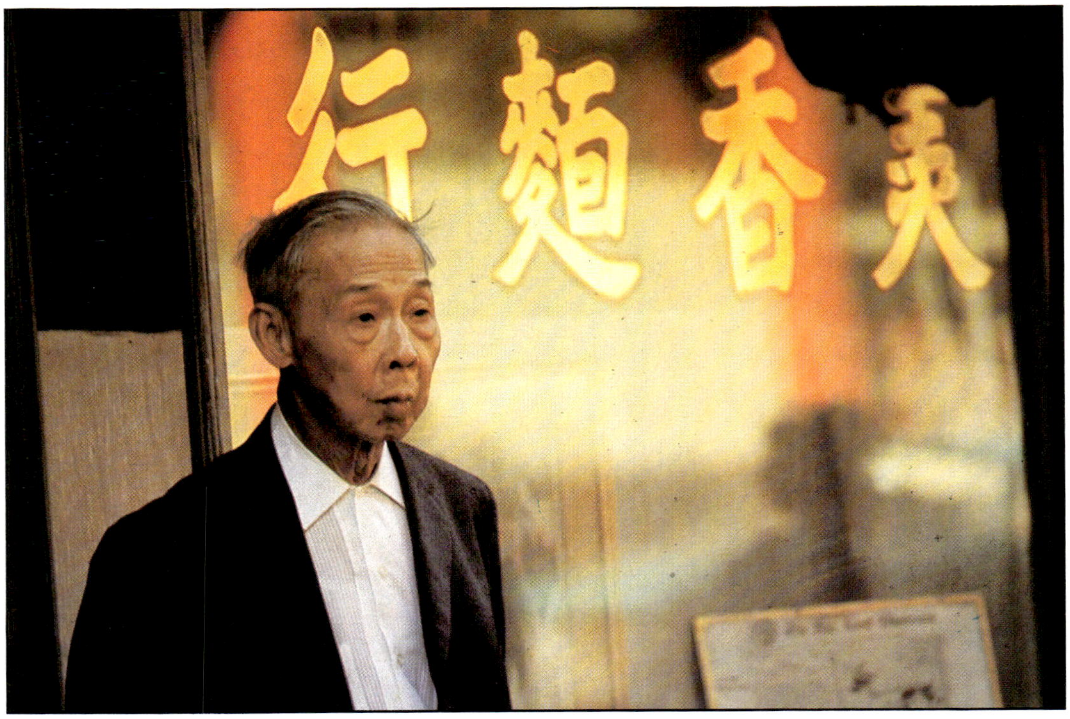

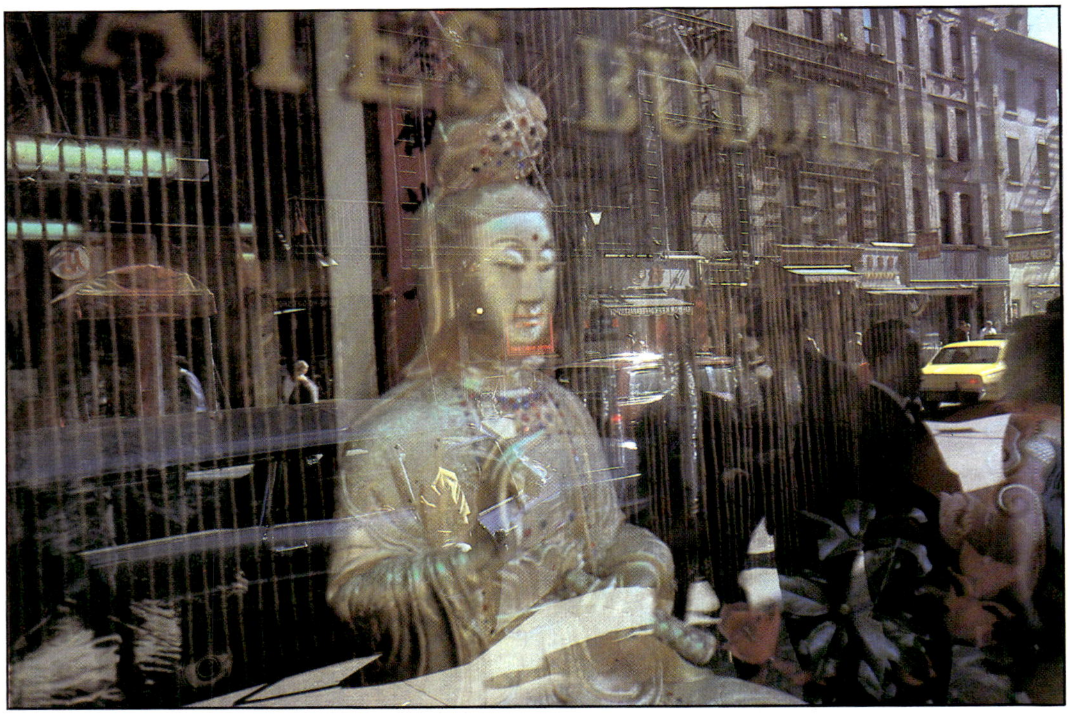

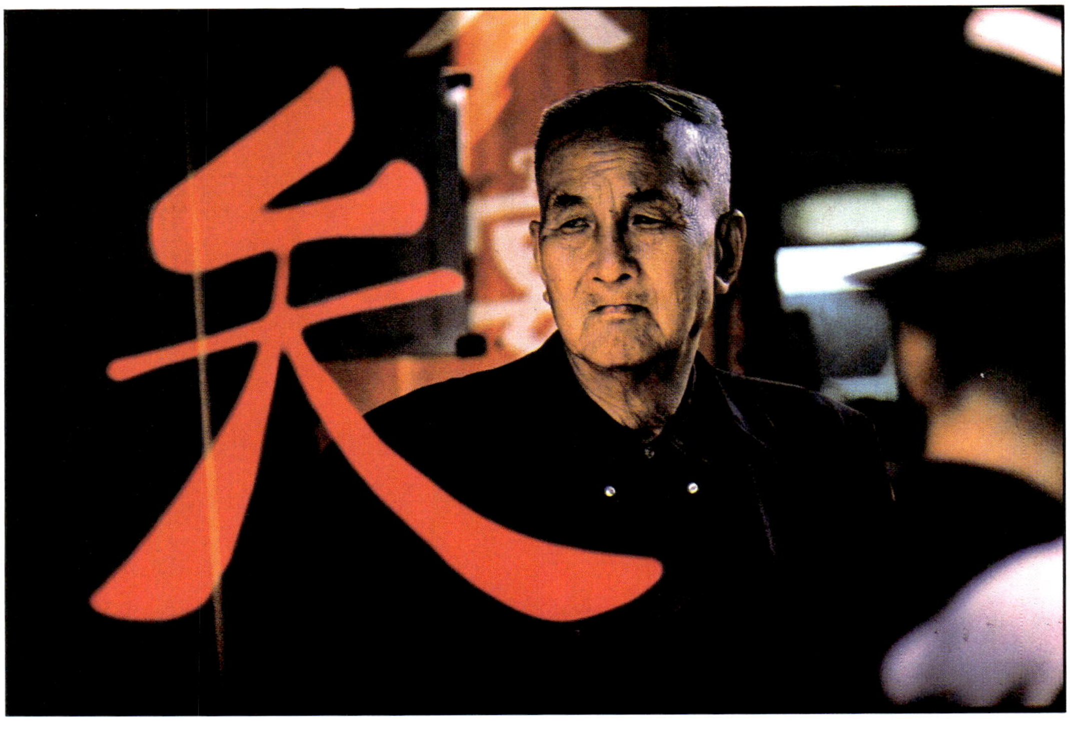

THE SOUNDS AND SCENTS
SWIRL IN THE EVENING AIR,
THE SKY SAD AND BEAUTIFUL
AS AN IMMENSE WAYSIDE SANCTUARY.
BAUDELAIRE

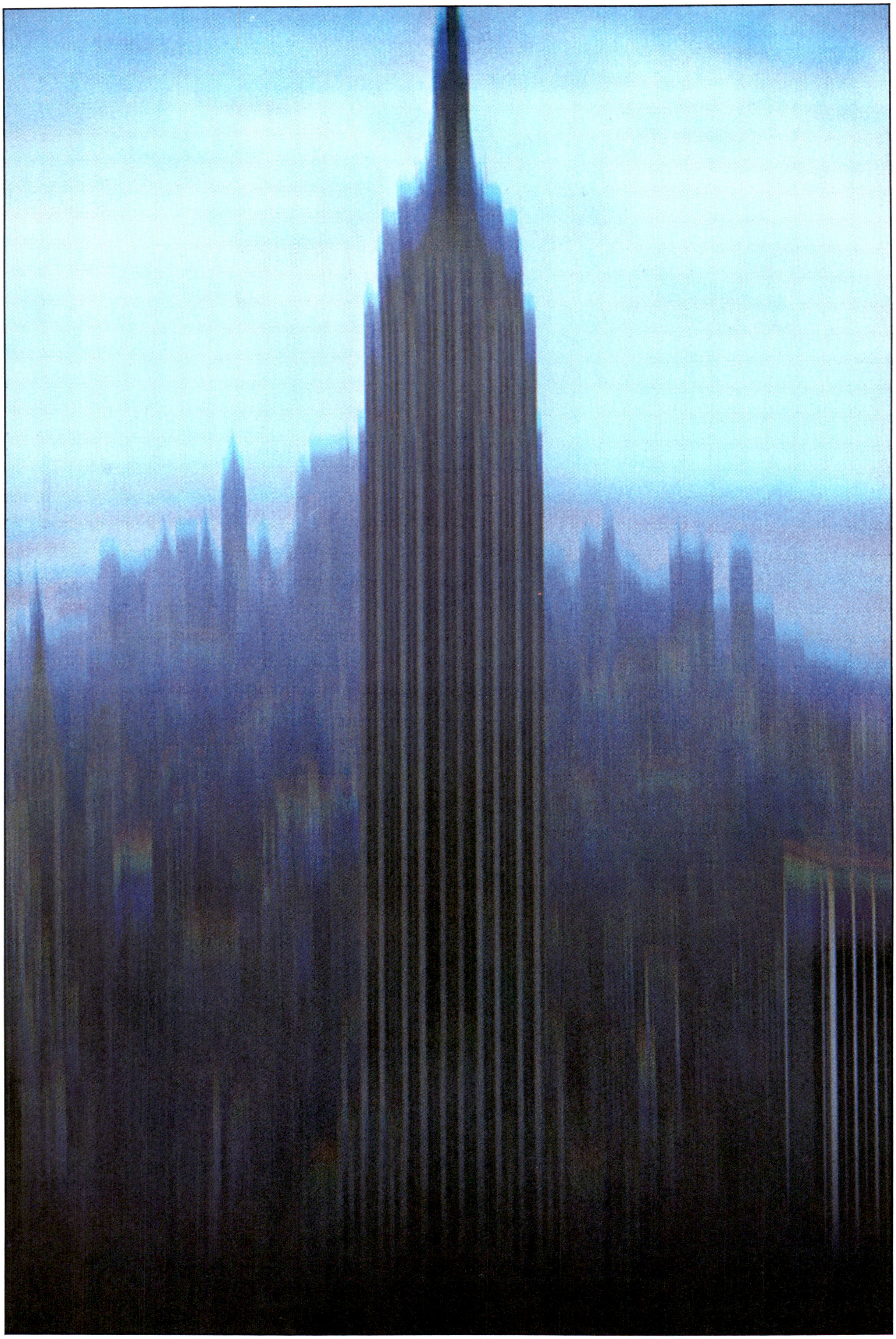

SEE, THE DAWN SHIVERS ROUND THE BLUE GILT-DIALLED TOWERS, AND THE RAIN
STREAMS DOWN EACH DIAMONDED PANE AND BLURS WITH TEARS THE WANNISH DAY.
OSCAR WILDE

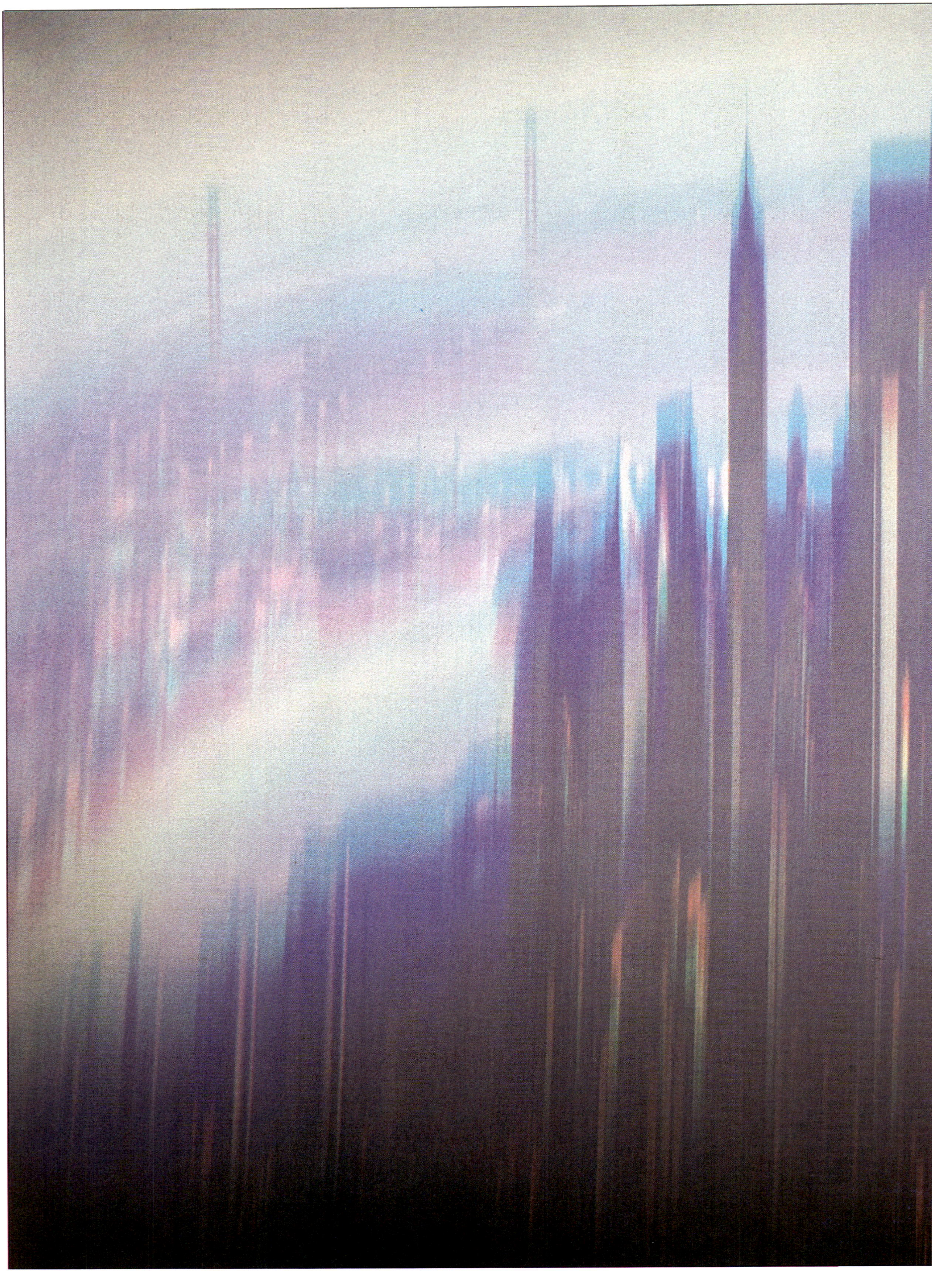

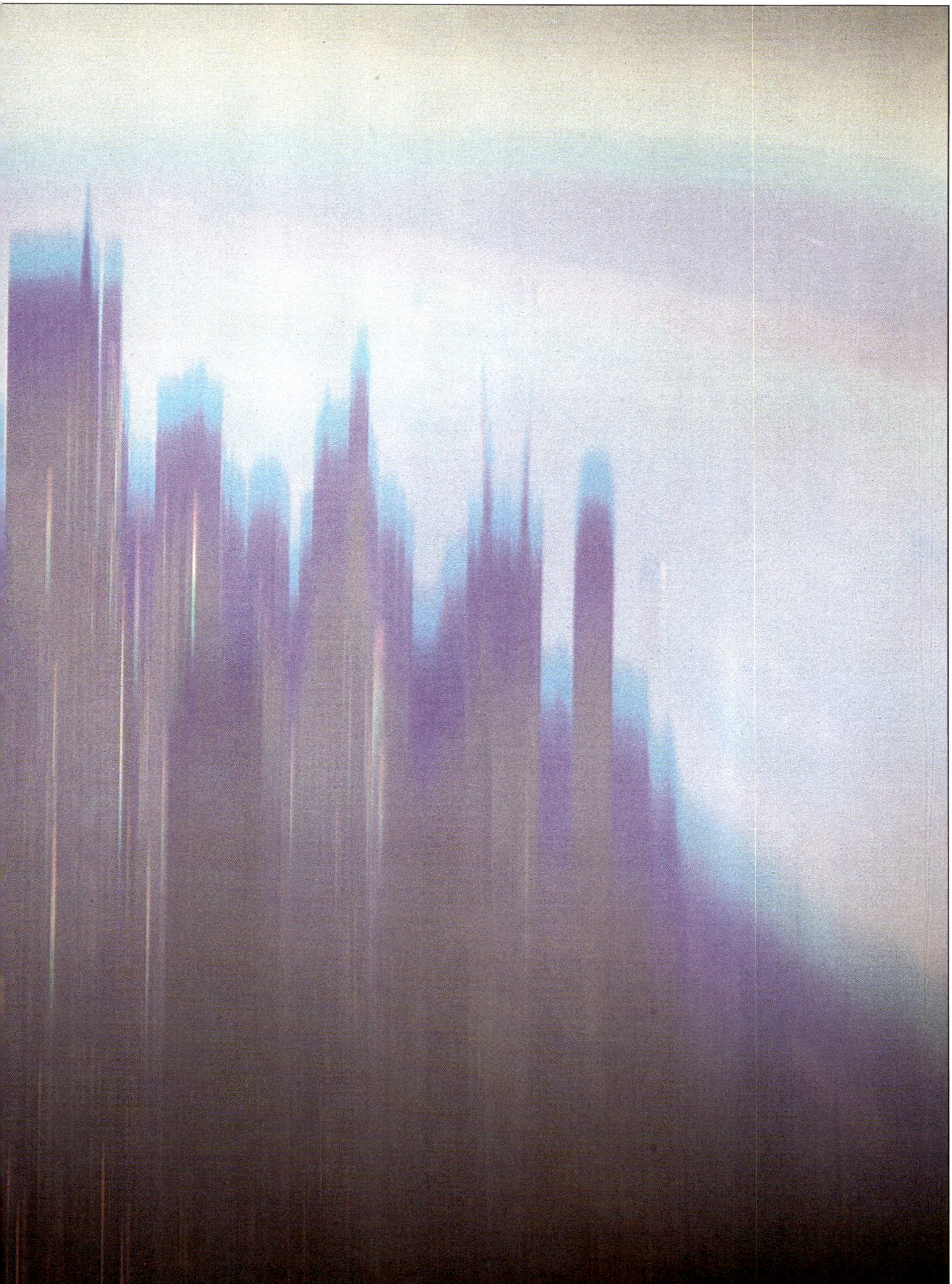

IN THE SUN TOGETHER ON THE RIVERSIDE STRAND
THE WATER TURNING TO MISTS AND MY THOUGHTS TO DREAMS.
VICTOR HUGO

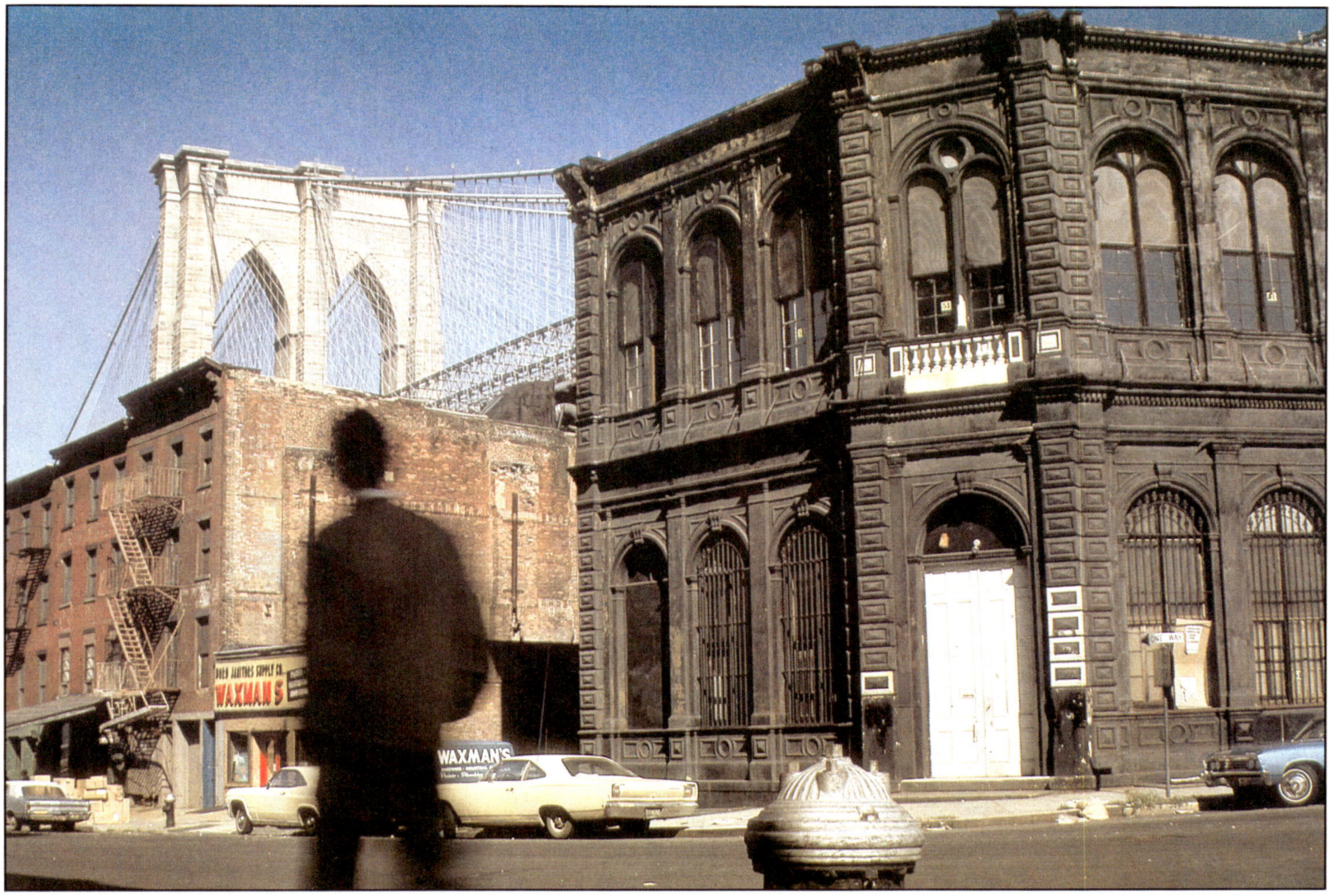
WAXMAN'S
WAXMAN'S

BANKSIDE
THEATRE
FRONT ST
ONE WAY
SNOW
EMERGENCY
STREET
LUNCH
FRONT ST
BANKSIDE BOON DOCK
ONE WAY
Schlitz
Schlitz

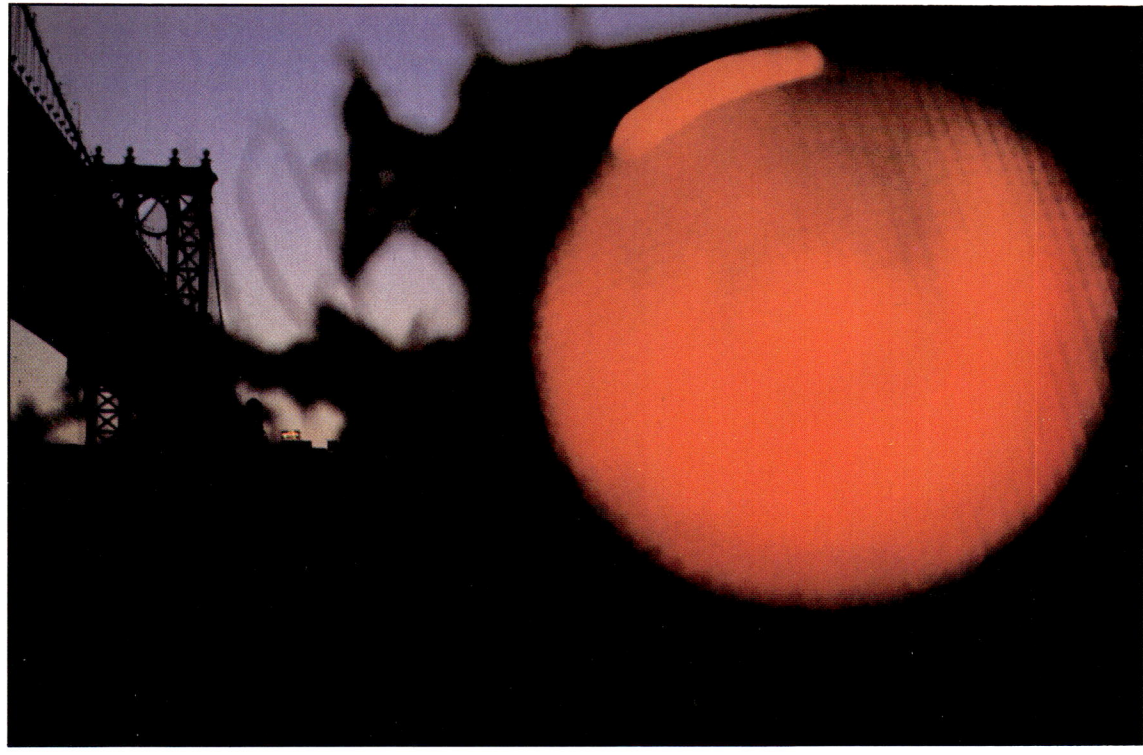

EVEN SO MY SUN ONE EARLY MORN DID SHINE
WITH ALL-TRIUMPHANT SPLENDOUR.
SHAKESPEARE

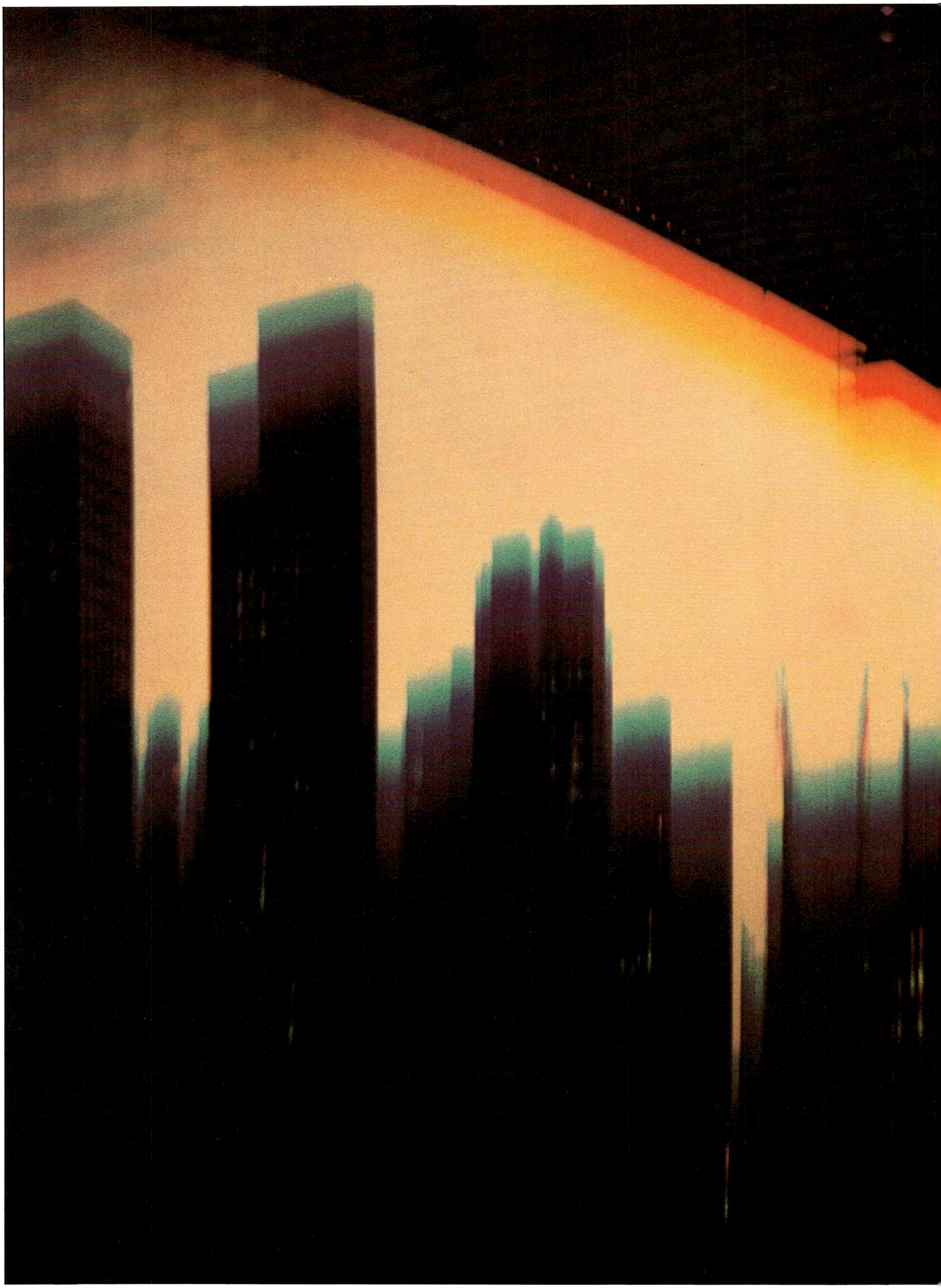

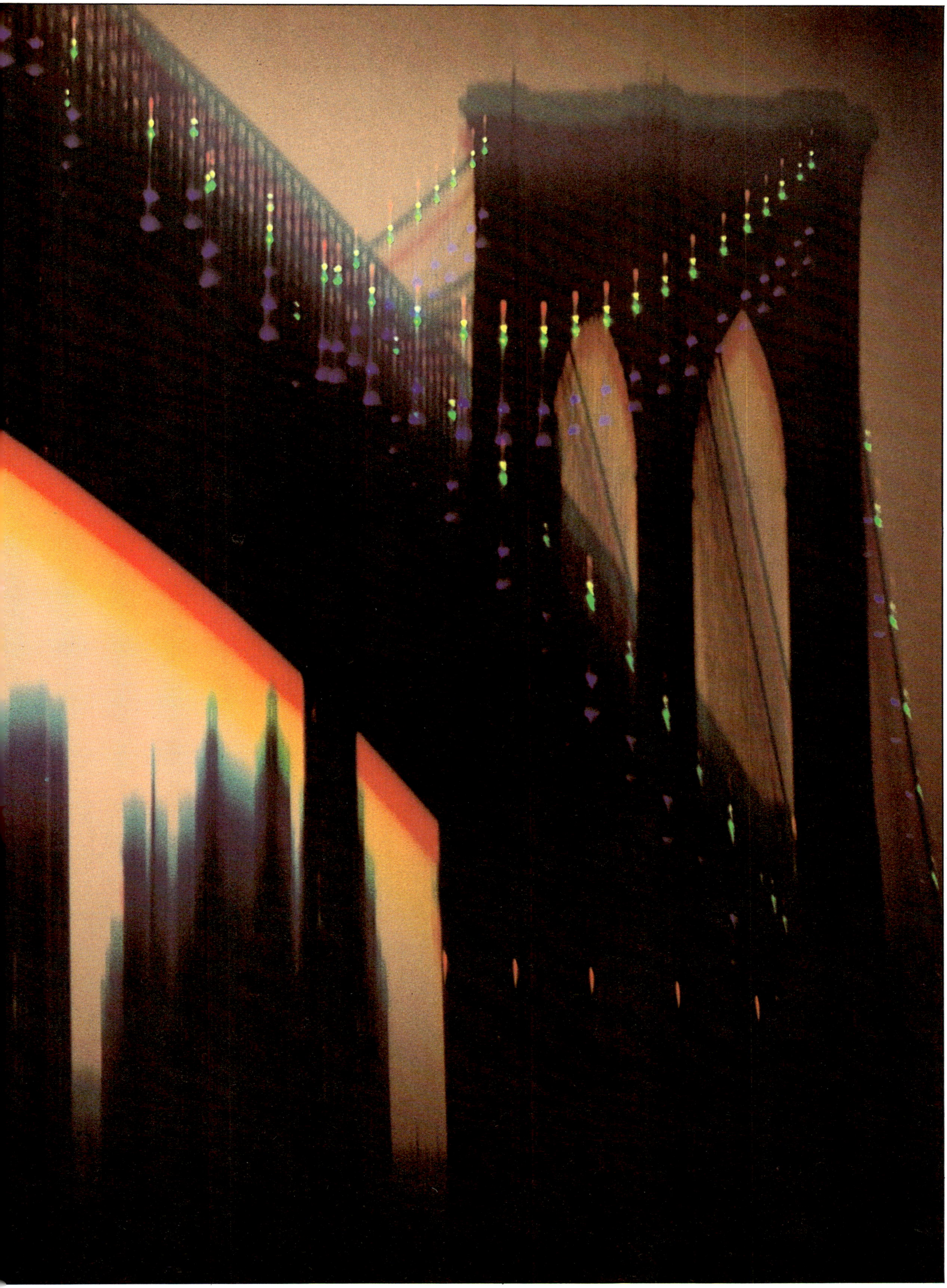

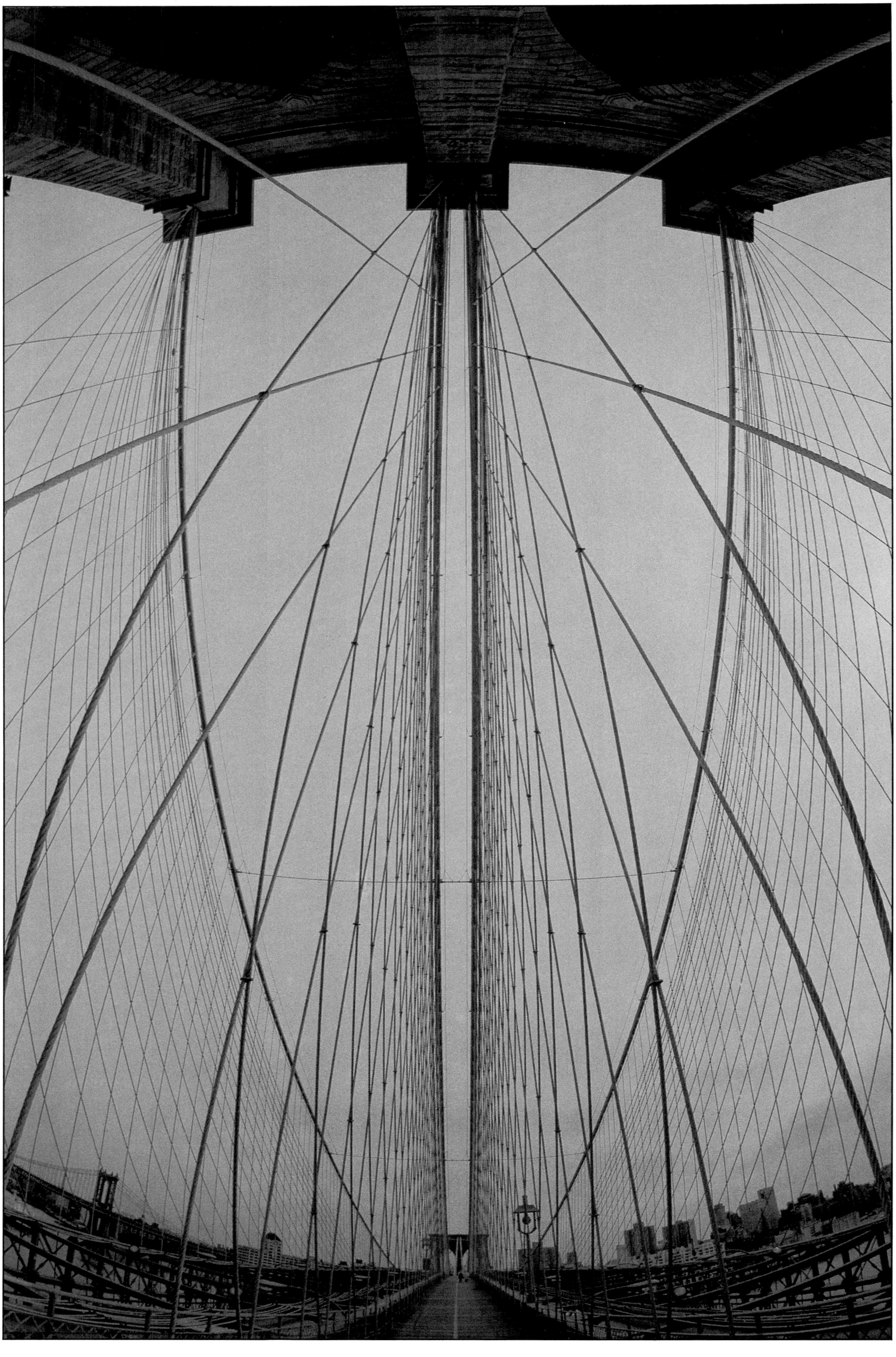

THE LOW SETTING SUNS
PAINT THE CITY'S WHOLE EXPANSE,
IN HYACINTH, GOLD.
BAUDELAIRE

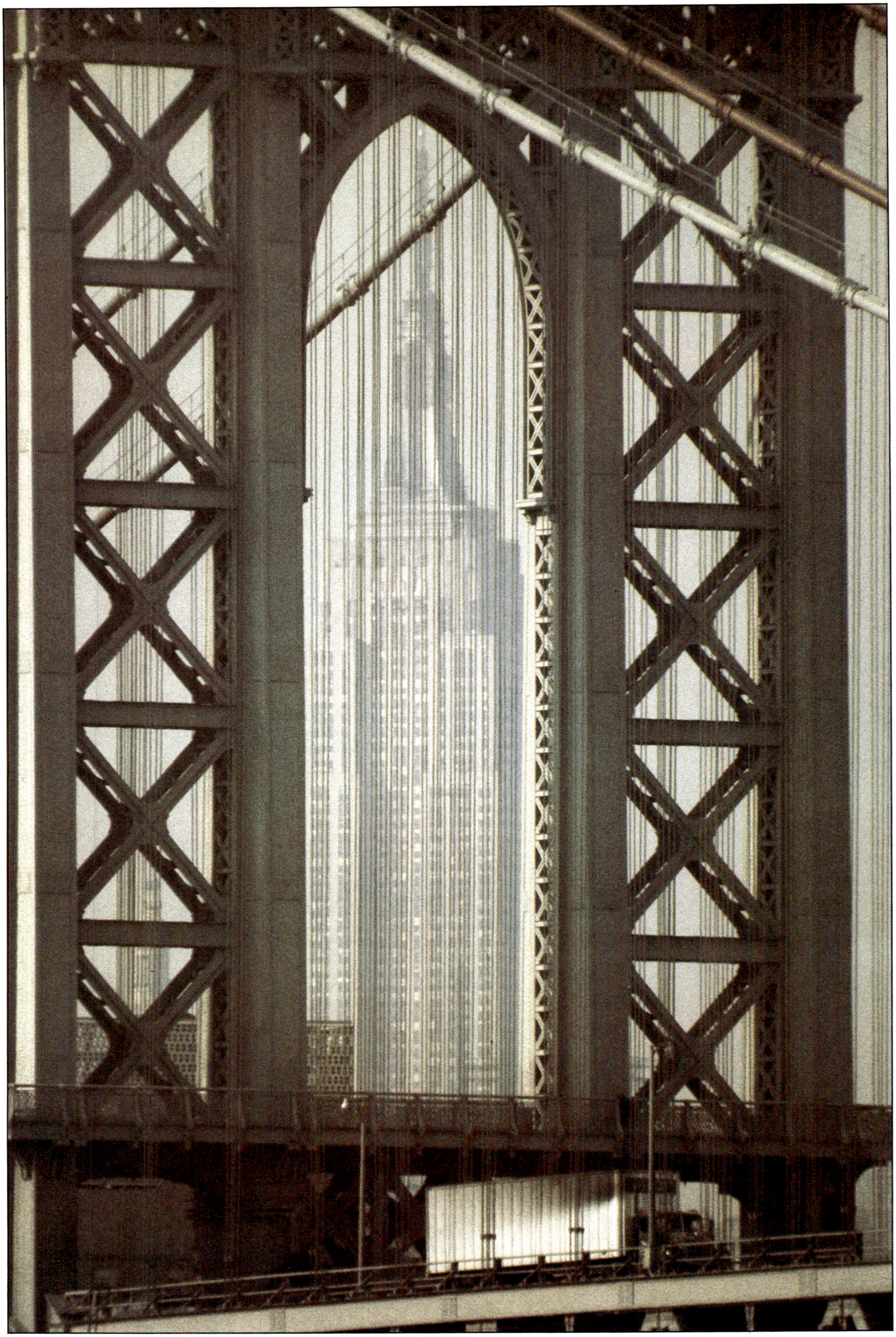

BOUNDLESS AS NIGHT ITSELF AND AS THE LIGHT
SOUNDS, FRAGANCES AND COLOURS CORRESPOND.
BAUDELAIRE

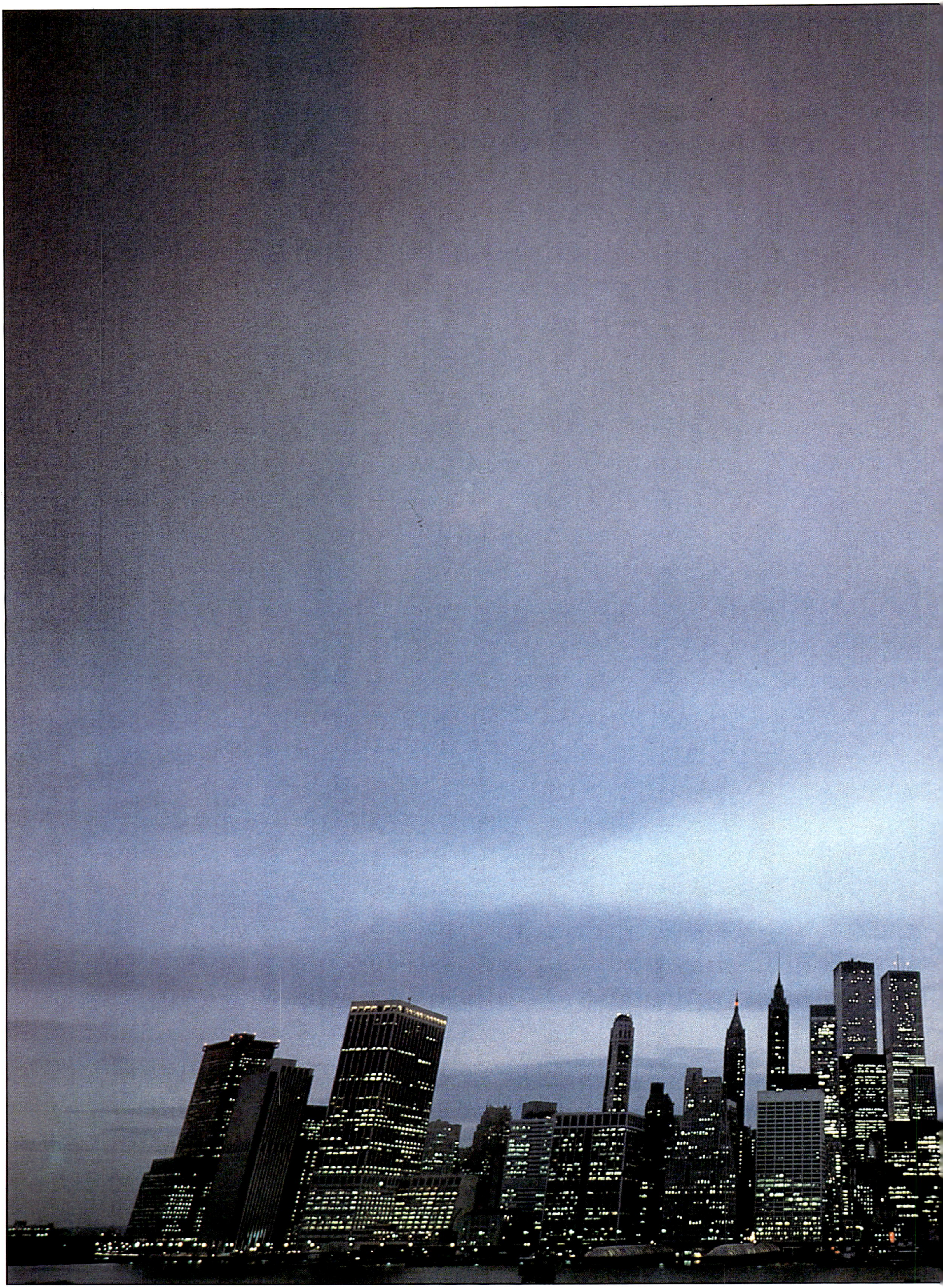

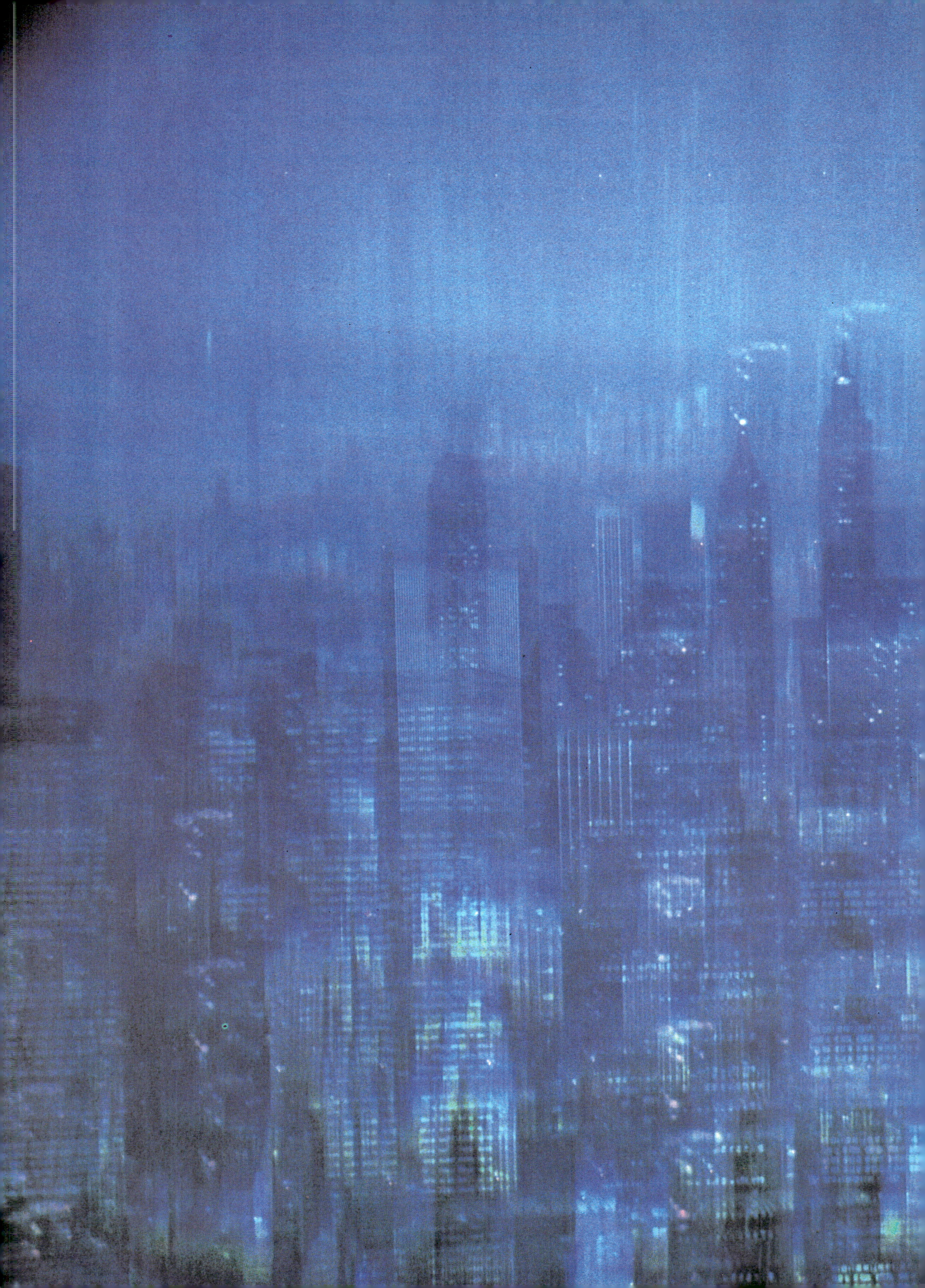

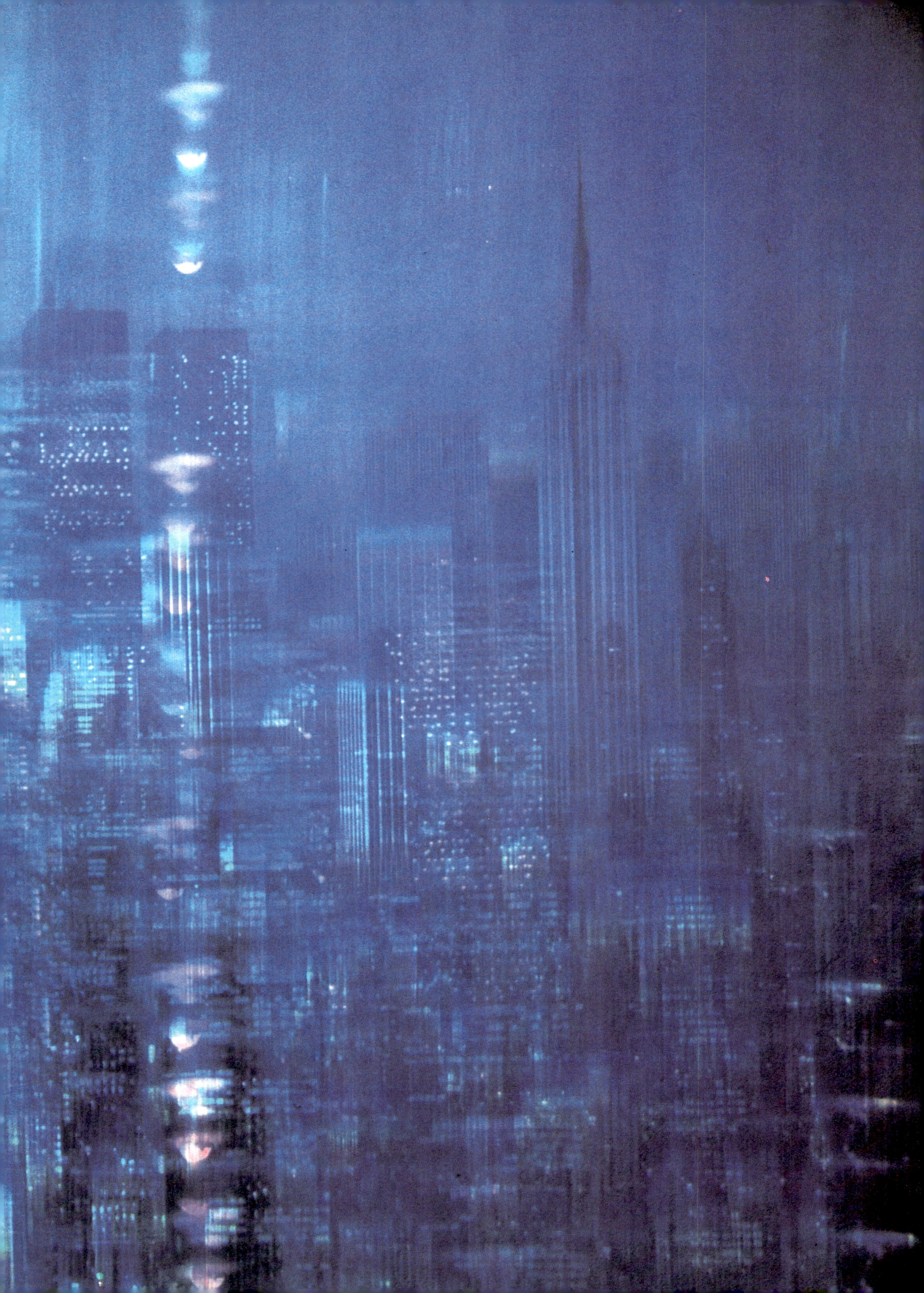

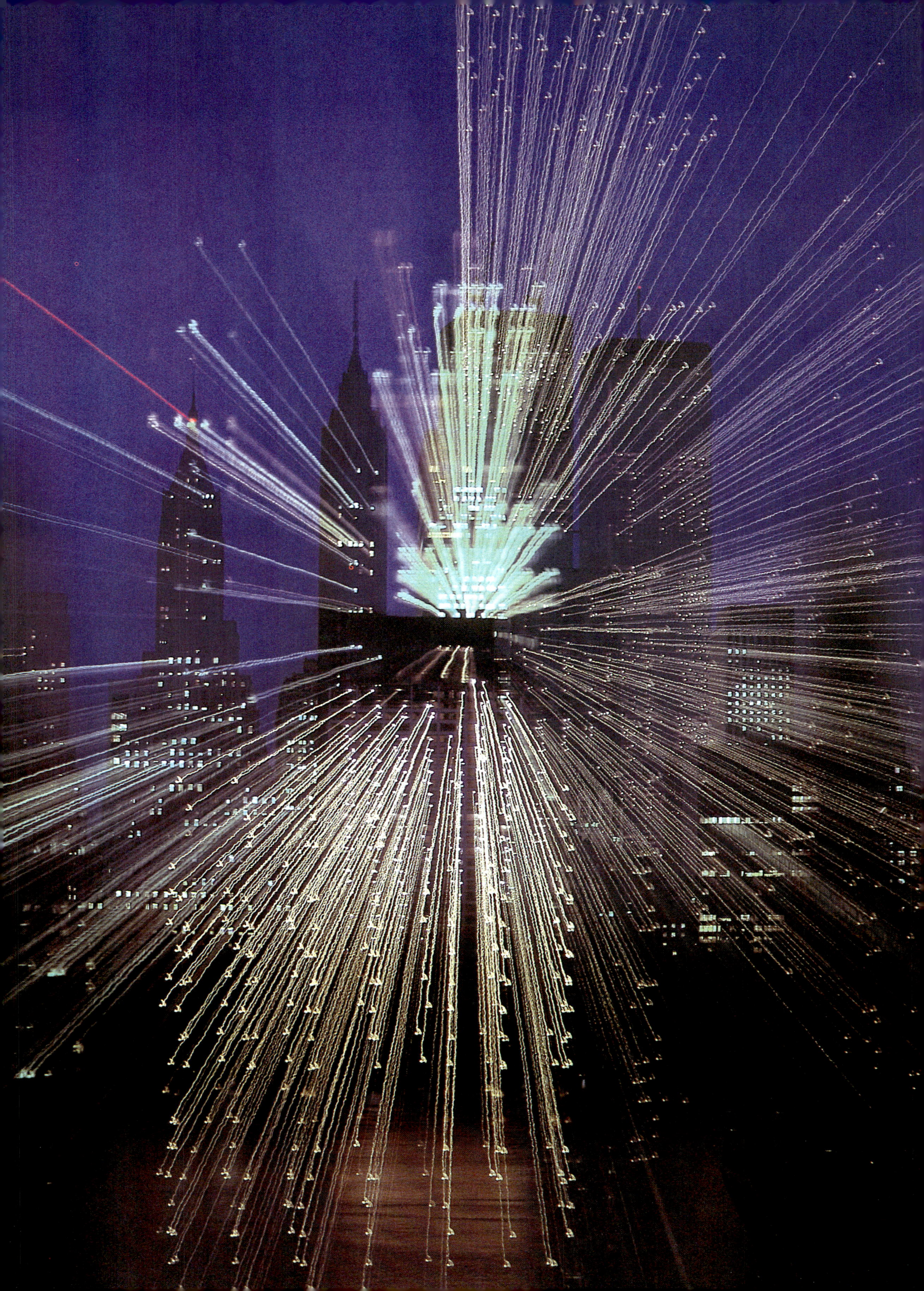

STARS, HIDE YOUR FIRES!
LET NOT LIGHT SEE MY BLACK
AND DEEP DESIRES!
SHAKESPEARE

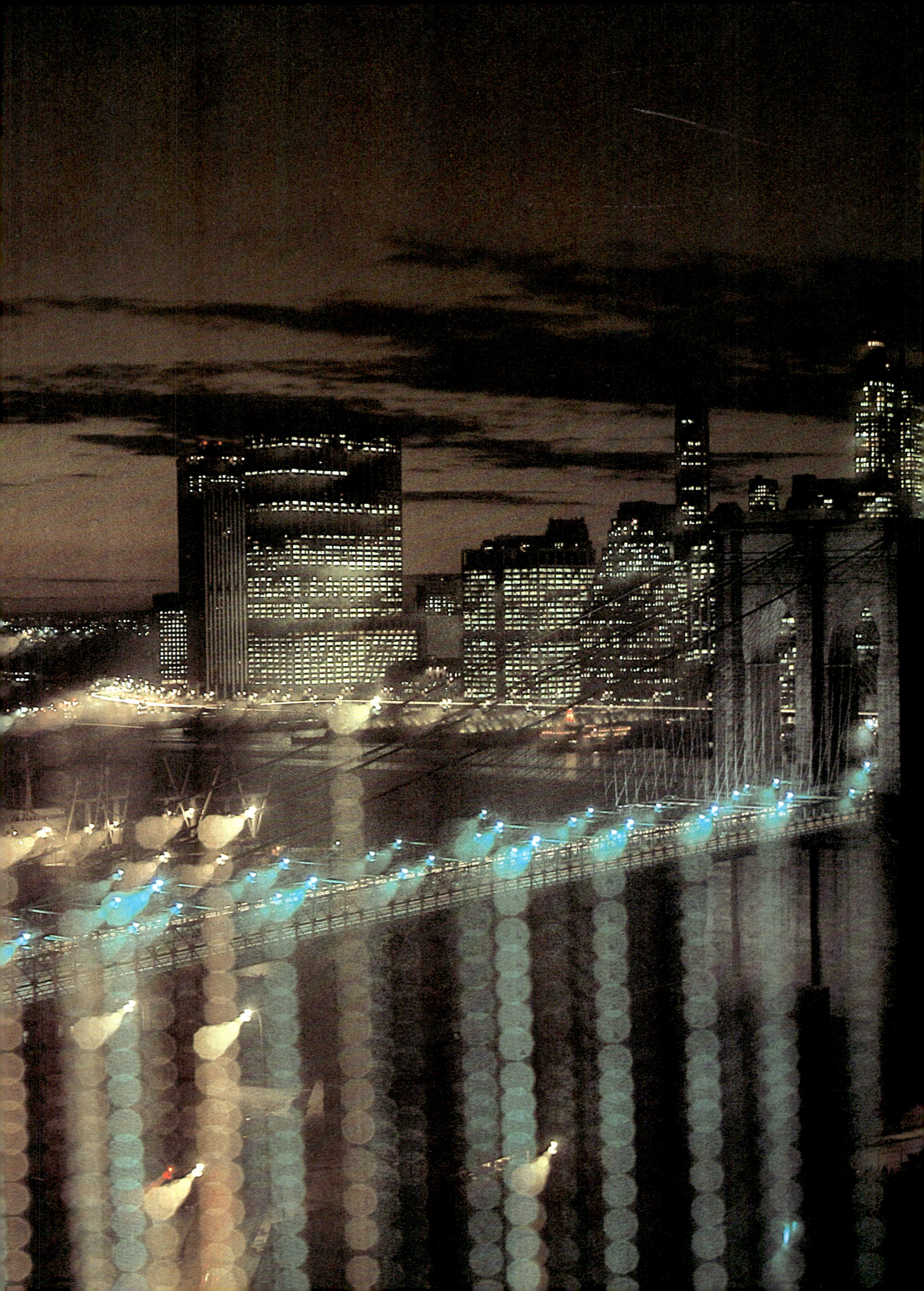

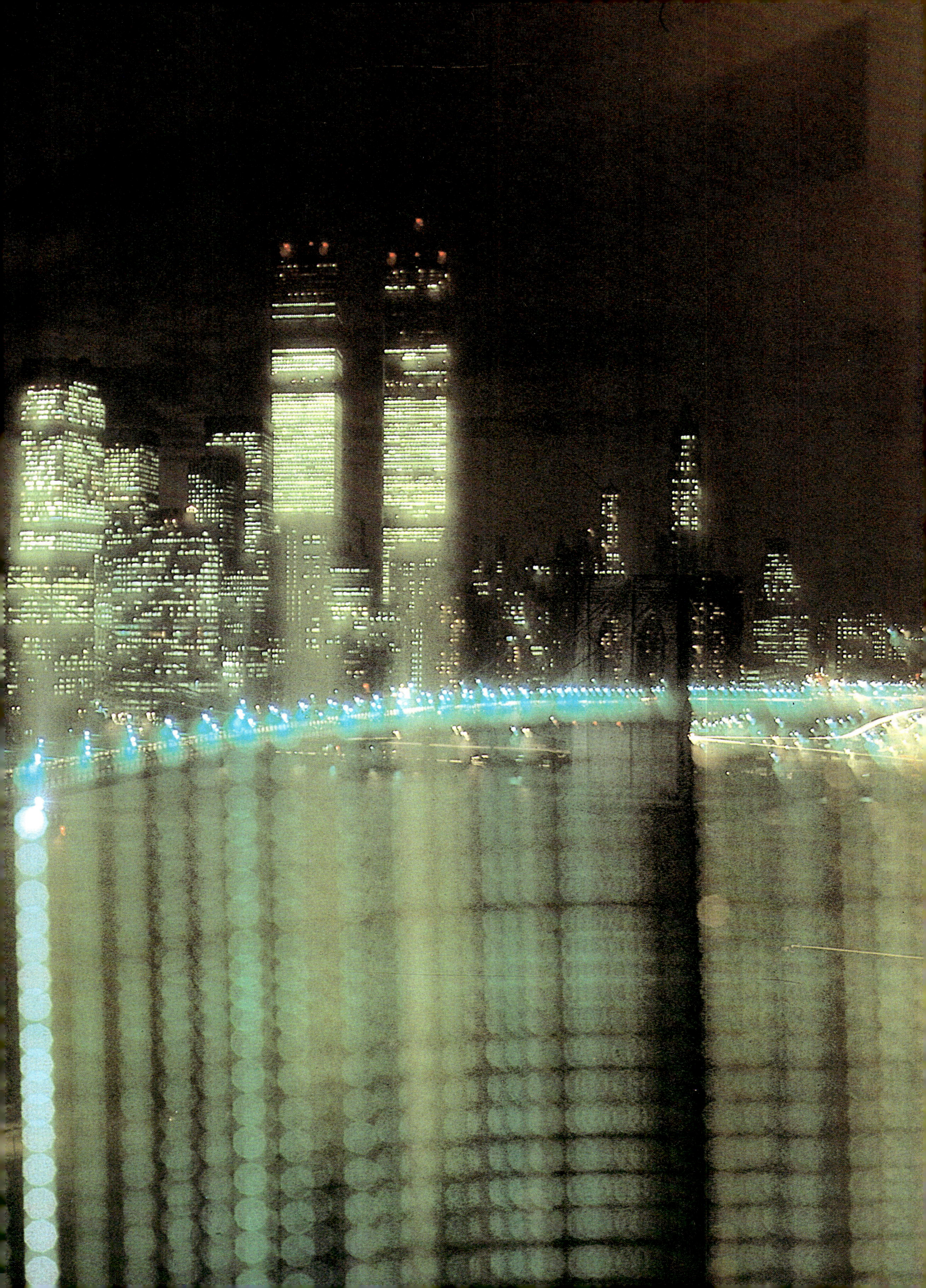

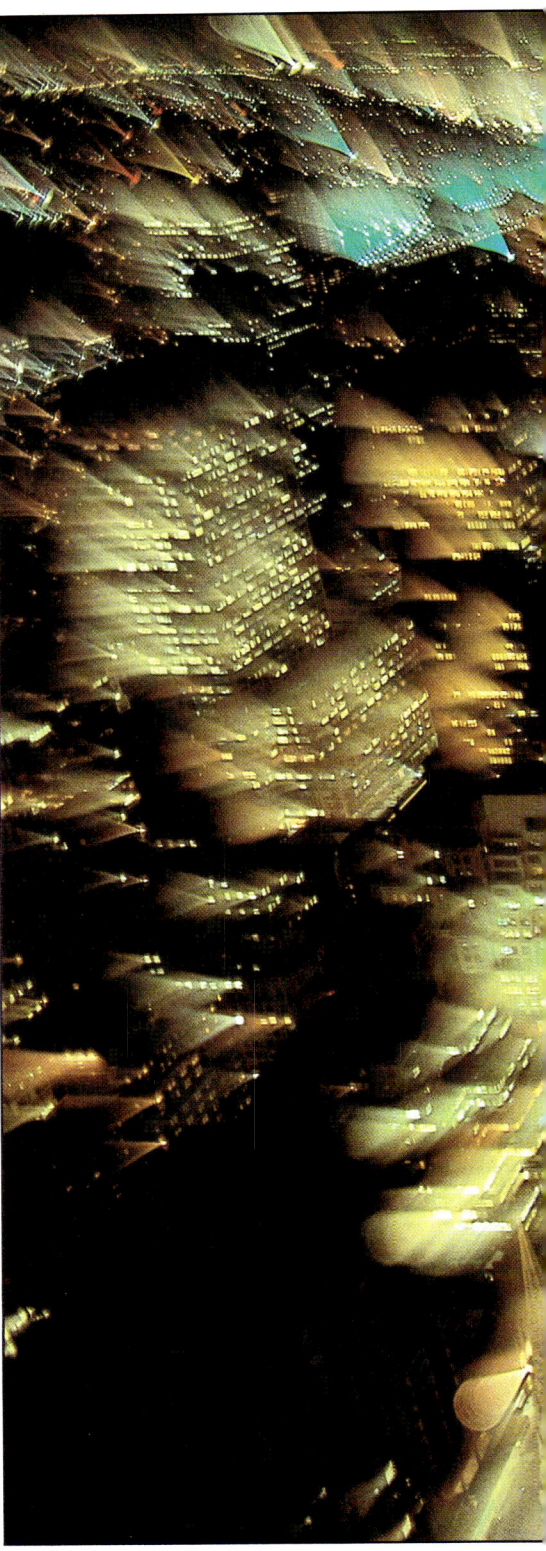

WHEN DUSK THROWS WIDE THE CONCEALING NIGHT,
THEN FLASHES FORTH EACH STAR IN BURNING TWINKLE BRIGHT.
VICTOR HUGO

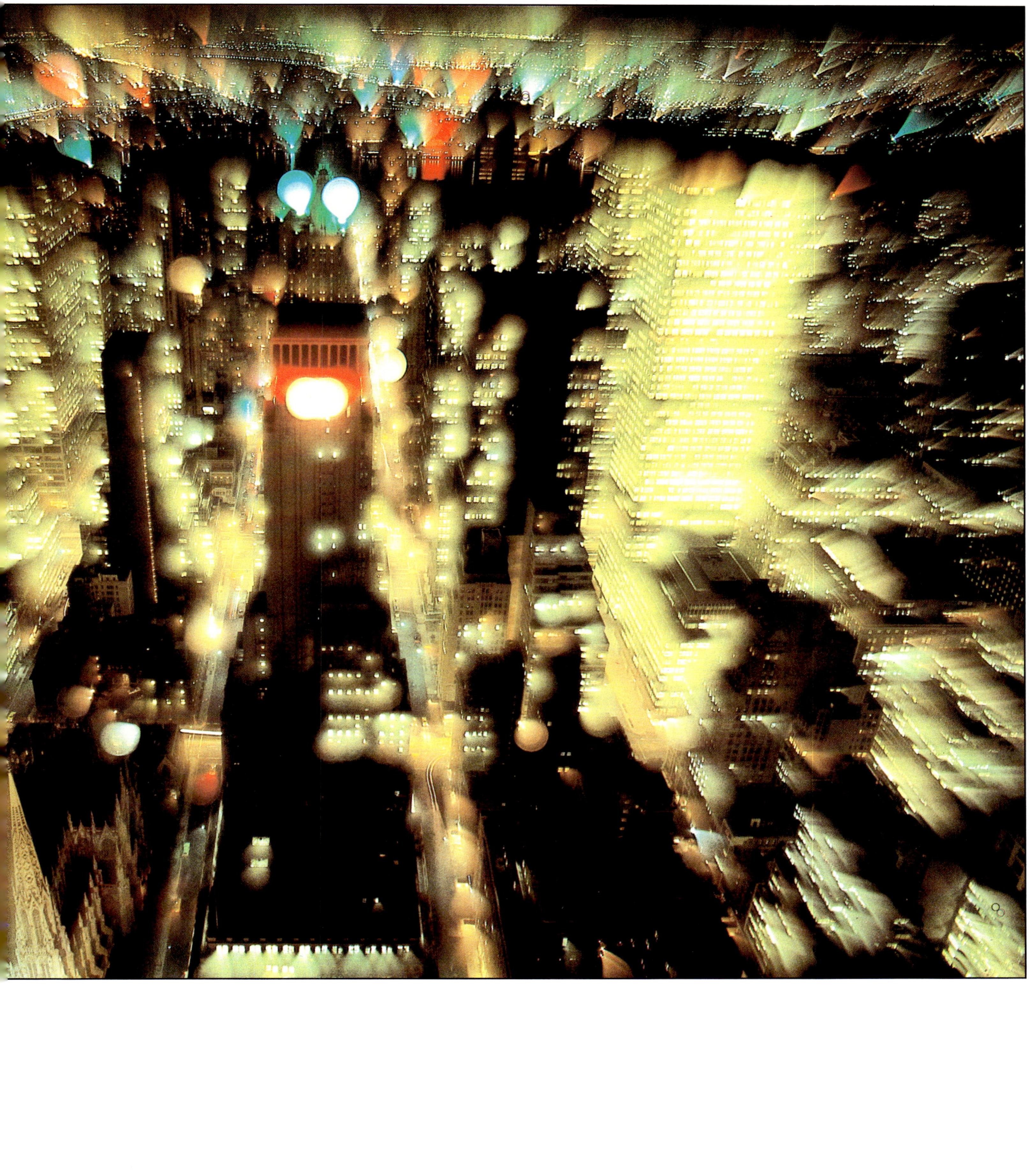

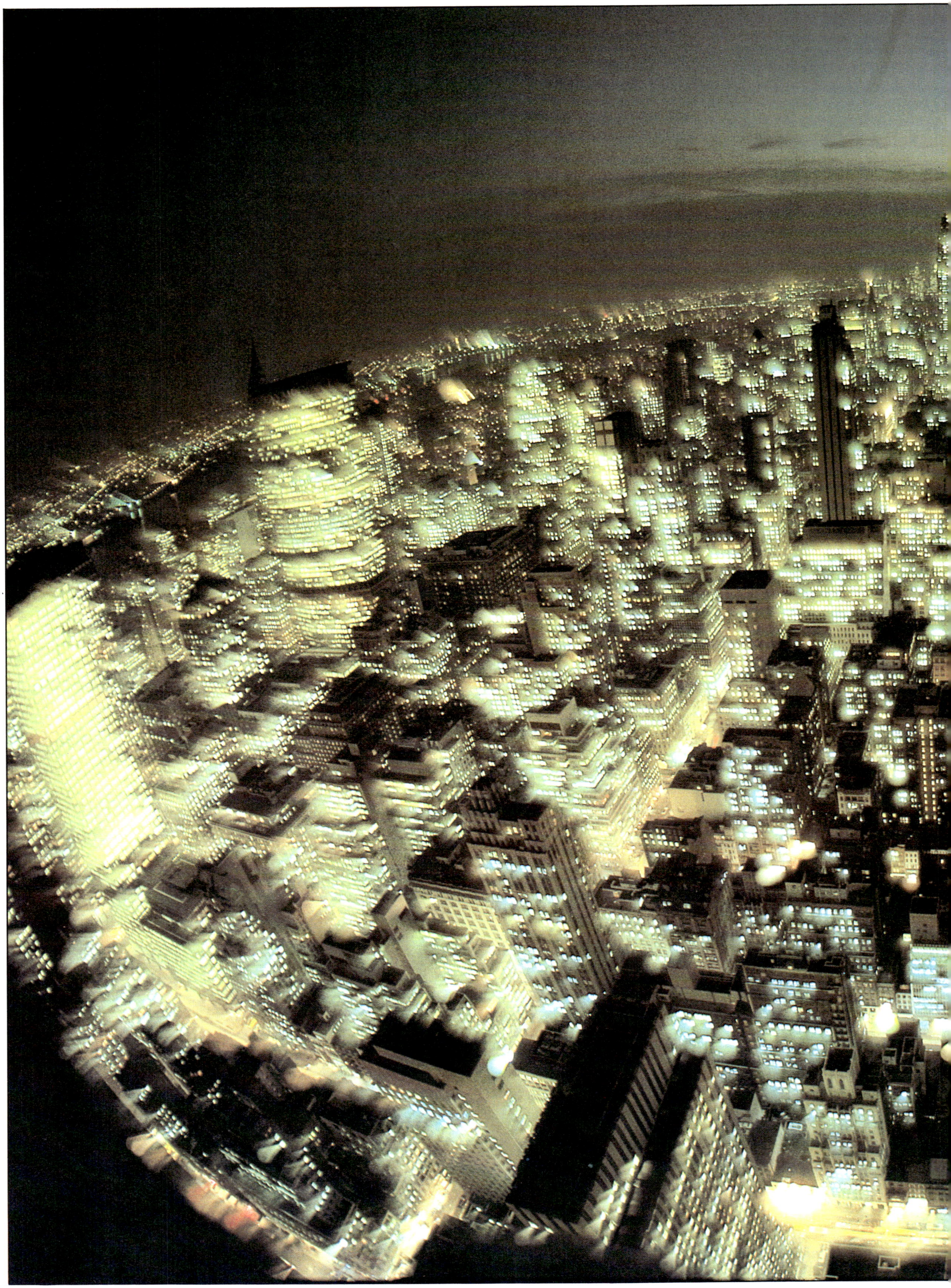

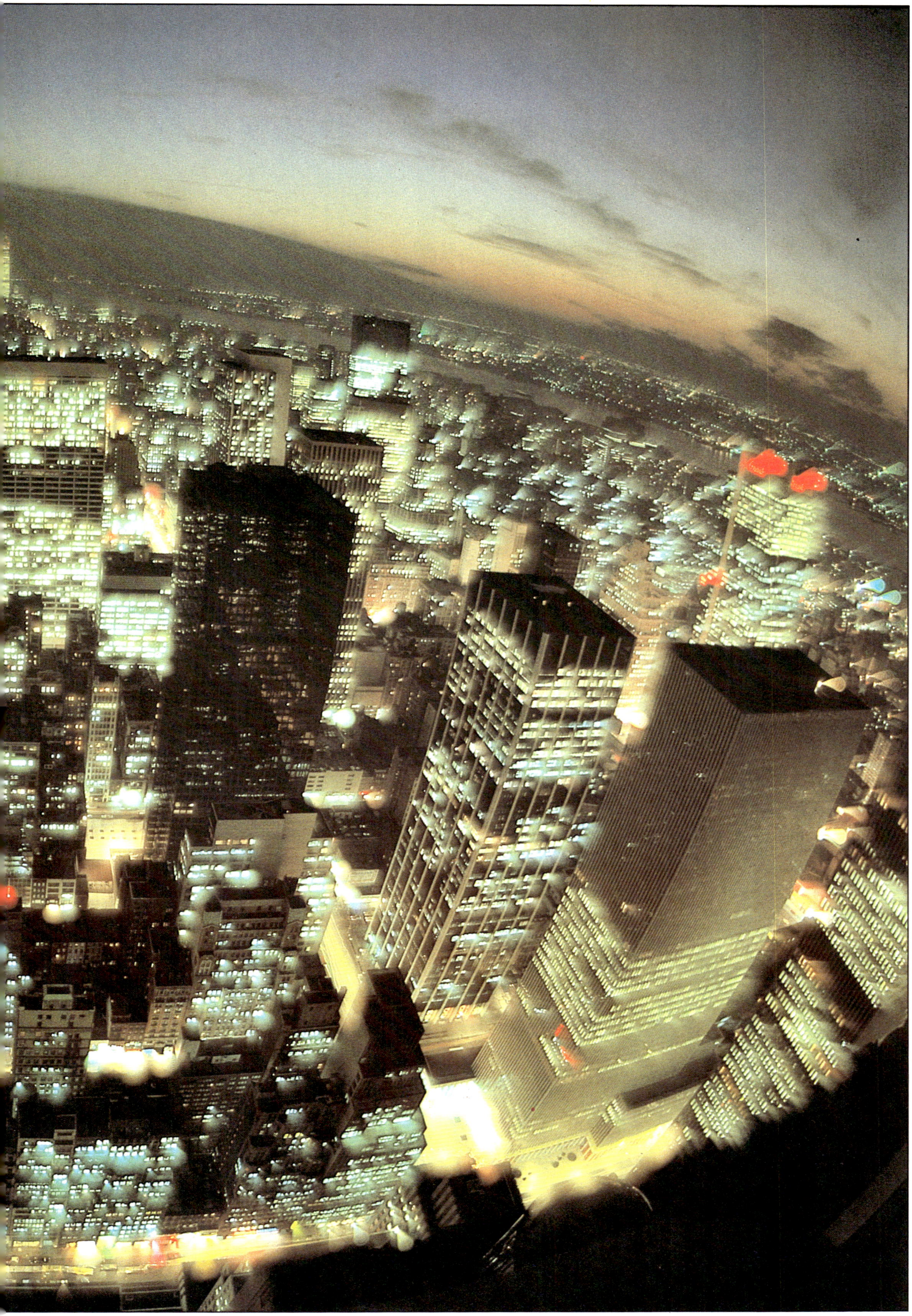

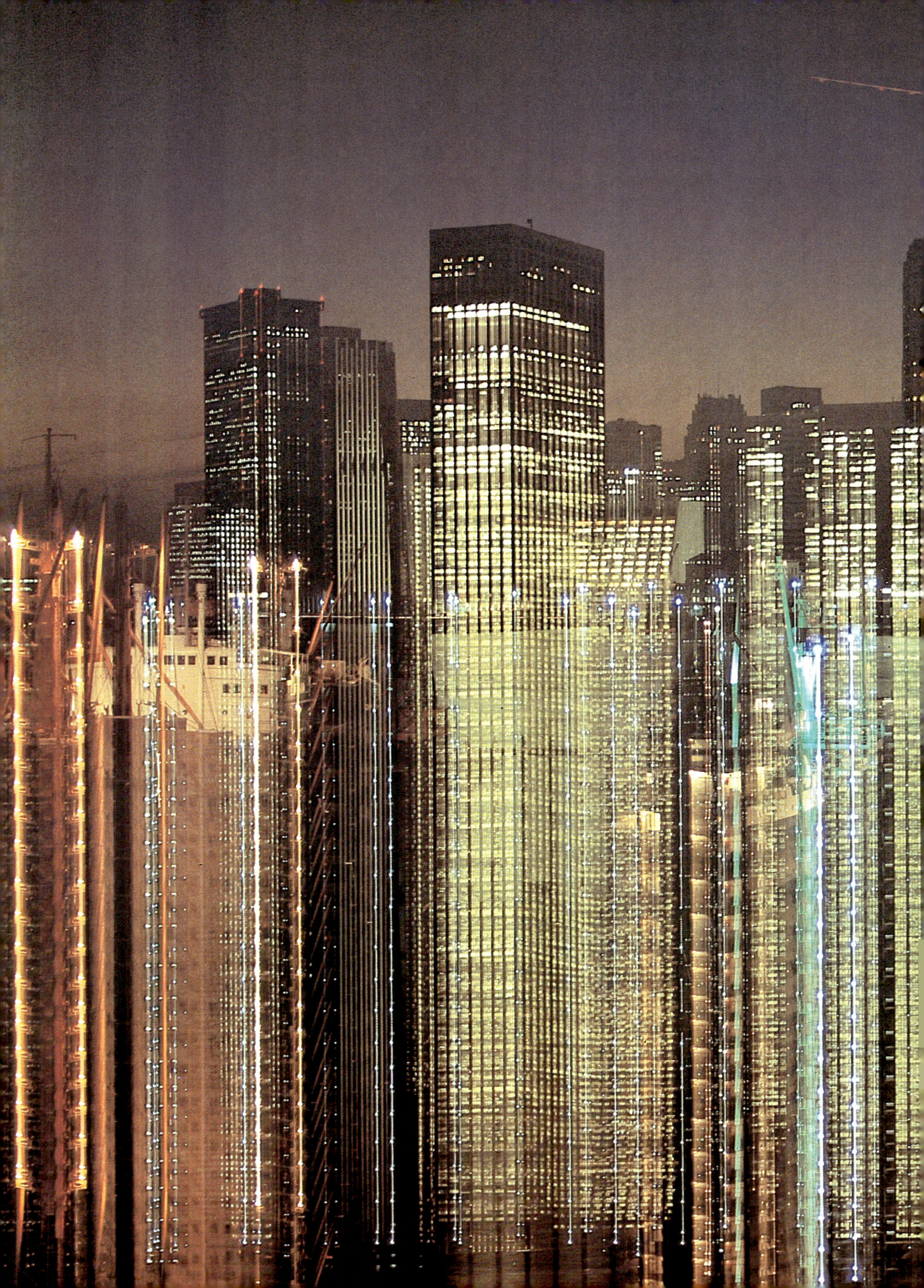

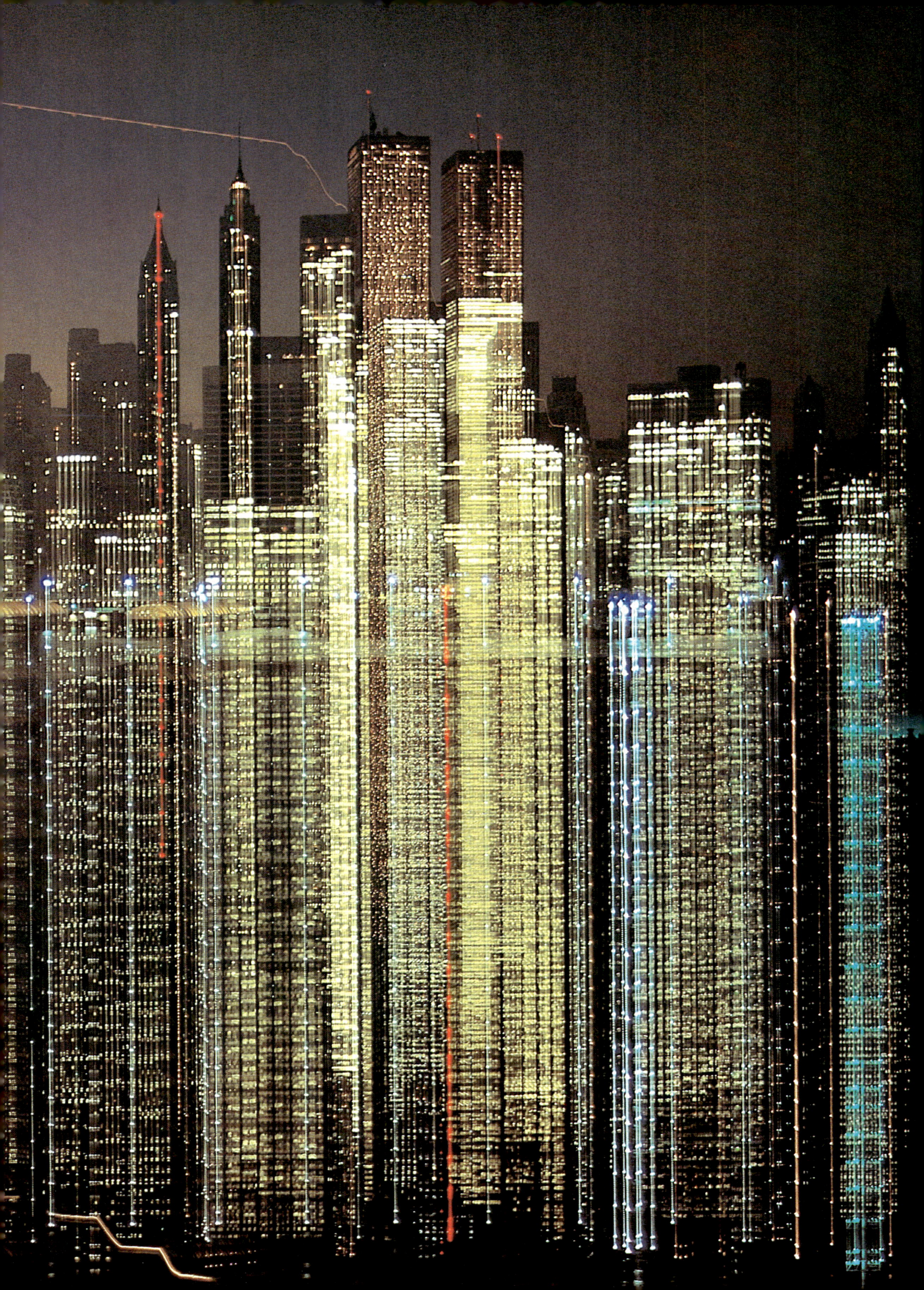

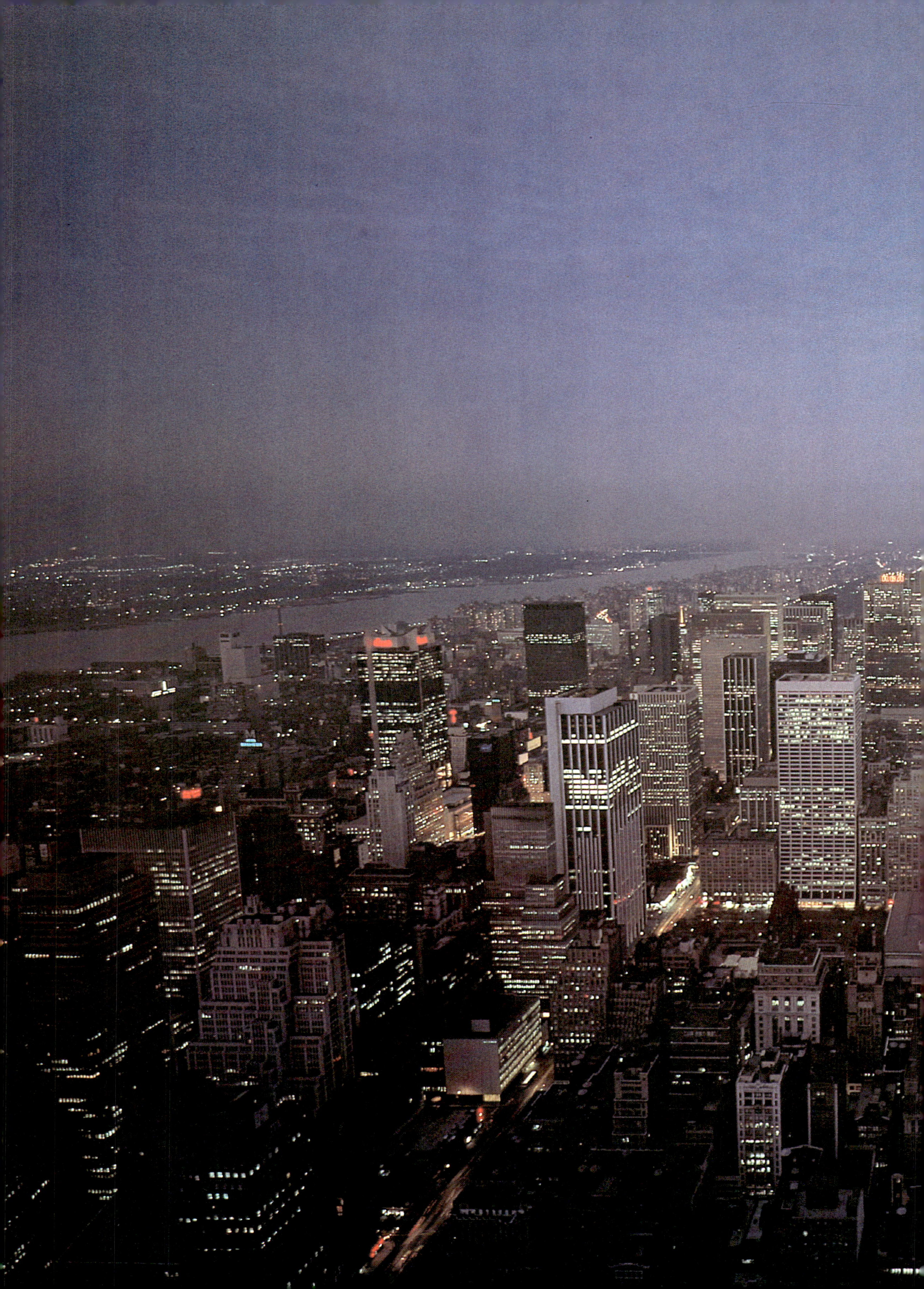

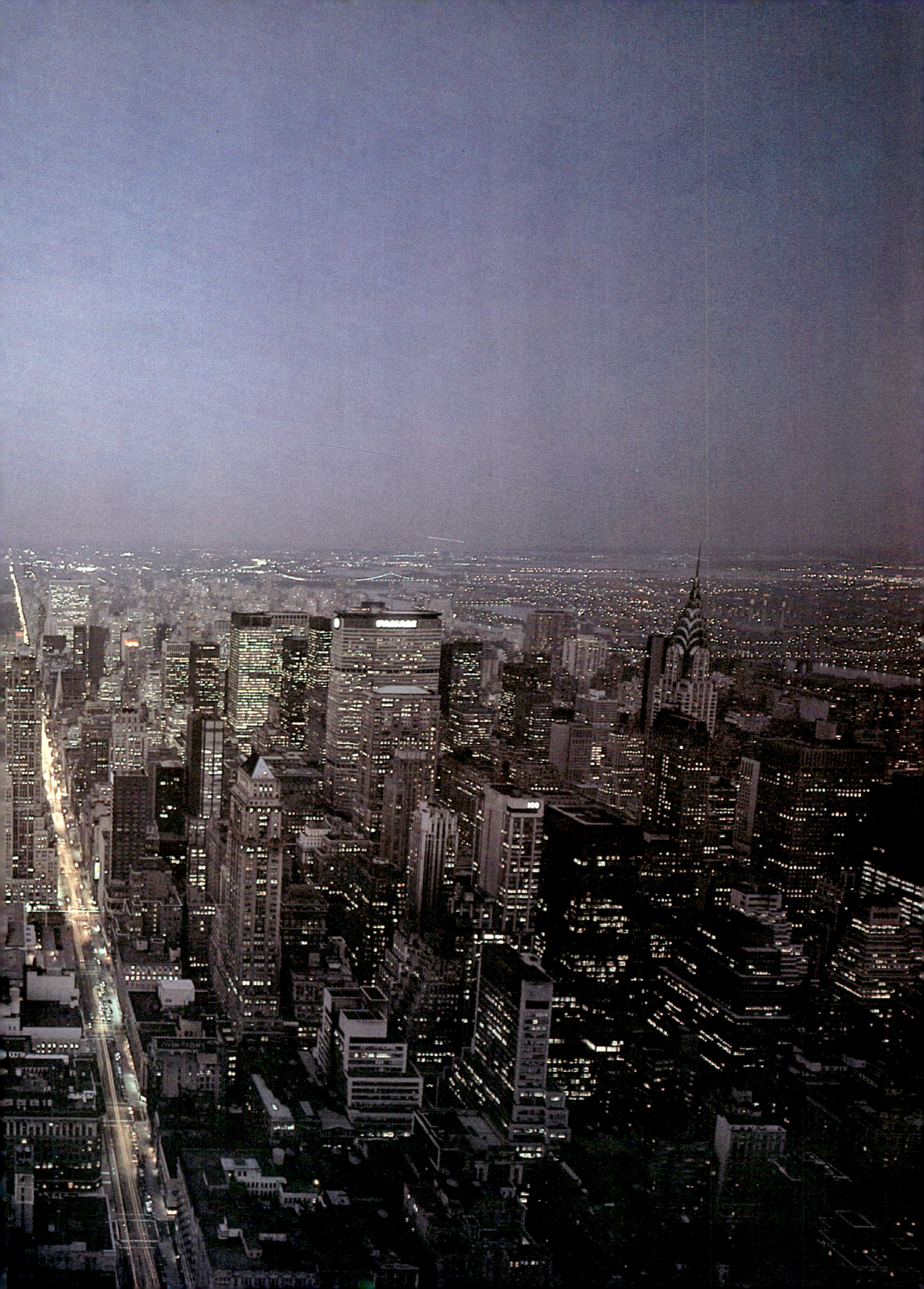

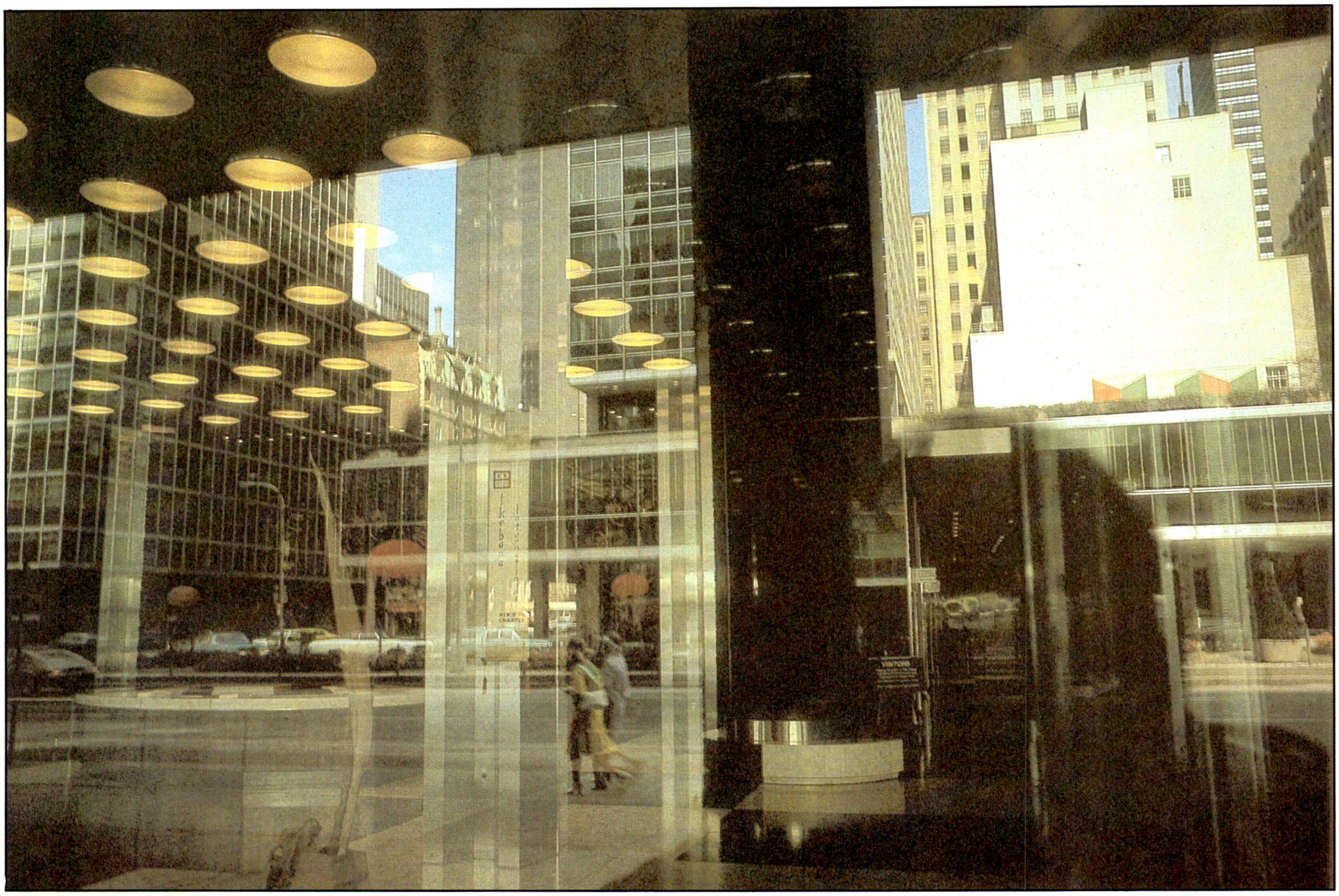

SWIFT AS A SHADOW, SHORT AS ANY DREAM
BRIEF AS THE LIGHTNING IN THE NIGHT.
SHAKESPEARE

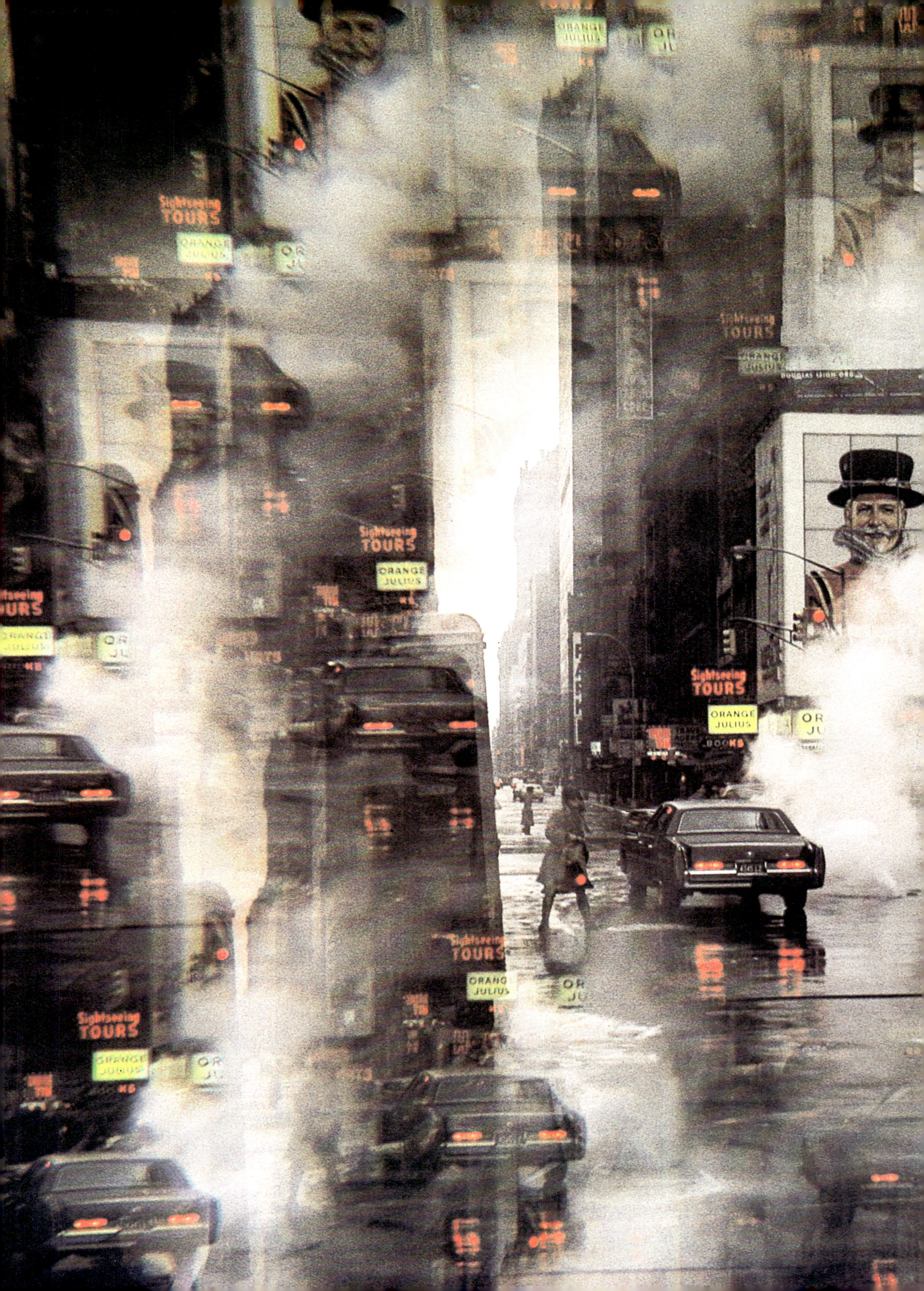
Sightseeing
TOURS
ORANGE
JULIUS

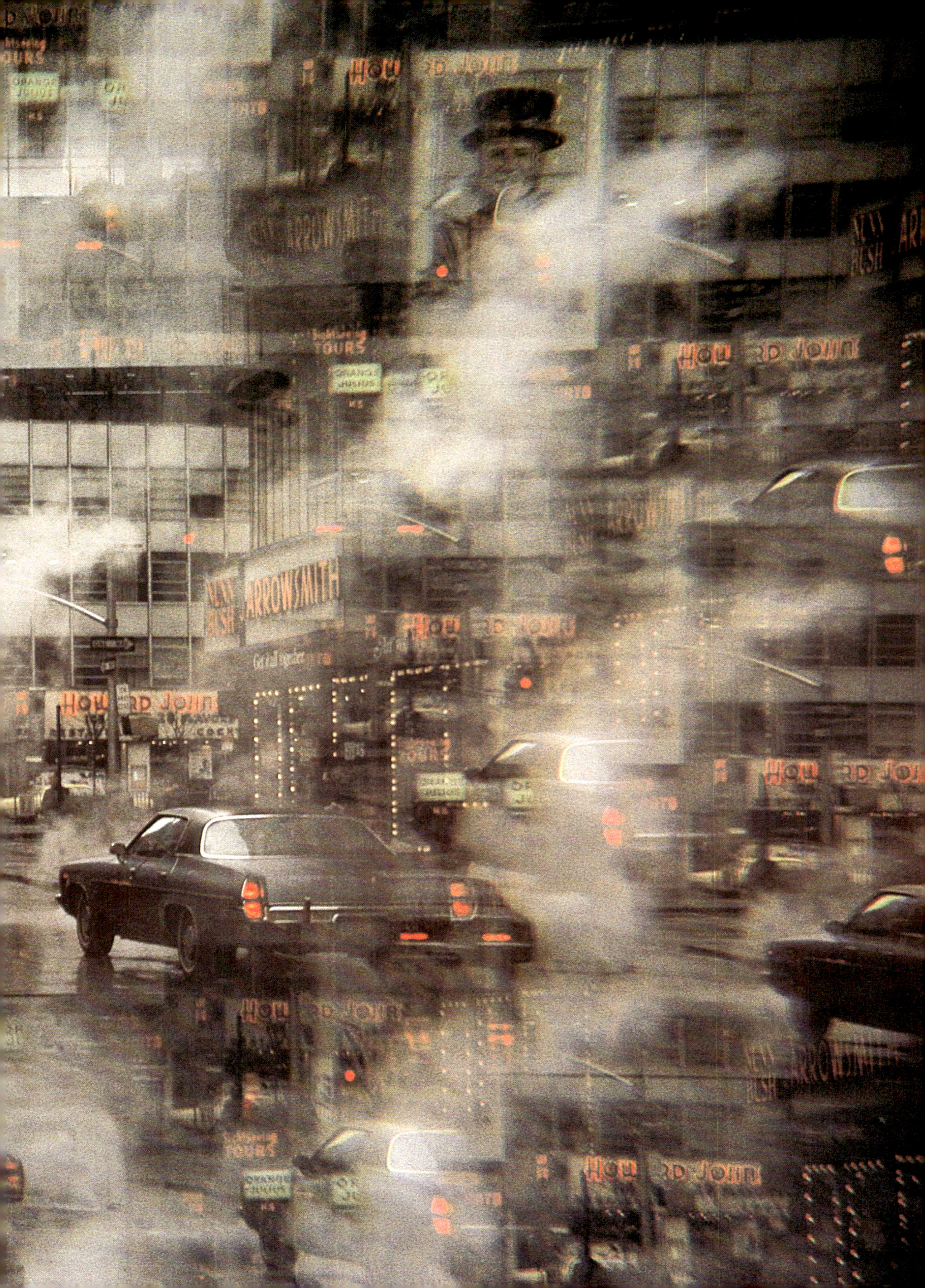
ARROWSMITH
TOURS

SONY
SONY
SONY
SAY
C.C.
HIRAM WALKER
Coca-Cola
"LET'S SCARE JESSICA TO DEATH"
HAM EGGS

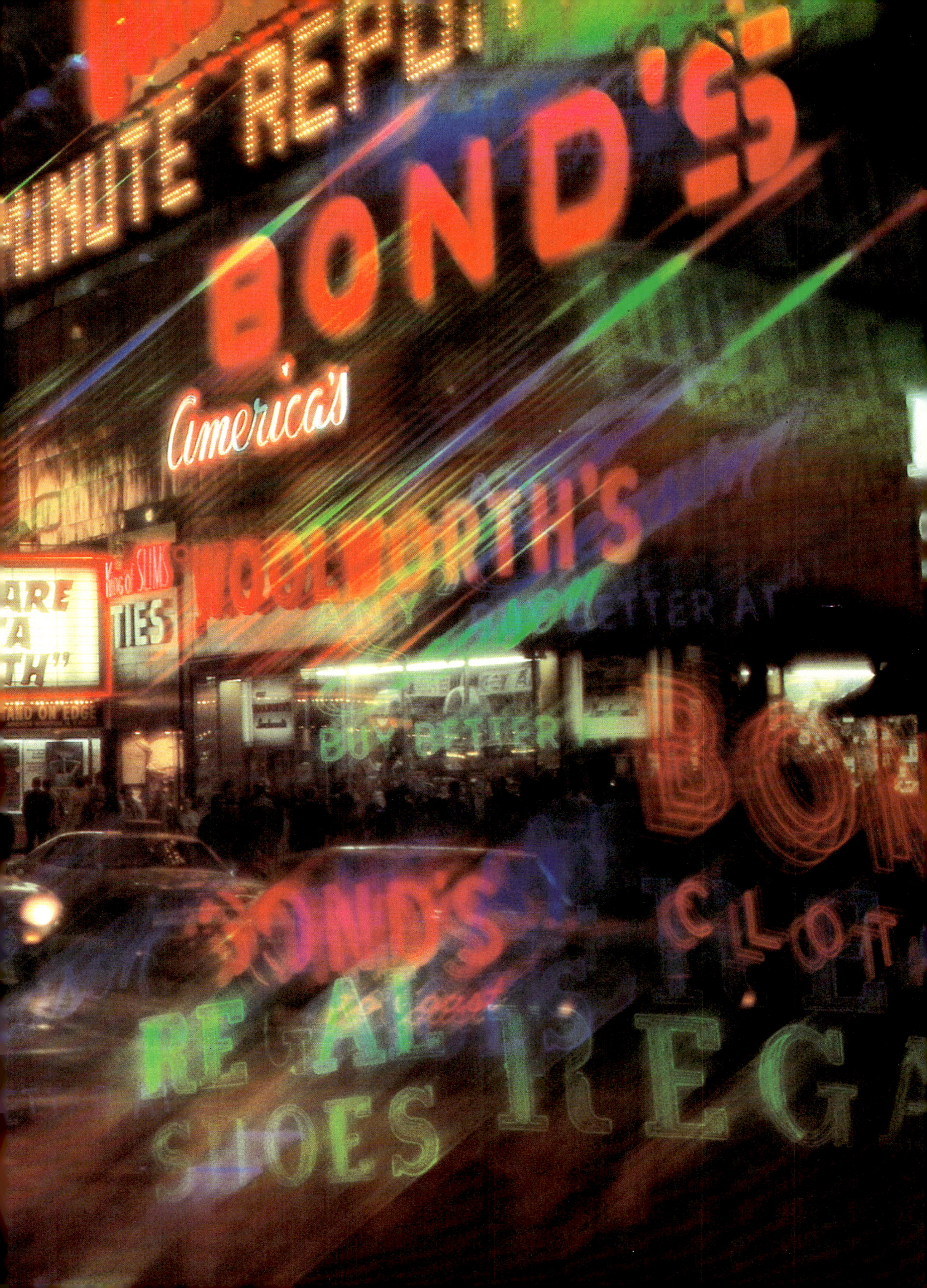
BOND'S
America's
TIES
BUY BETTER
BOND'S
SHOES

HOW I LOVED THOSE GREY DAYS, THOSE PASSERS-BY...
ALFRED DE MUSSET

THE RAIN SLIPPED AWAY FROM THE REFLECTED CHARMS.

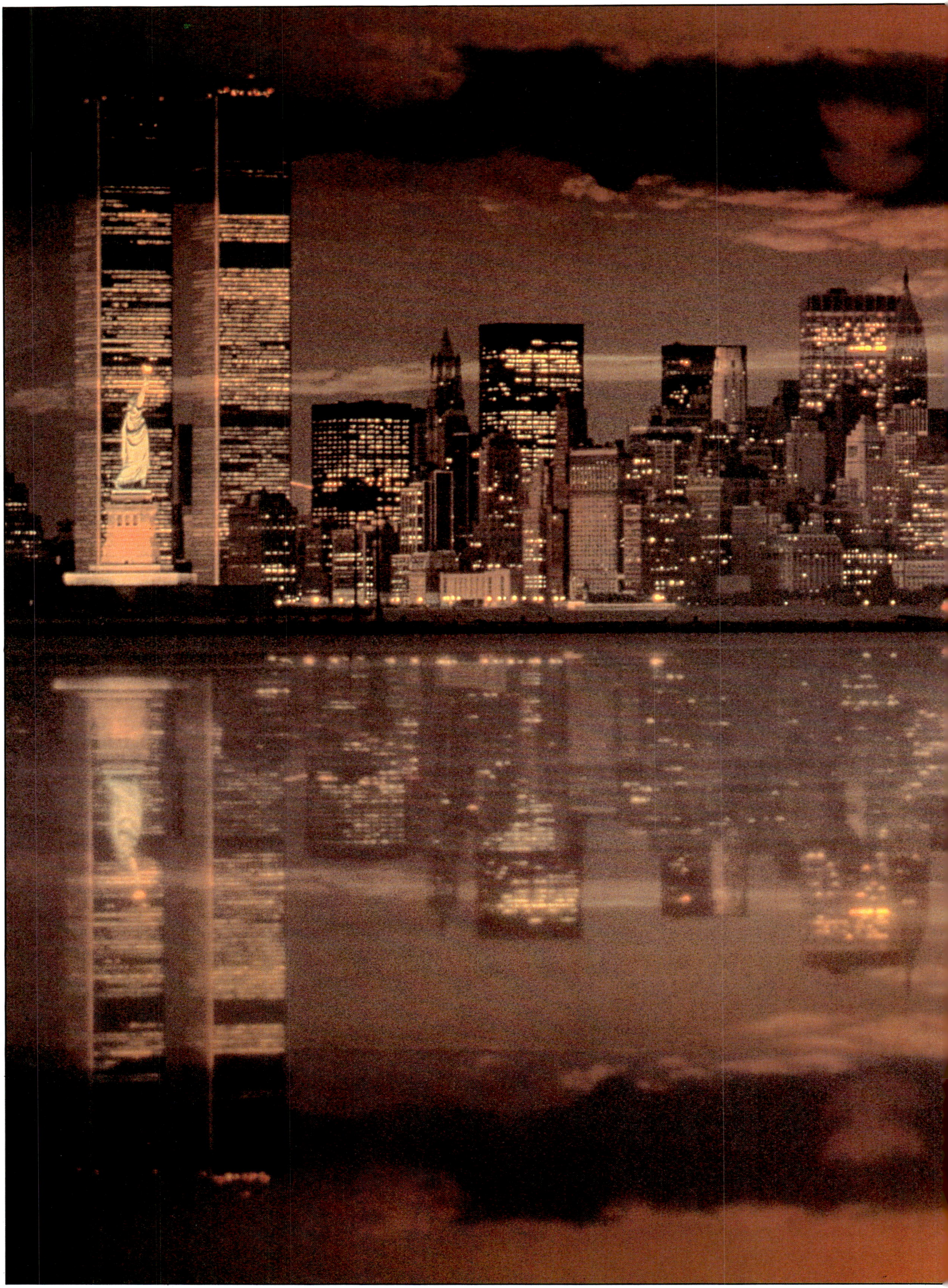

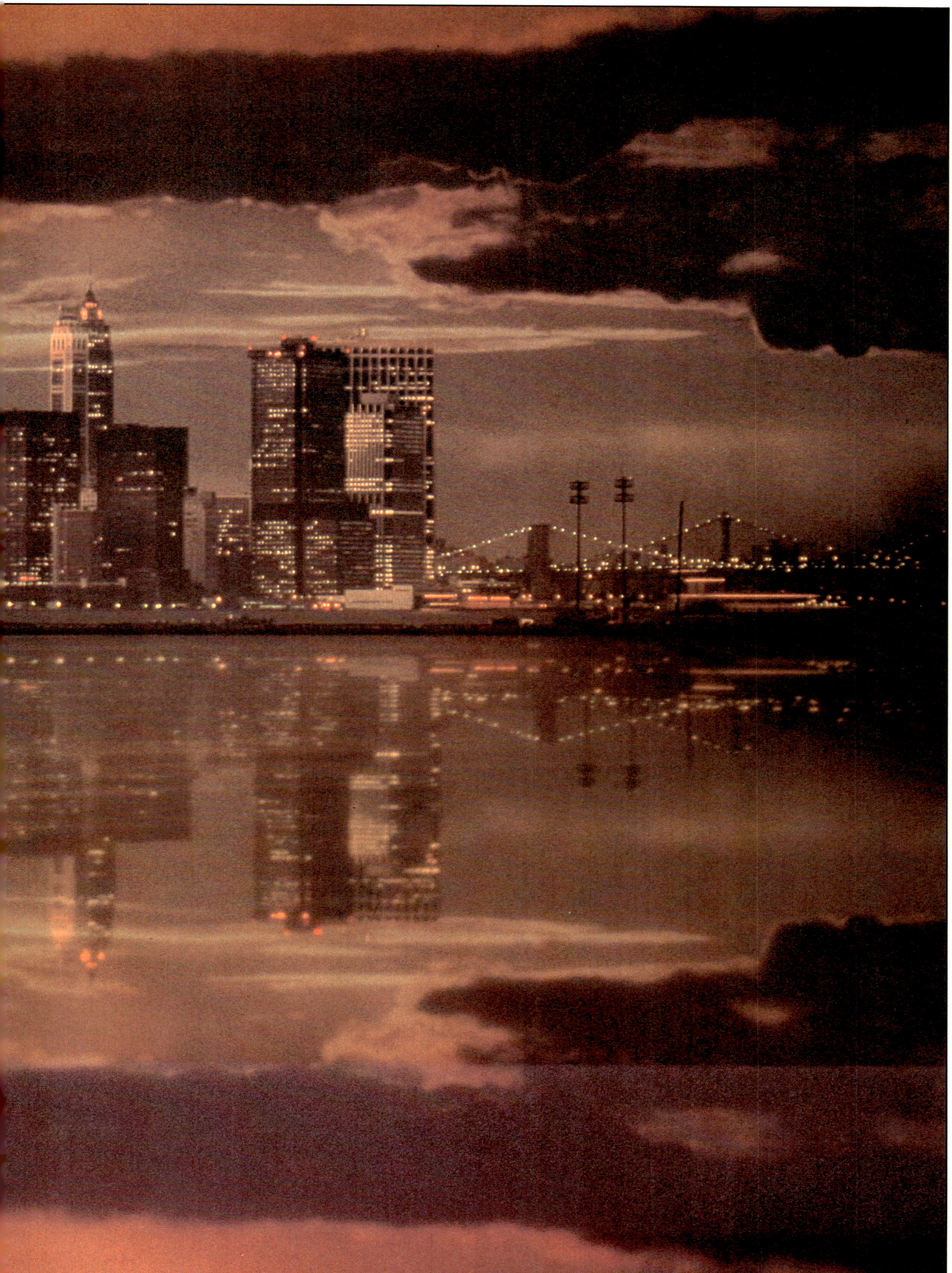

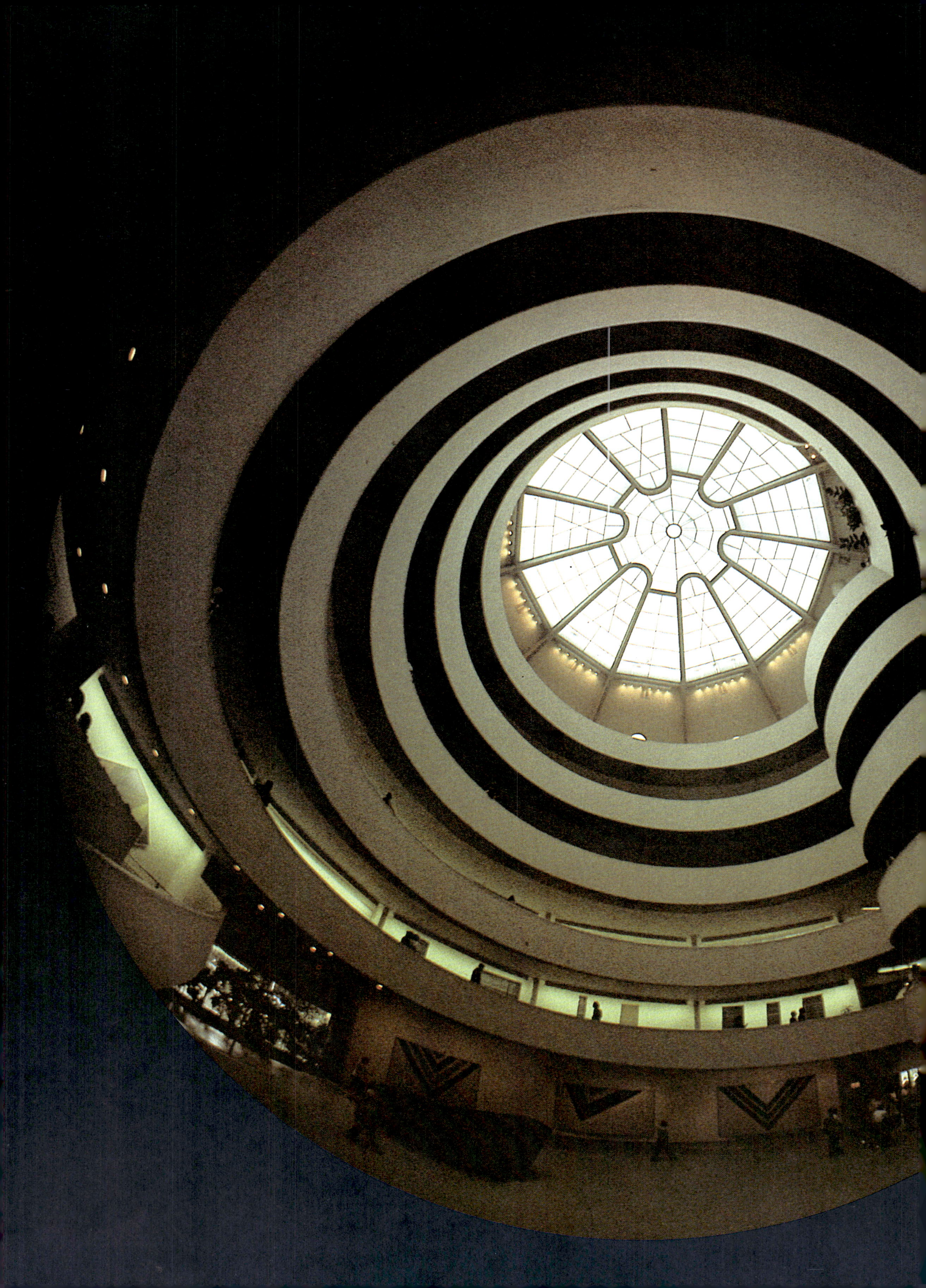

I WATCHED THE MINGLING OF THEIR DIVERSE FORMS
PAINTED A HUNDRED HUES, RED, GOLD AND BLUE.
RONSARD

LIKE DISTANT ECHOS BLURRING FROM AFAR
THE SOUNDS AND COLOURS SO REVERBERATE.
BAUDELAIRE

MAIL COLLECTION TIMES
LETTER BOX
U.S.MAIL
CUTLER~MAIL~CHUTE~CO.
ROCHESTER.N.Y.U.S.A.
CUTLER-MAILING-SYSTEM

DAY BREAKS,
THE FIRST LIGHTS INVADE THE TOWN
ON SHIMMERING SURFACES, THE OUTLINES OF HORSEMEN
AND OF MADDENED BEASTS.

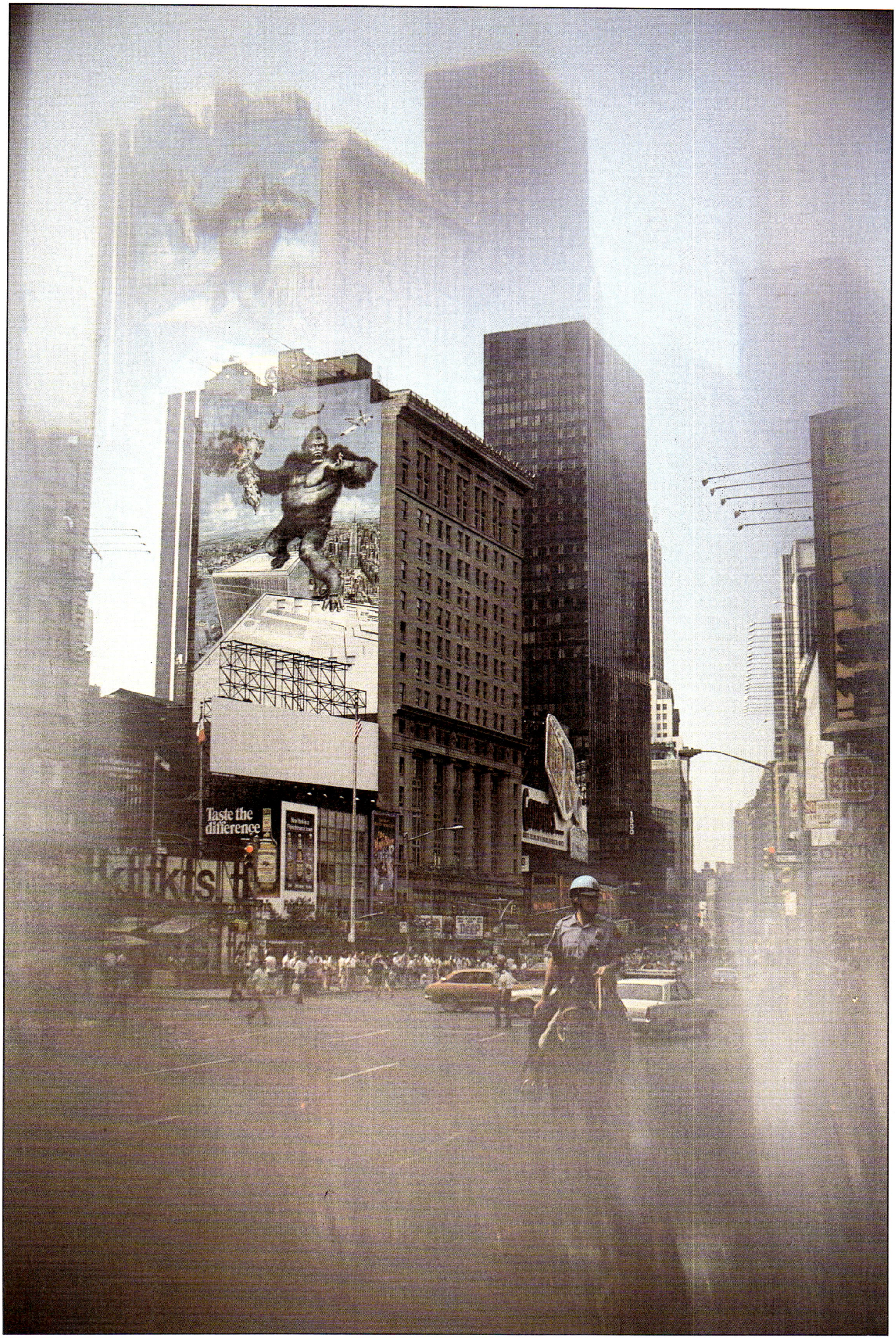
Taste the
difference
DEEP
FORUM

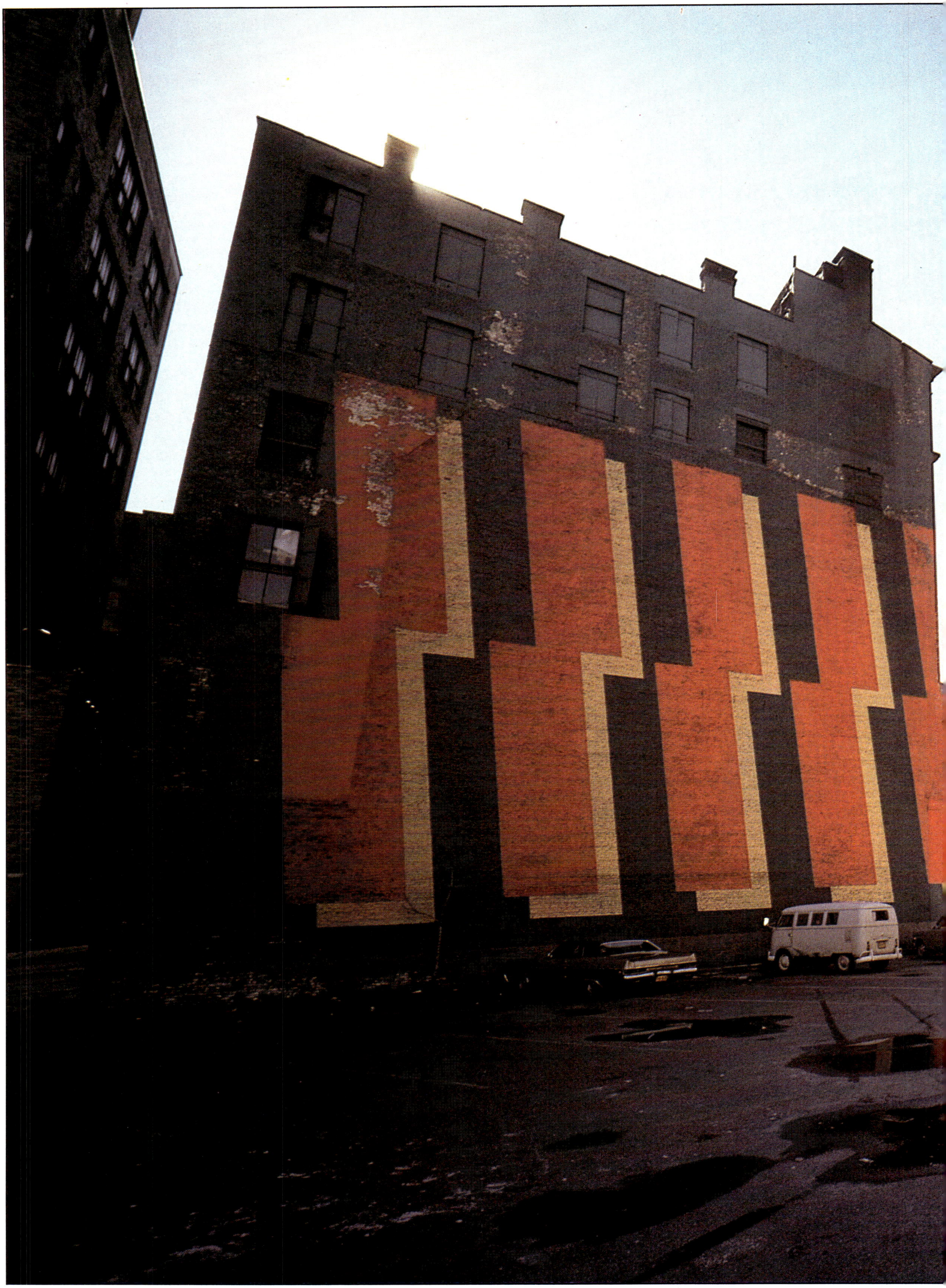

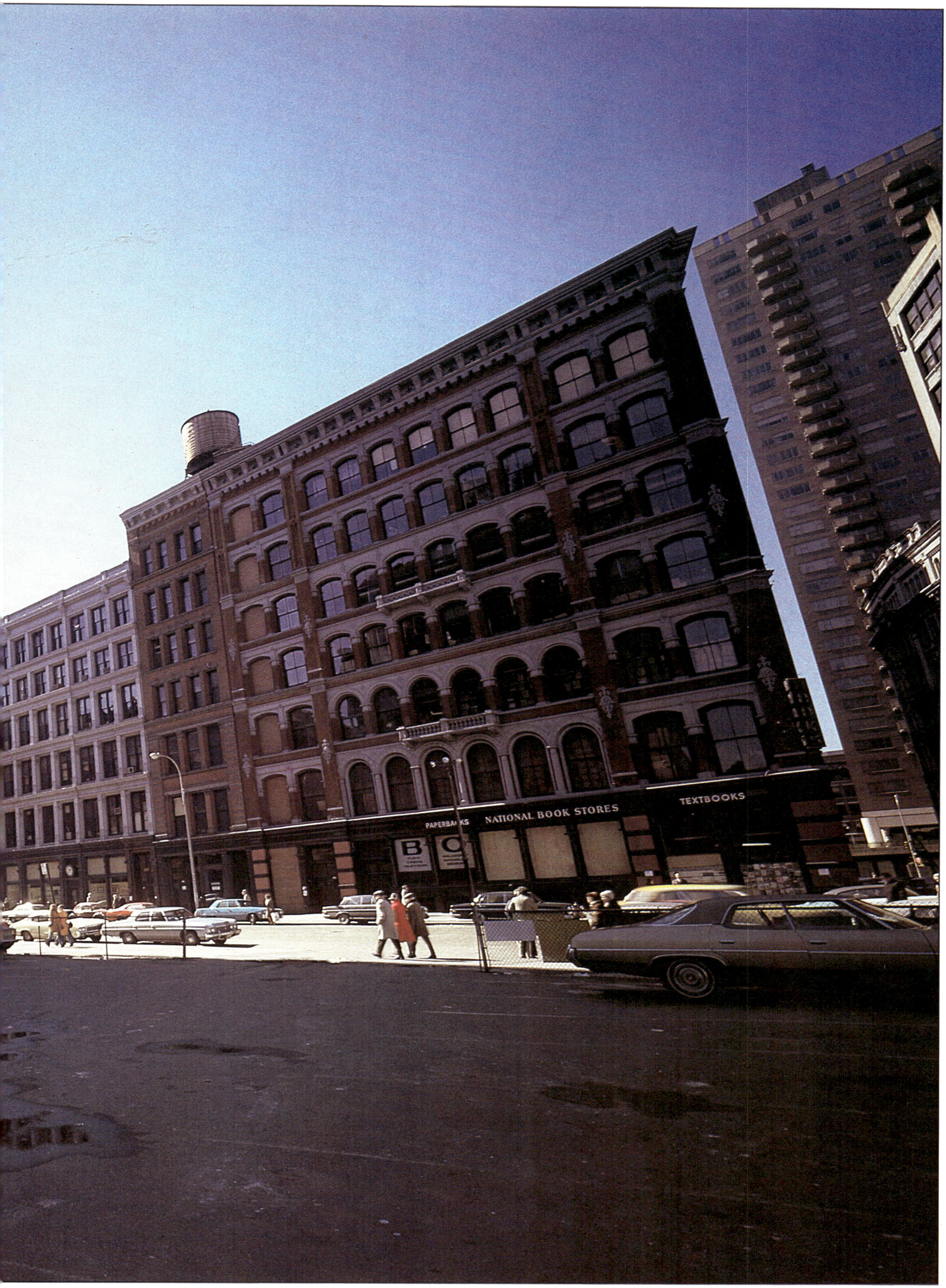
PAPERBACKS
NATIONAL BOOK STORES
TEXTBOOKS

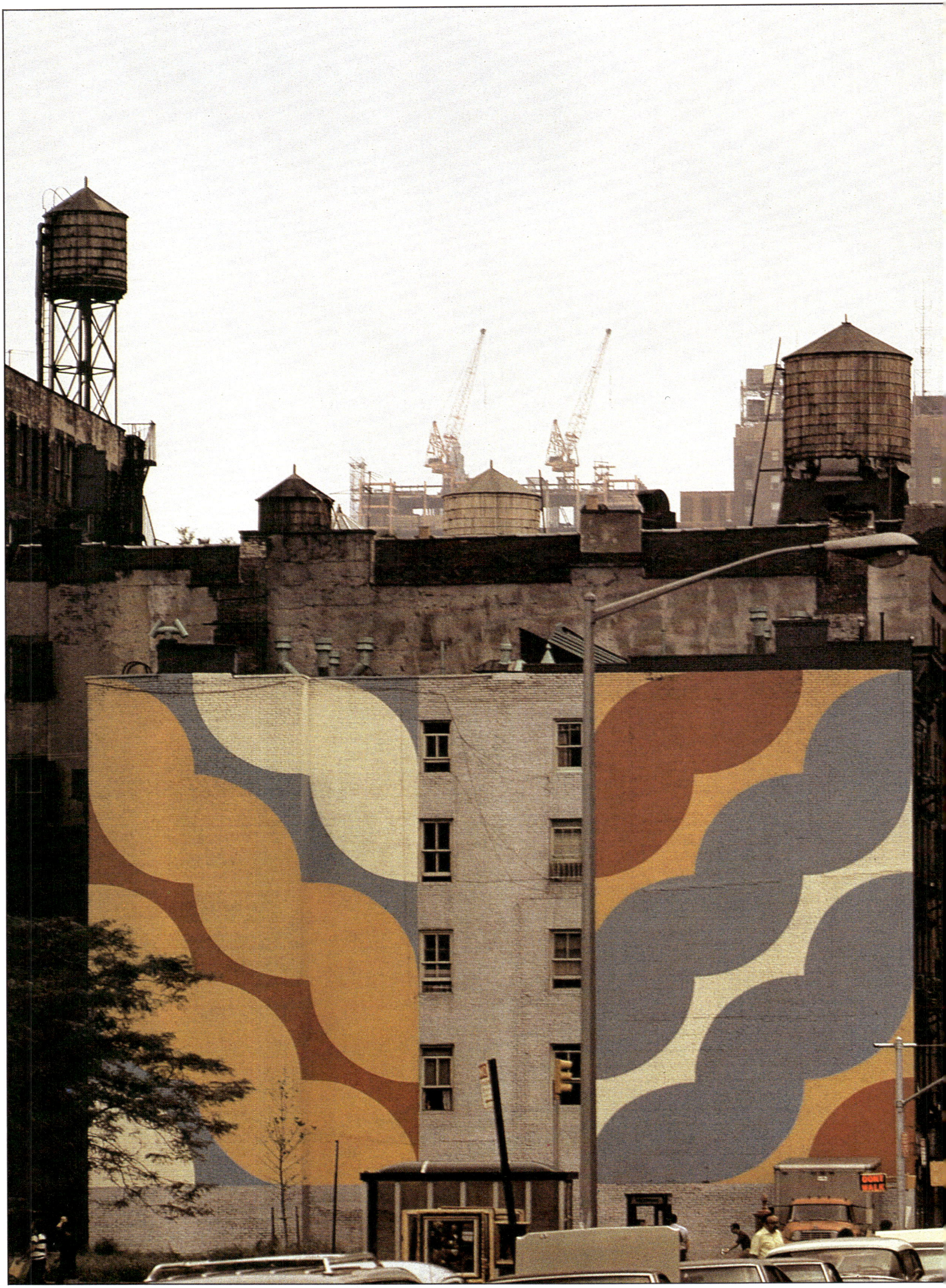

MANY THE BOUQUET THAT
WASTES ITS FRAGRANCE
IN THE DEEPEST SOLITUDE.
BAUDELAIRE

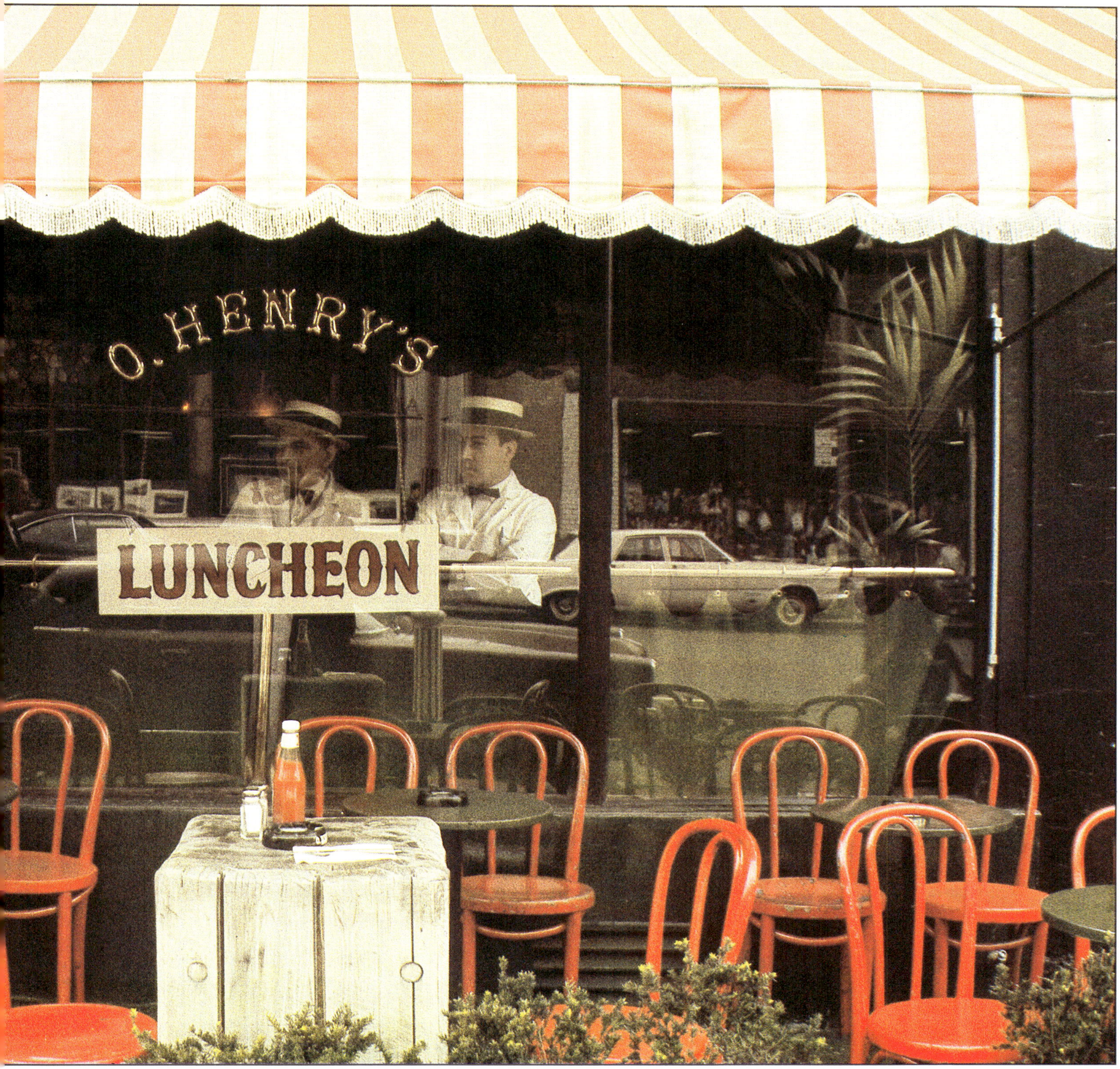
O. HENRY'S
LUNCHEON

WIRE-PULLED AUTOMATONS,
WENT SIDLING THROUGH THE SLOW QUADRILLE.
OSCAR WILDE

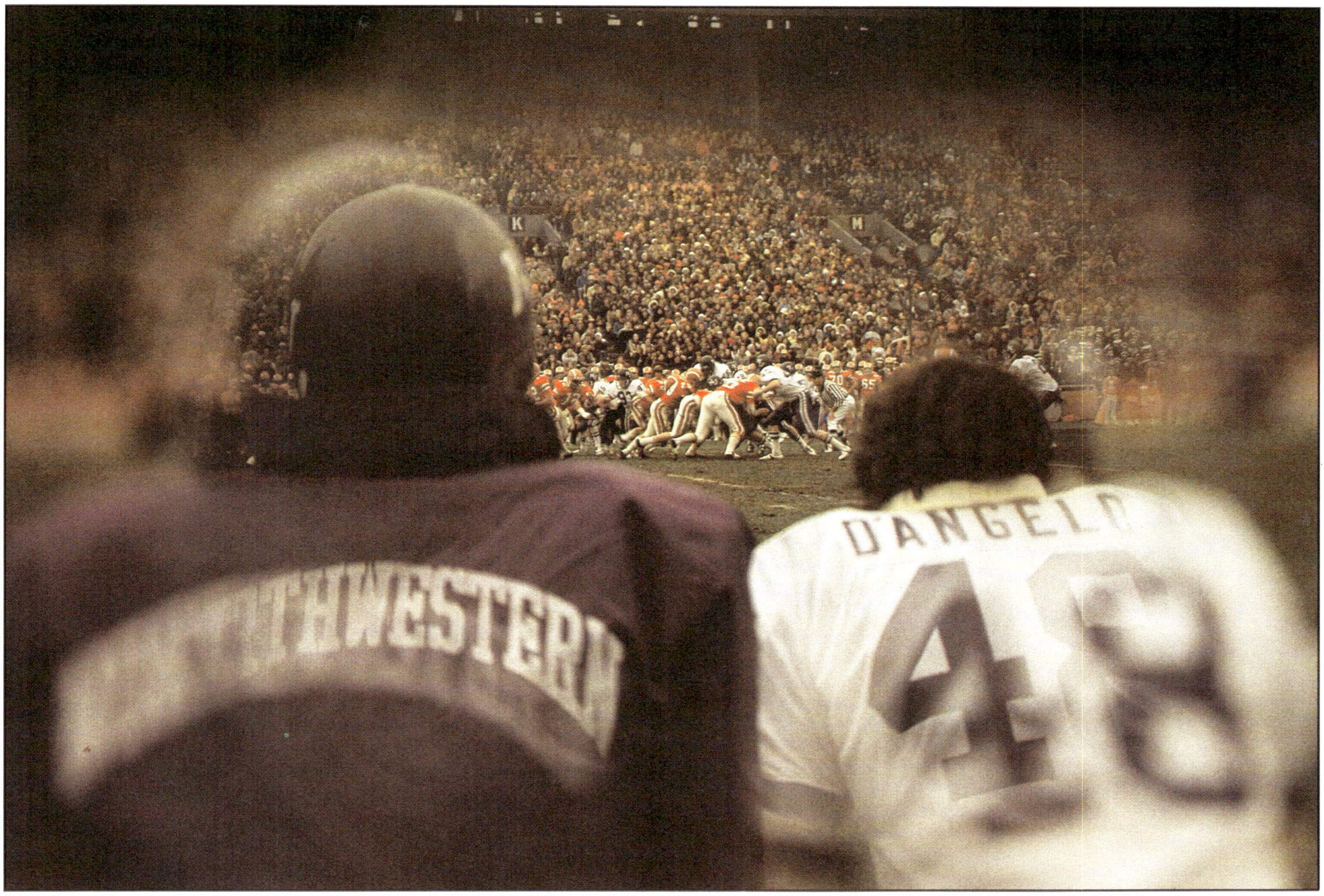
DANGELO
48

AGAINST THESE TURBID TURQUOISE SKIES
THE LIGHT AND LUMINOUS BALLOONS
DIP AND DRIFT LIKE SATIN MOONS.
OSCAR WILDE

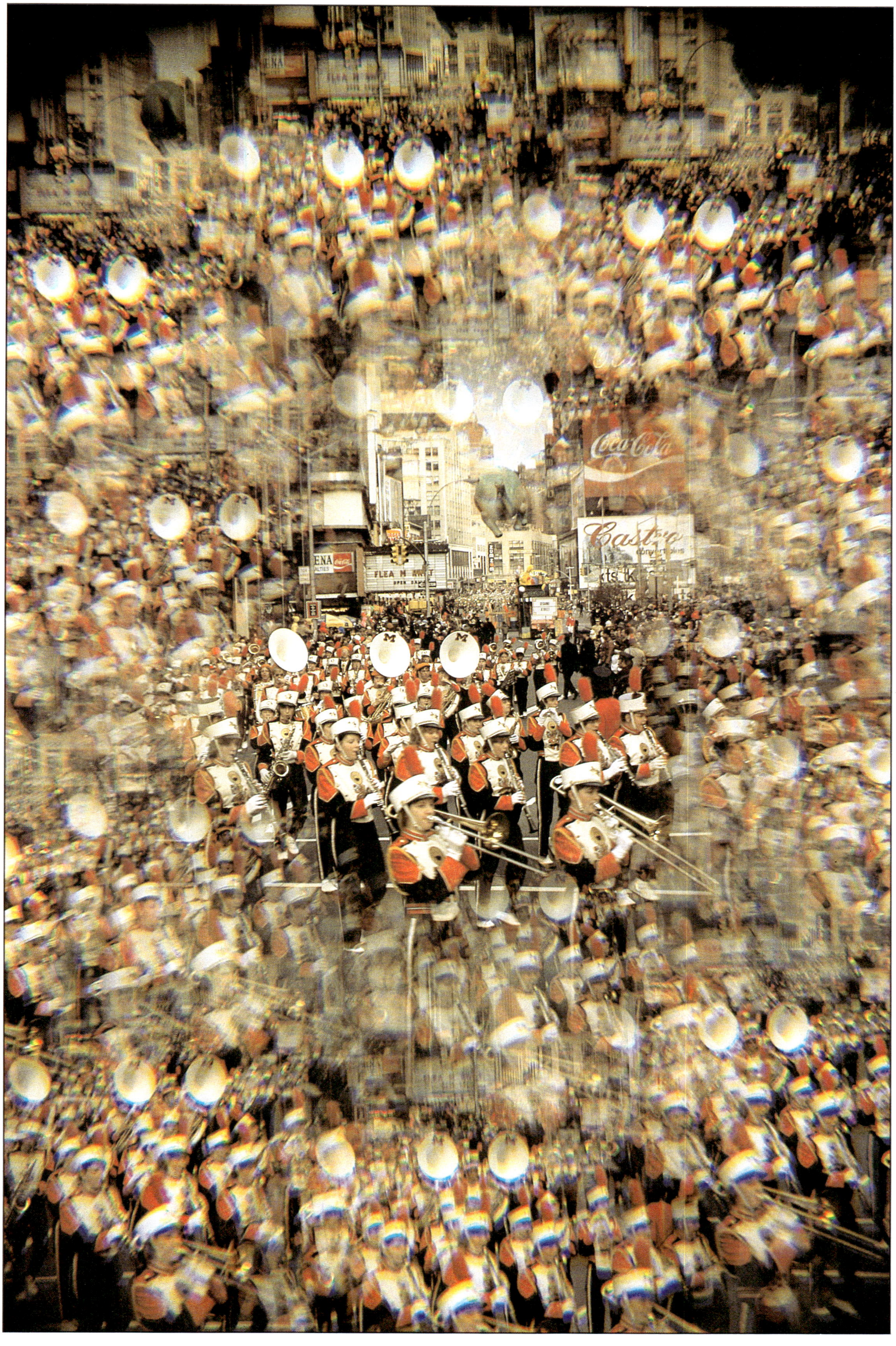
Coca-Cola

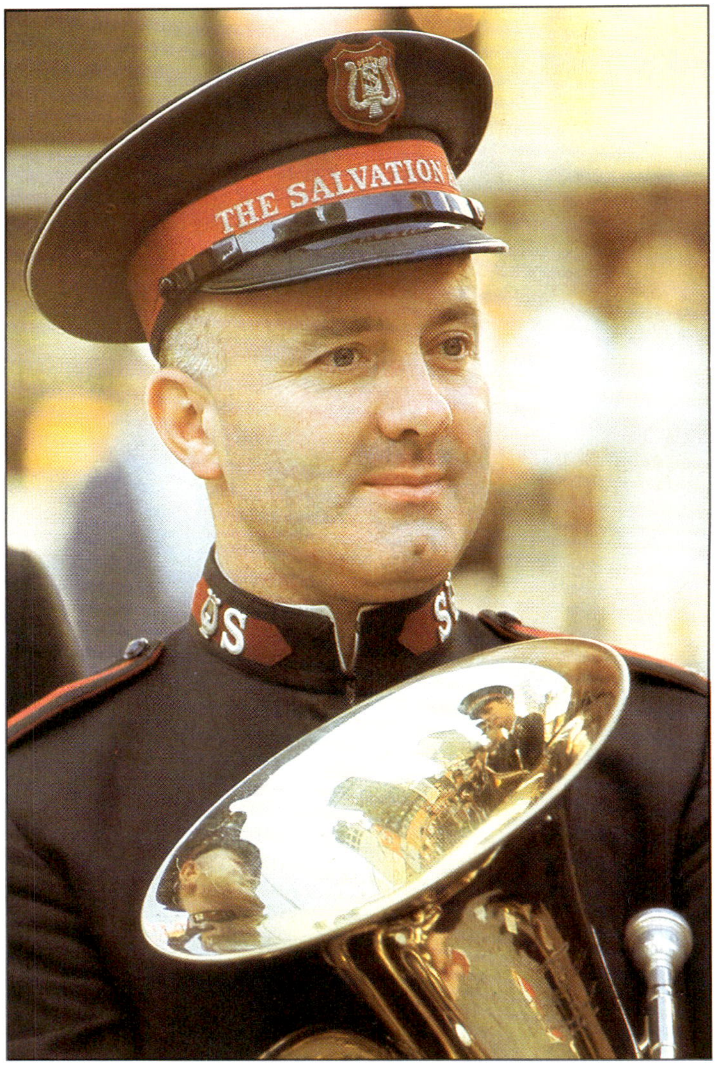
THE SALVATION

IN THE DANCING SHADE
STAND SOME LITTLE FIGURES
PULLING THE SHIMMERING GOLD.
OSCAR WILDE

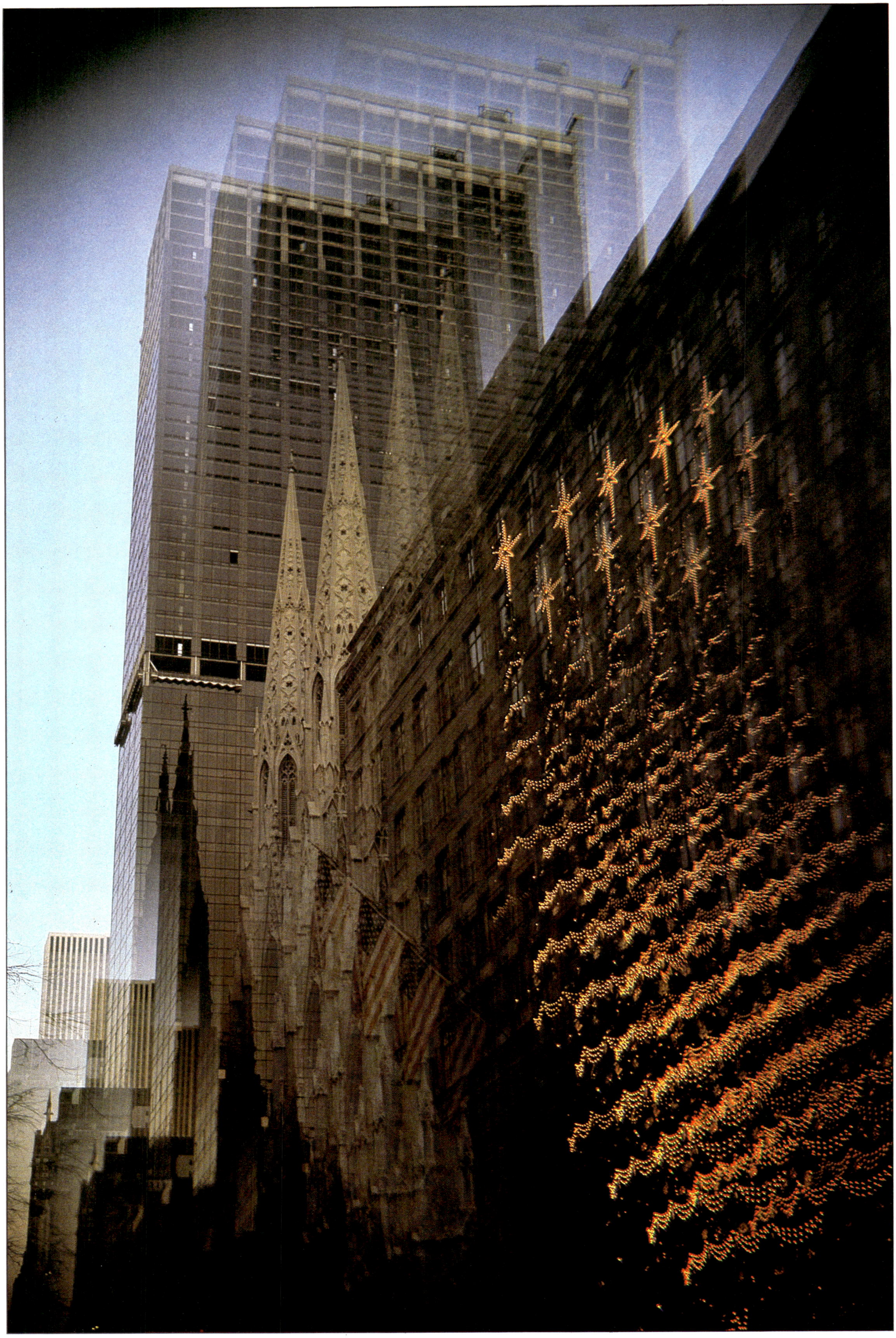

AND IN A CRYSTAL SKY
EACH POINT OF LIGHT
BECAME A STAR,
THE CITY TO ILLUMINATE.

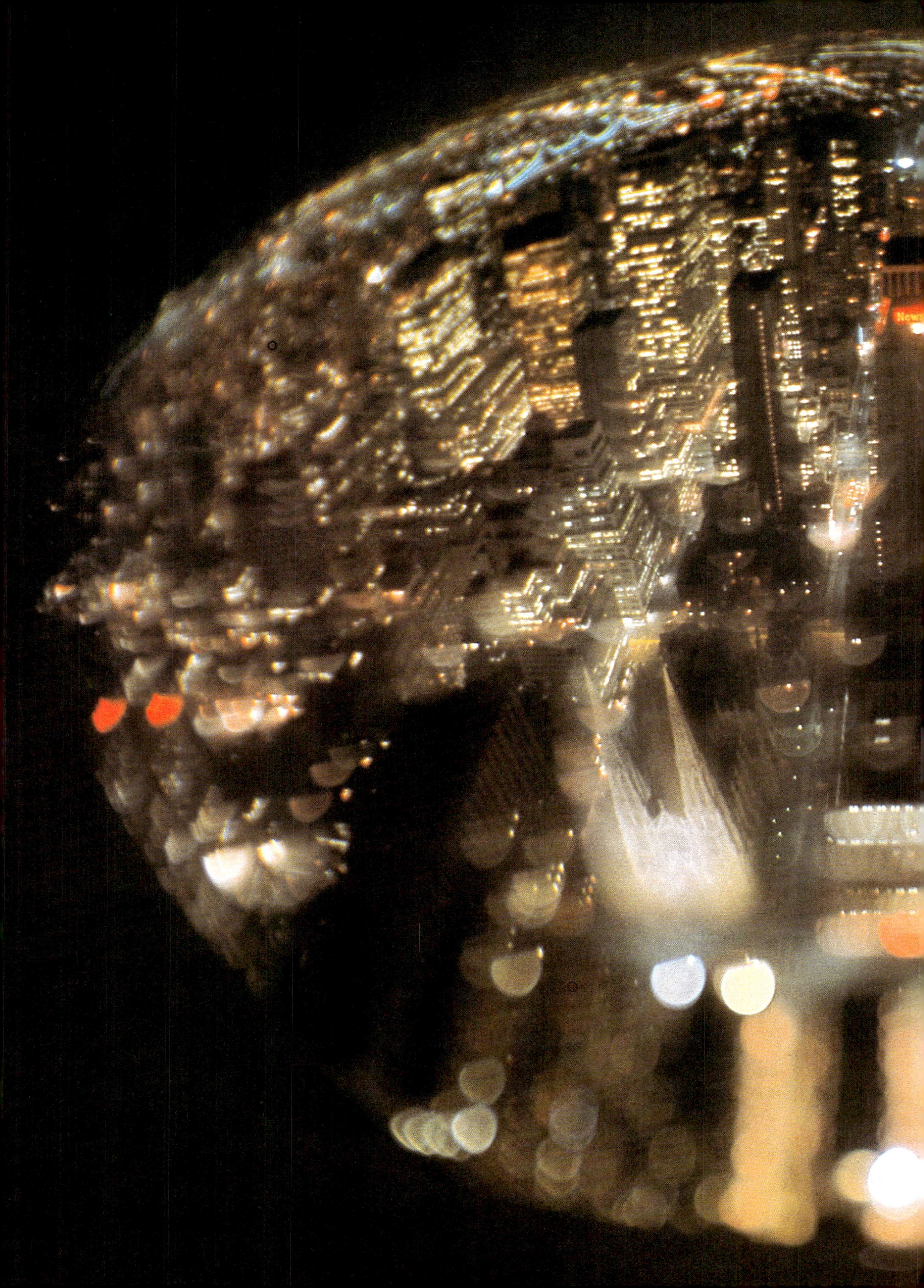

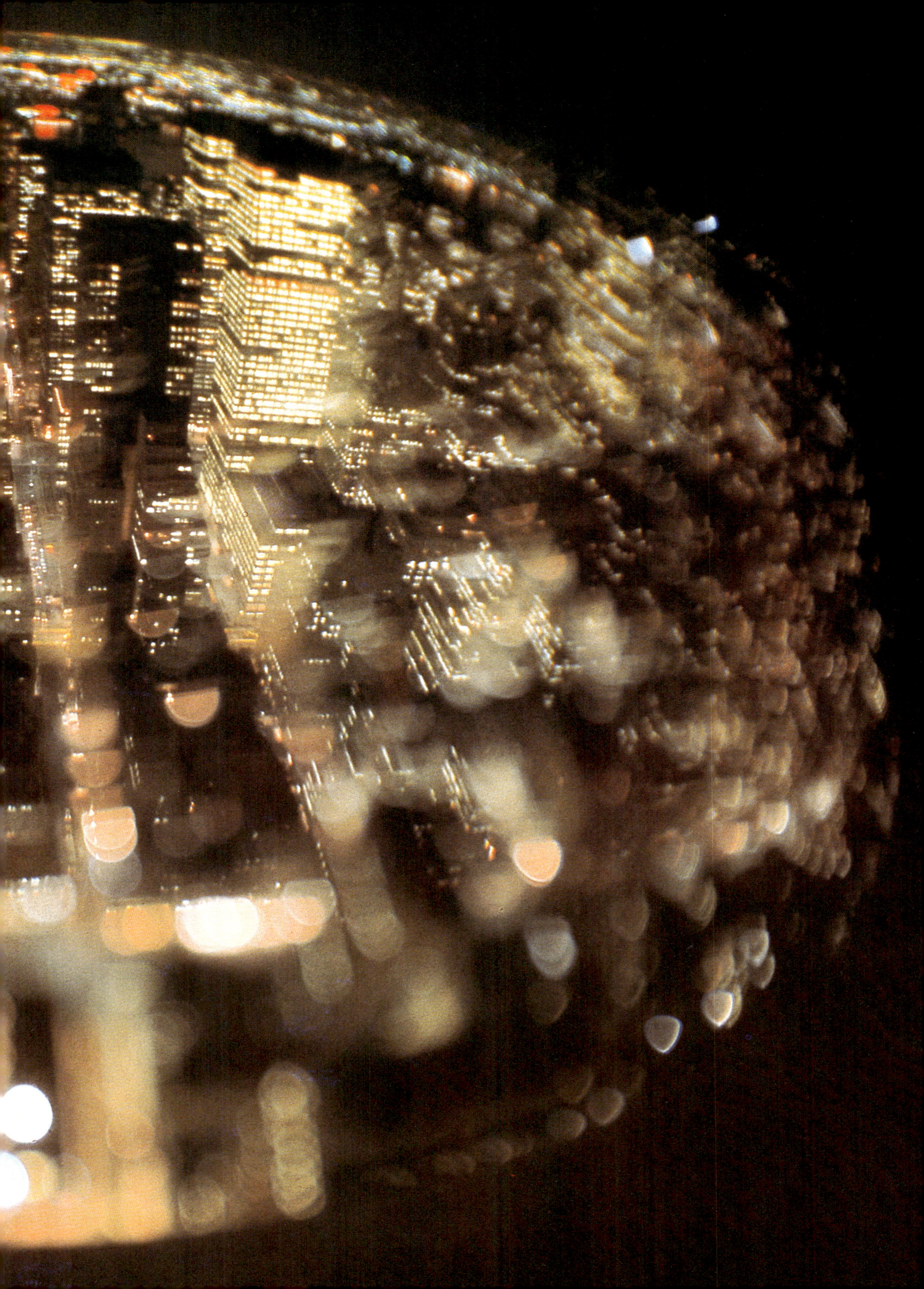

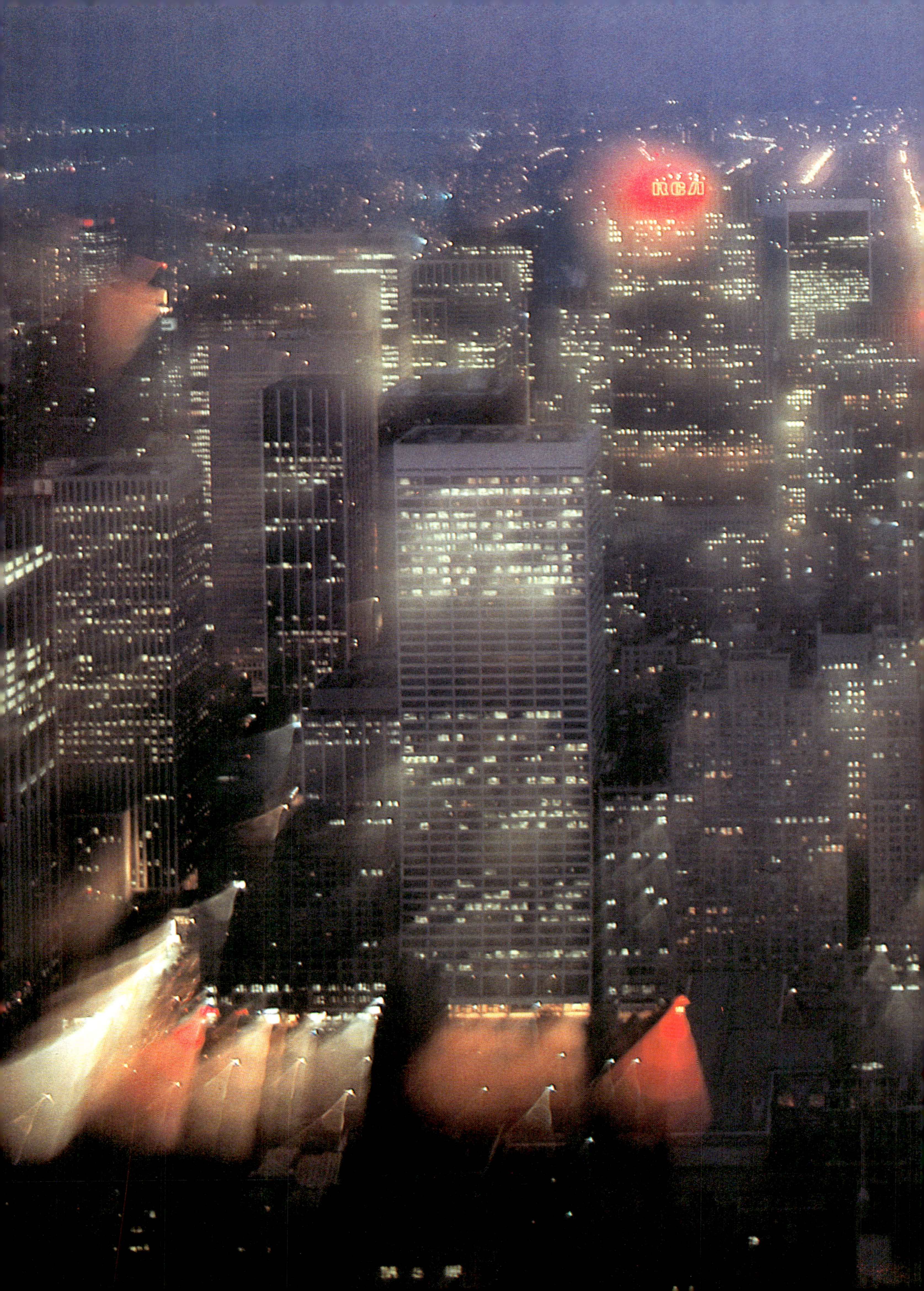
RCA

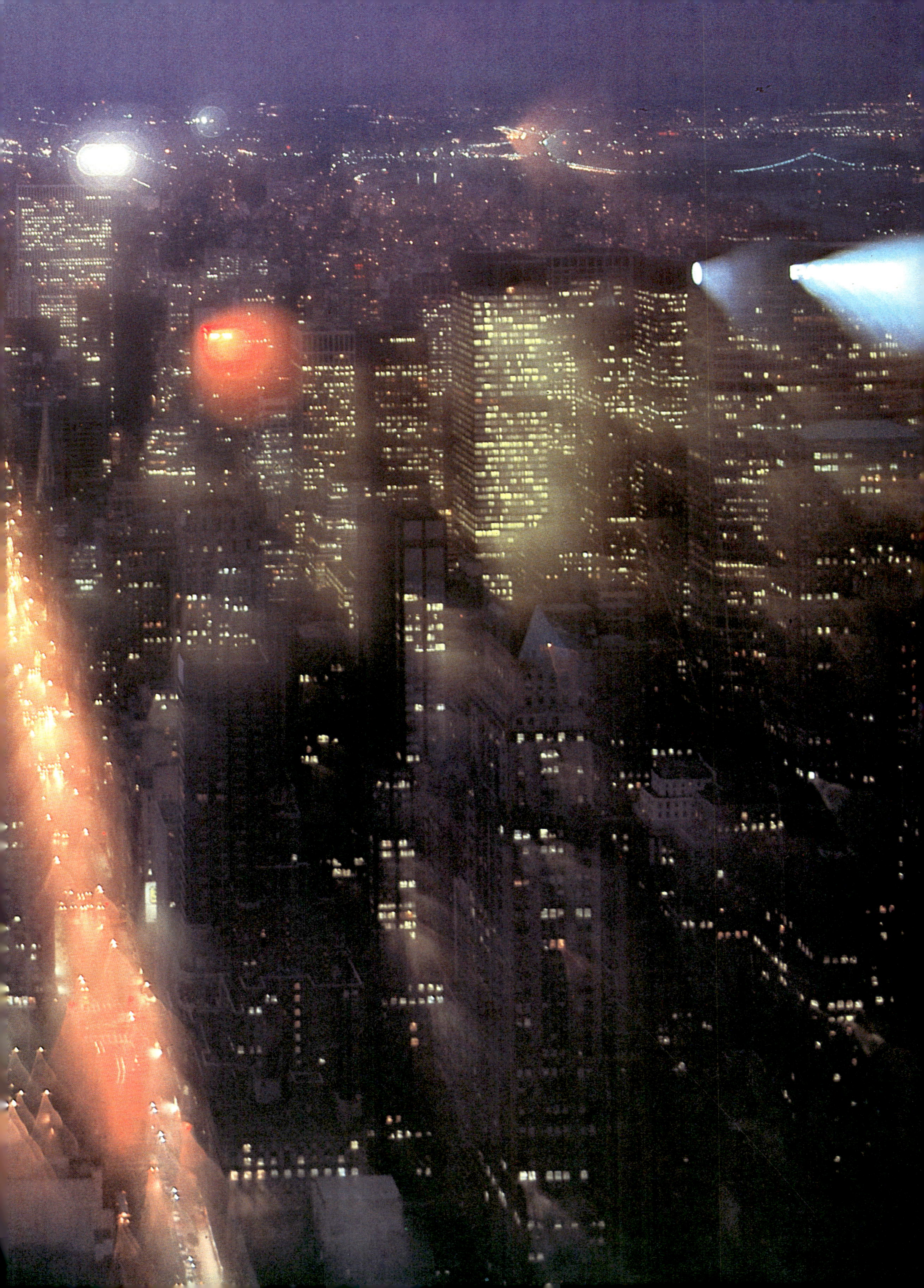

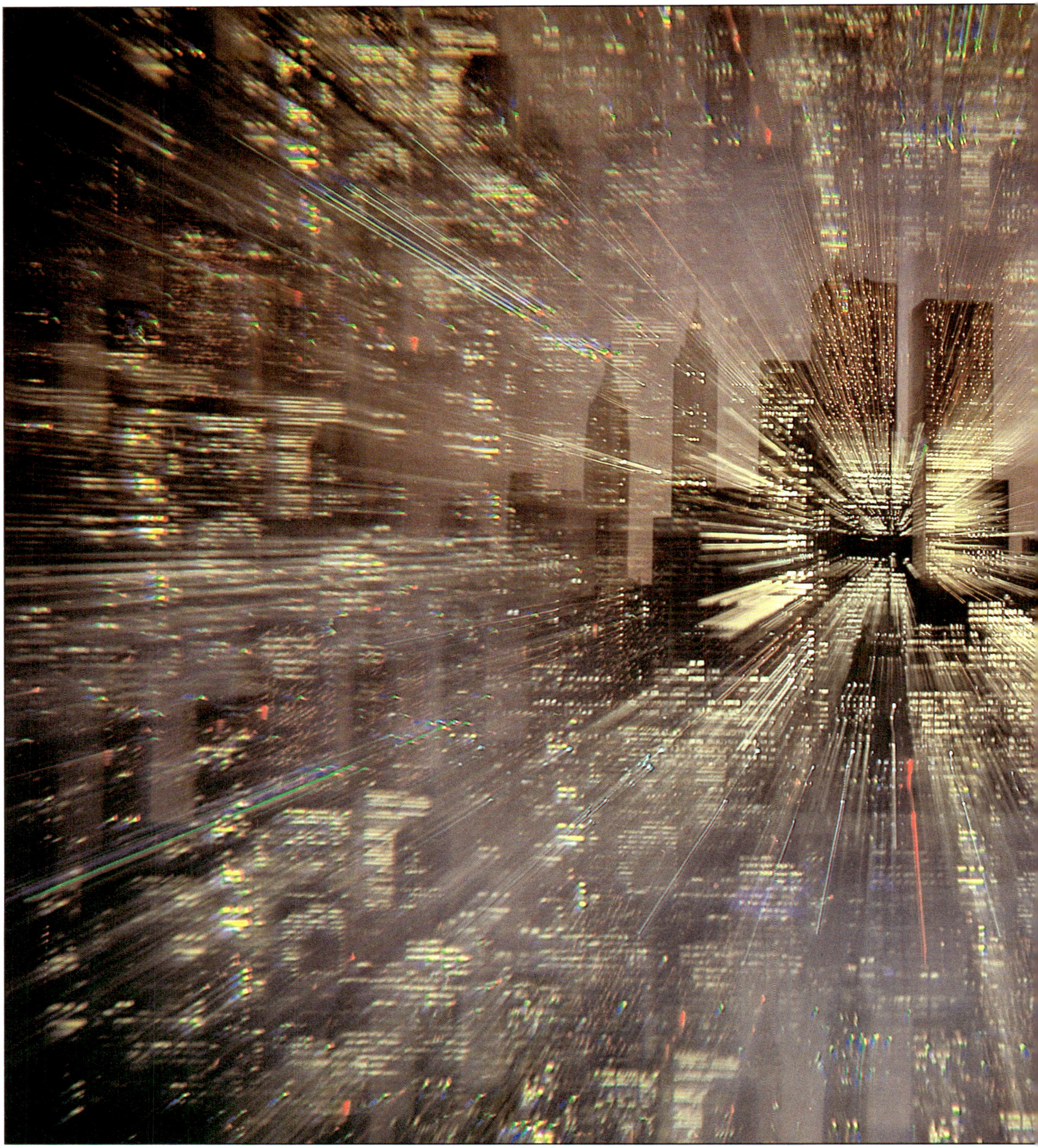

FROM MY DESIRE ARISING
IN THE GOLDEN NIGHT,
A THOUSAND-WINDOWED SKY.

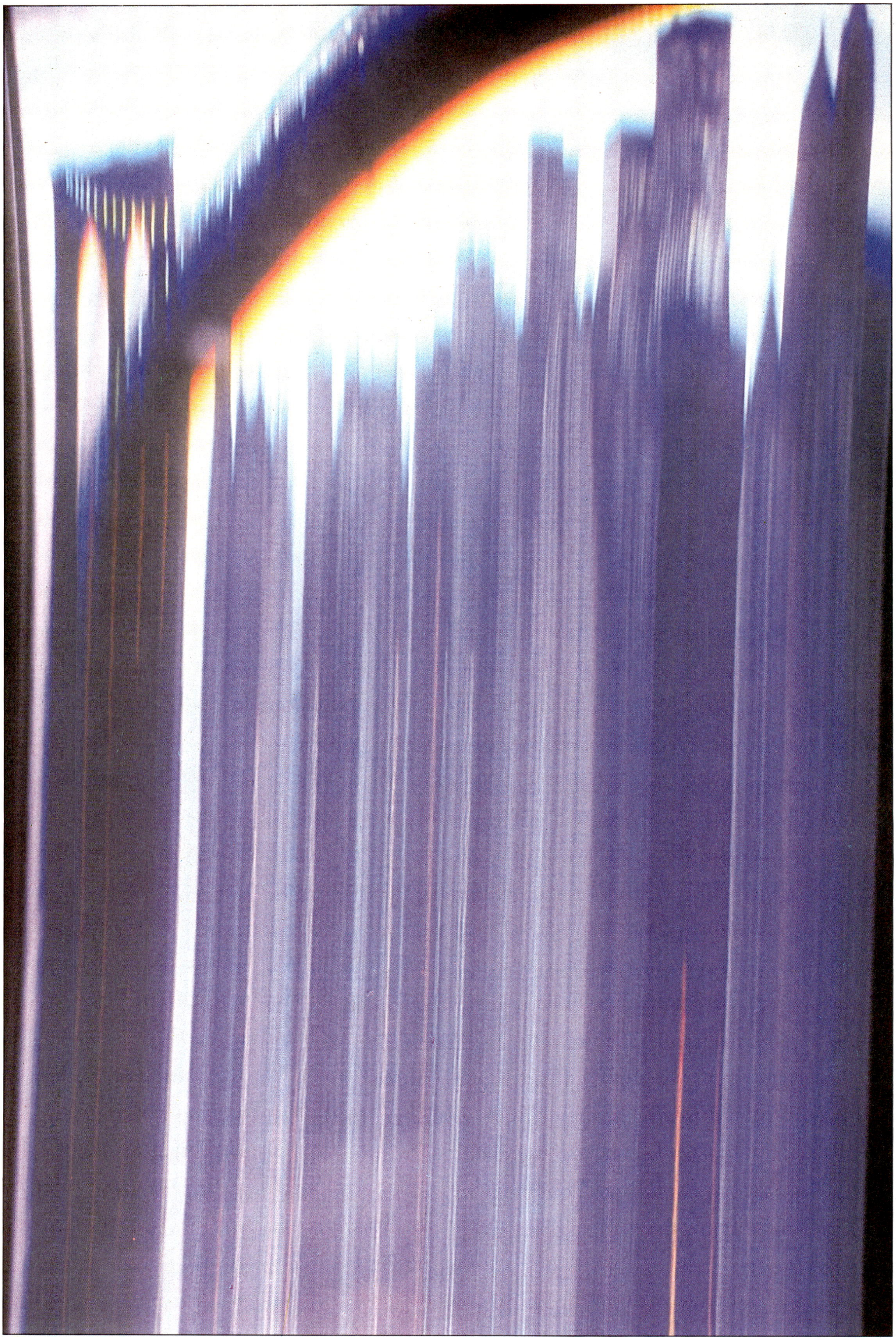

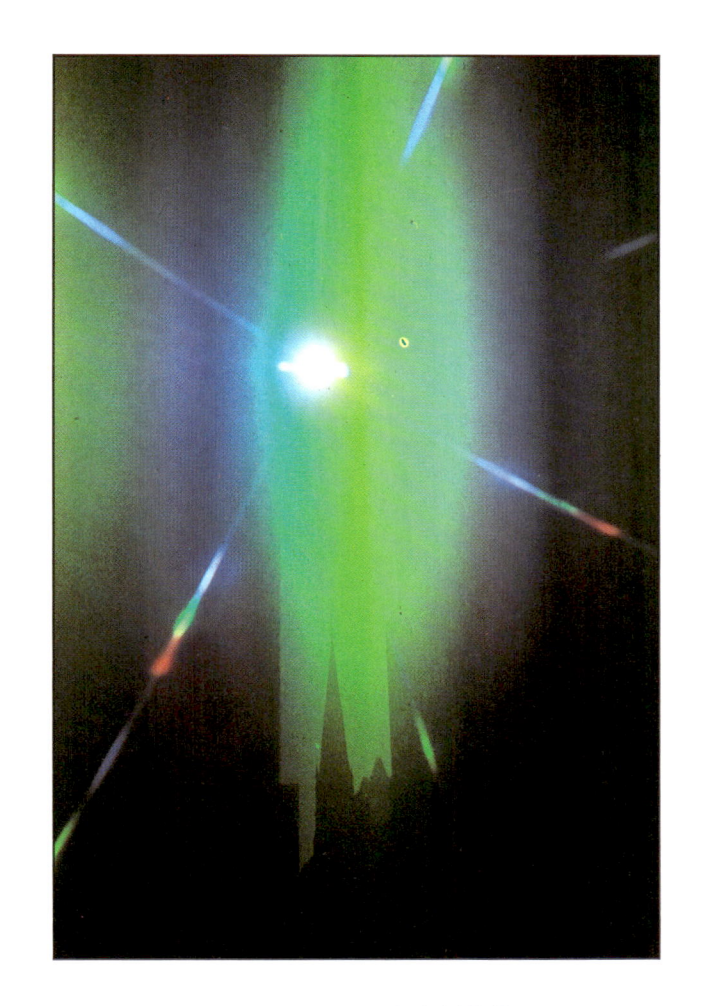

FOR IT WILL BE MADE
OF PURE LIGHT ALONE,
DRAWN FROM THE SACRED
SOURCE OF EVERY LIGHT.
BAUDELAIRE

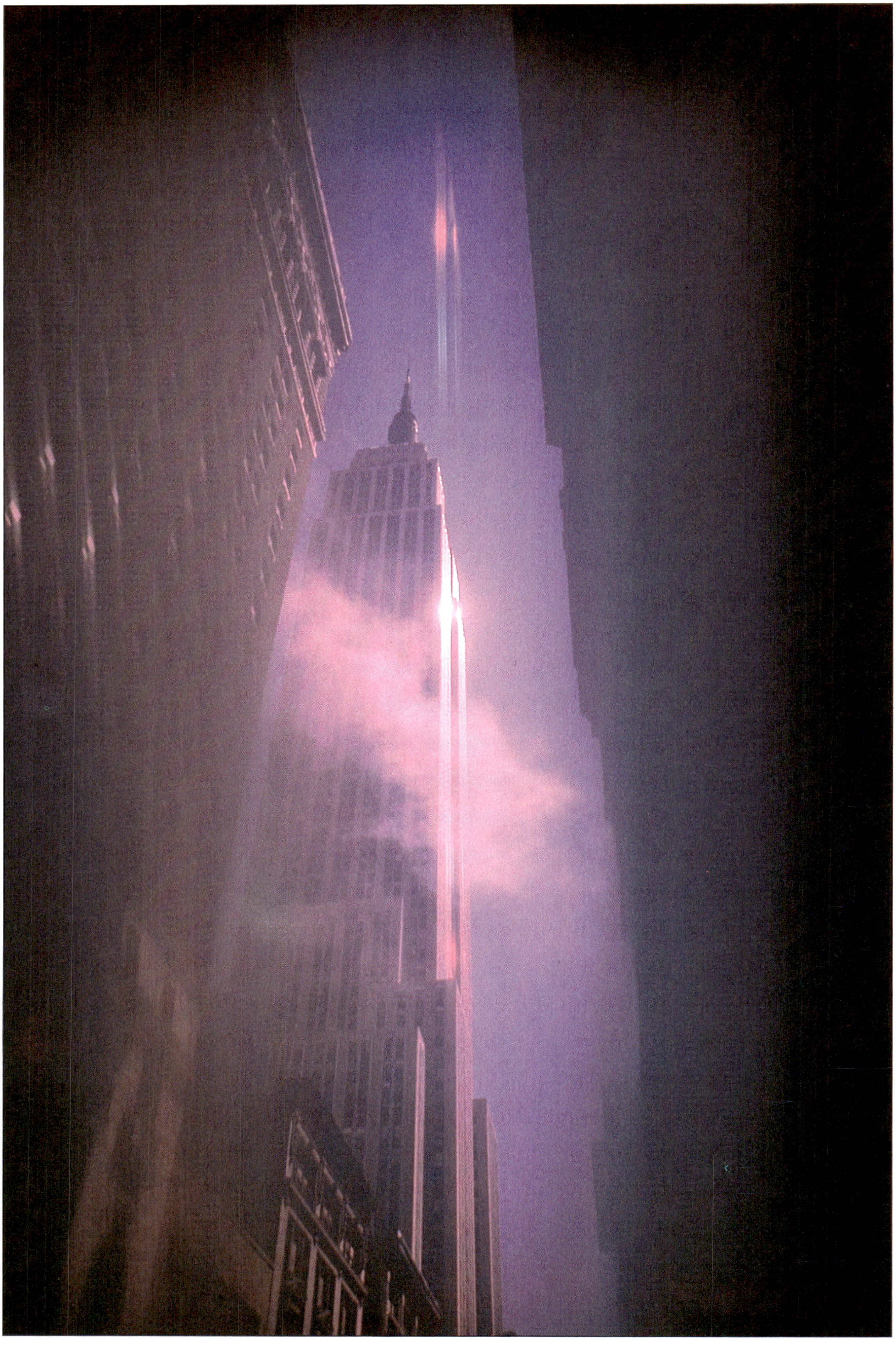

AND THE SKY WATCHING
THE SUPERB CLOUDS
BLOSSOM LIKE FLOWERS.
BAUDELAIRE

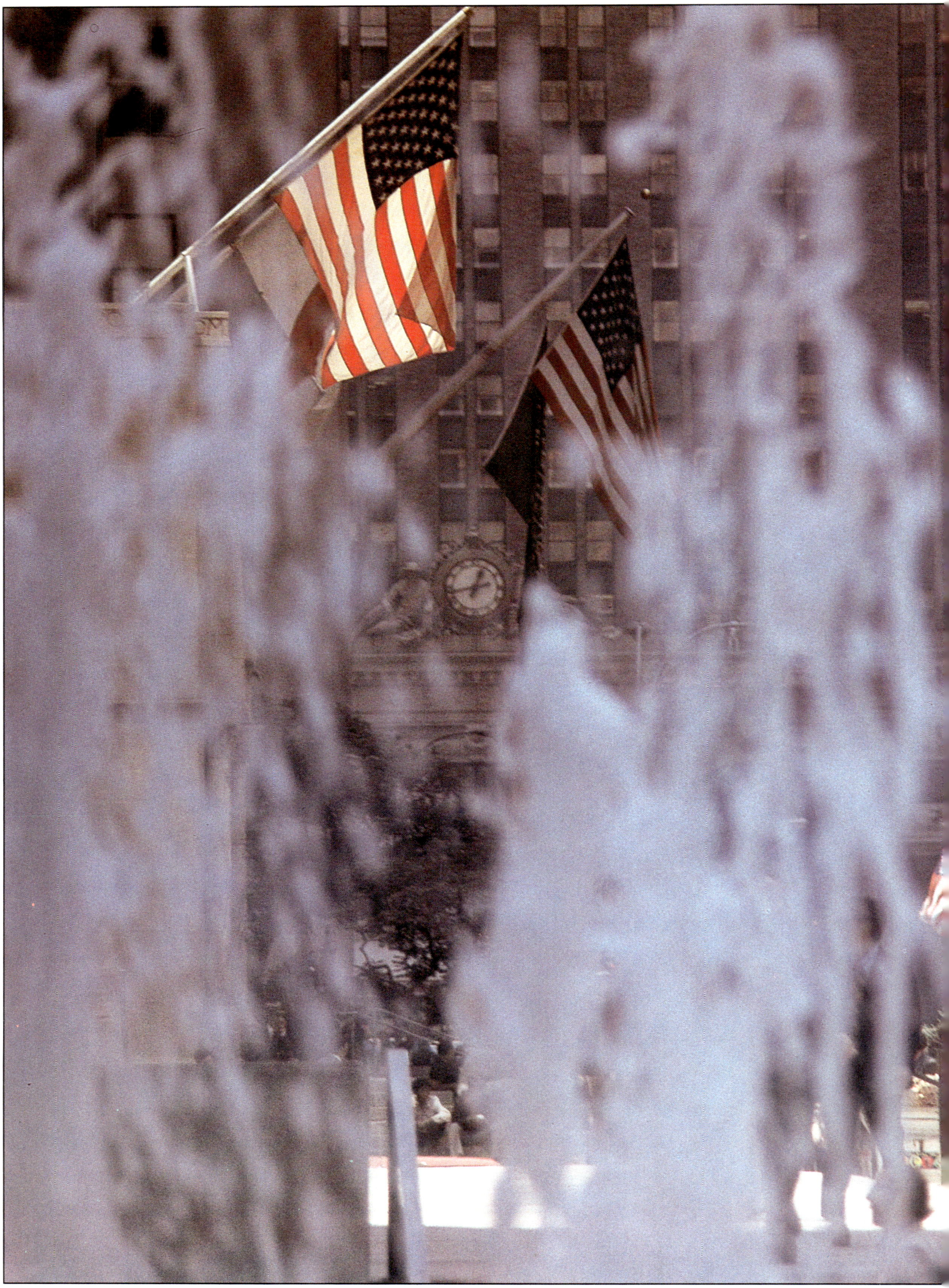

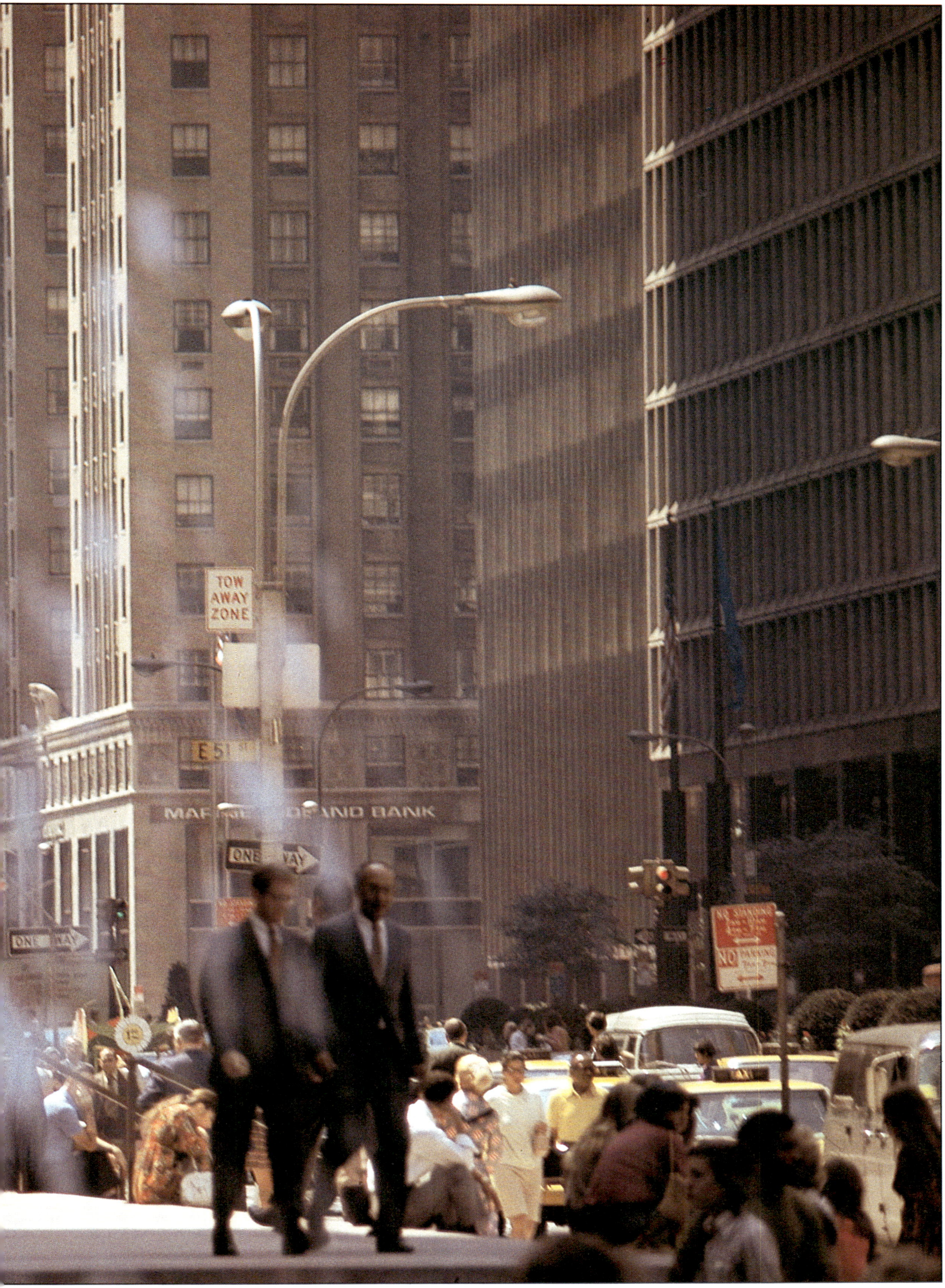
TOW
AWAY
ZONE
ONE WAY

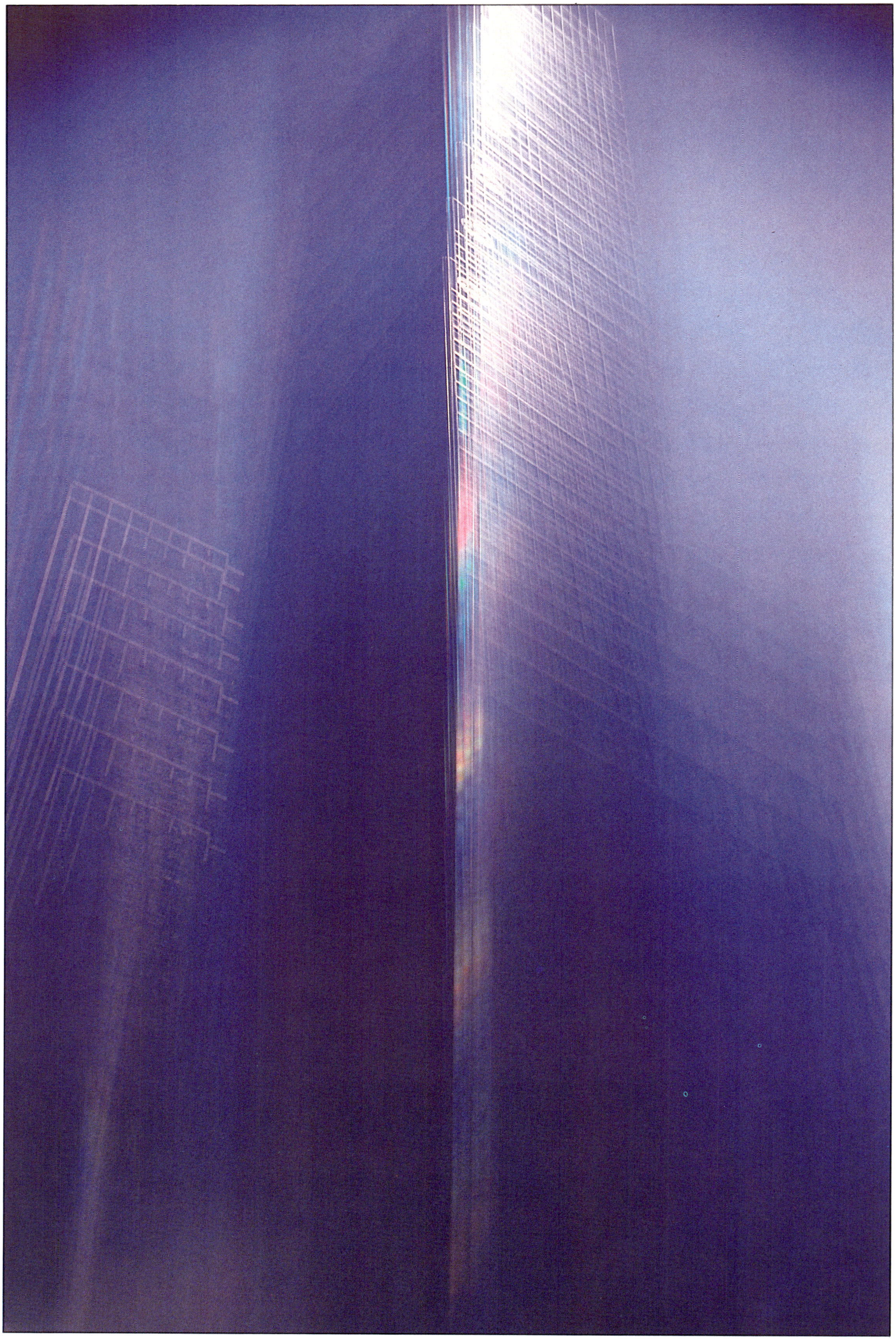

ALL DRIFTED INTO MY SIGHT RICHLY LIT BY THAT BEWITCHING STAR
WHOSE RAYS GLOW DIAMOND BRIGHT.
VICTOR HUGO

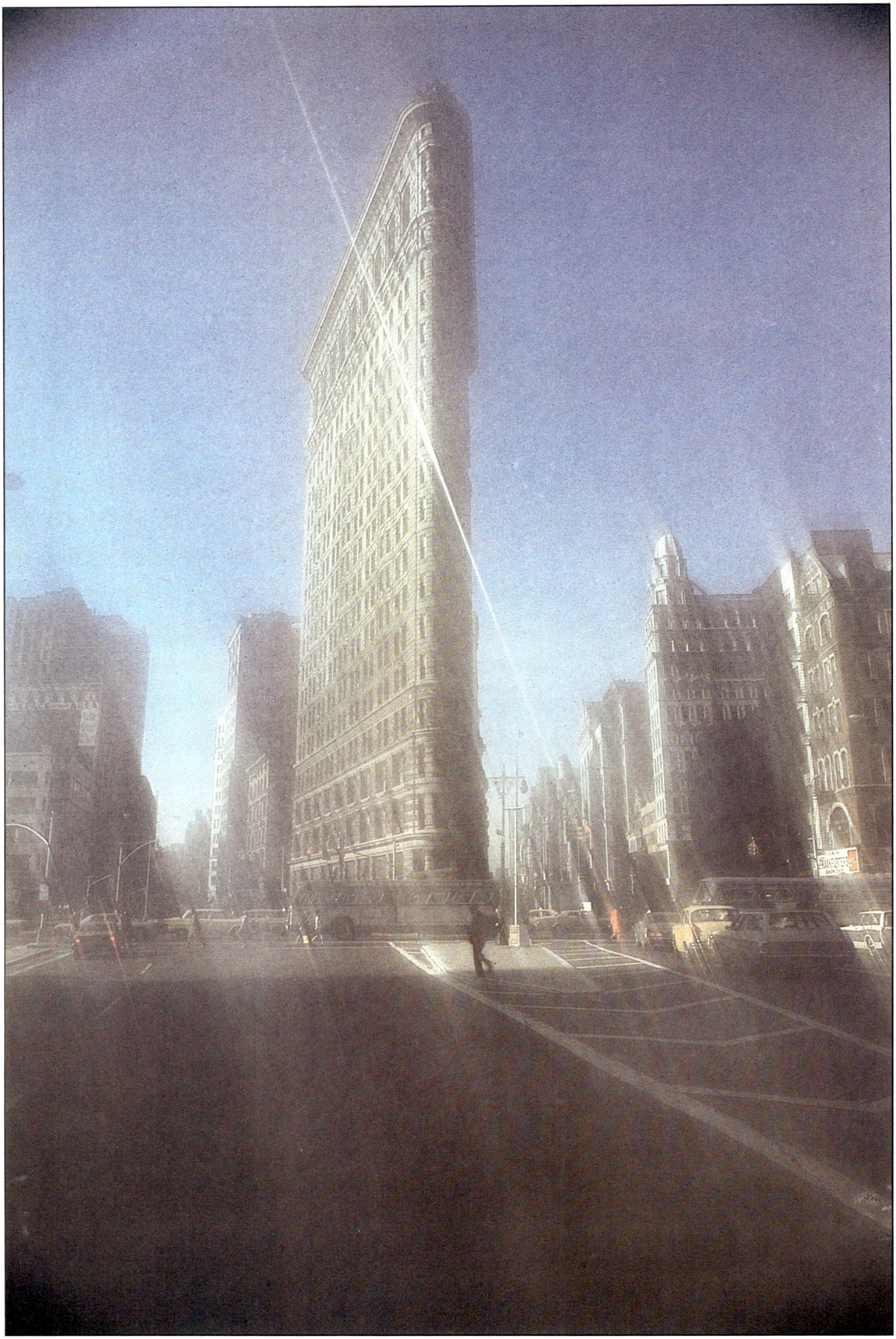

NEW YORK DAWN STIRS,
SEARCHING ROUND SHARP CORNERS,
ITS LIGHT CONCEALED.

THE STRANGEST VISIONS,
AS SUN-LIKE HOSTS
SETTING O'ER THE TOWN,
BRIGHT-RED GHOSTS
IN RESTLESS PROCESSION.
VERLAINE

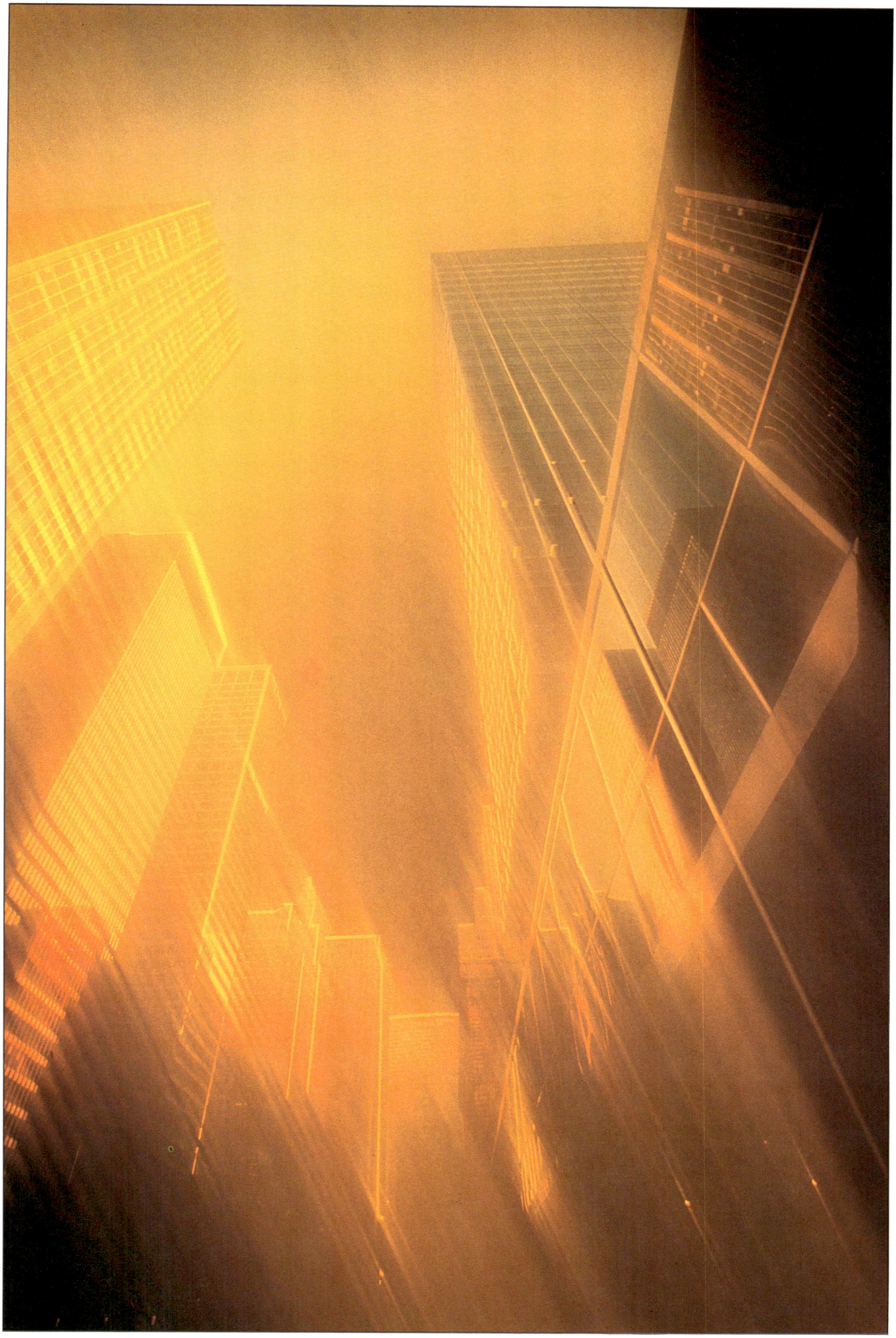

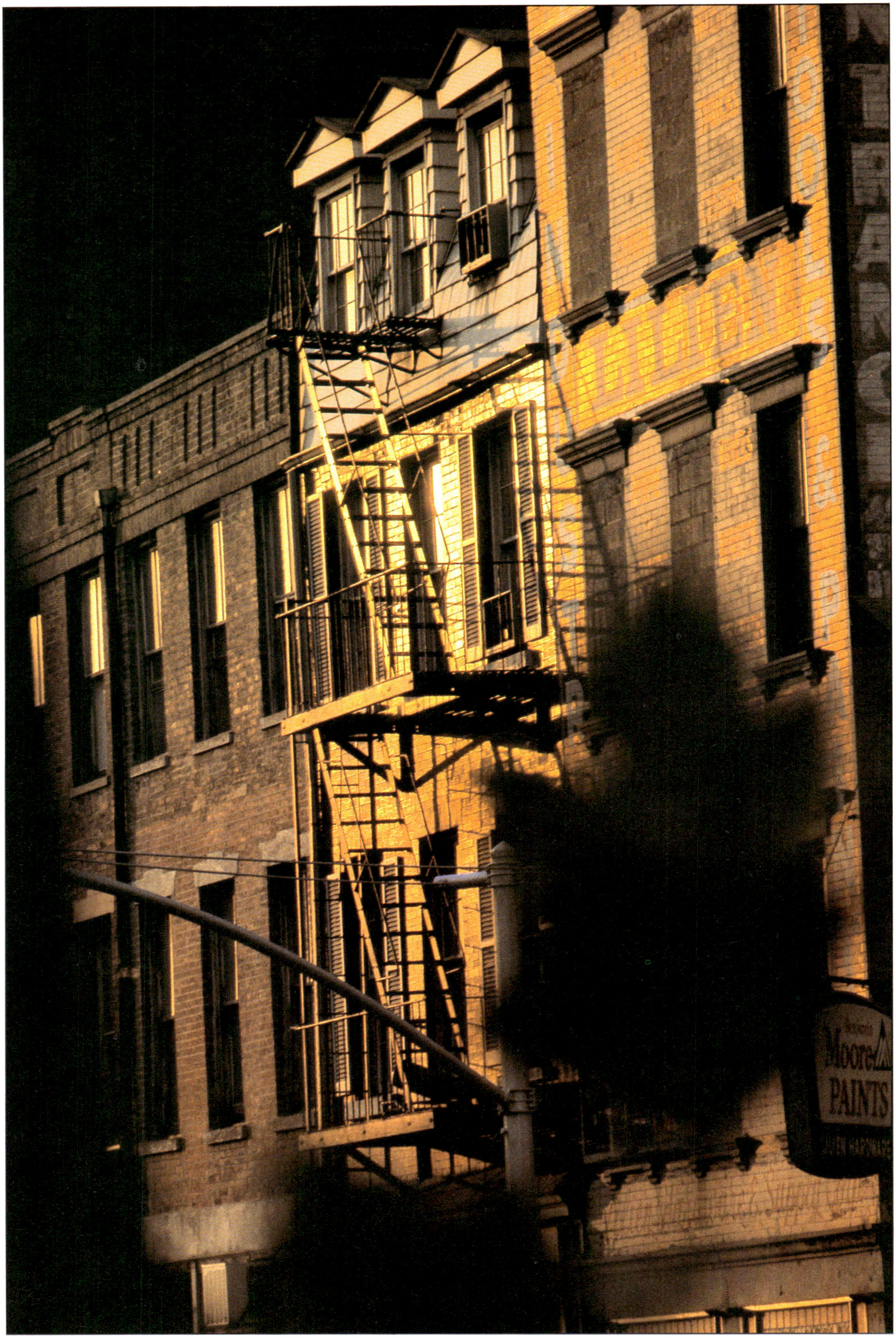
Moore
PAINTS

THE SPLENDID SUN AT EVENING,
STREAMING DOWN,
A VAST WIDE EYE
IN THE ENQUIRING SKY.
BAUDELAIRE

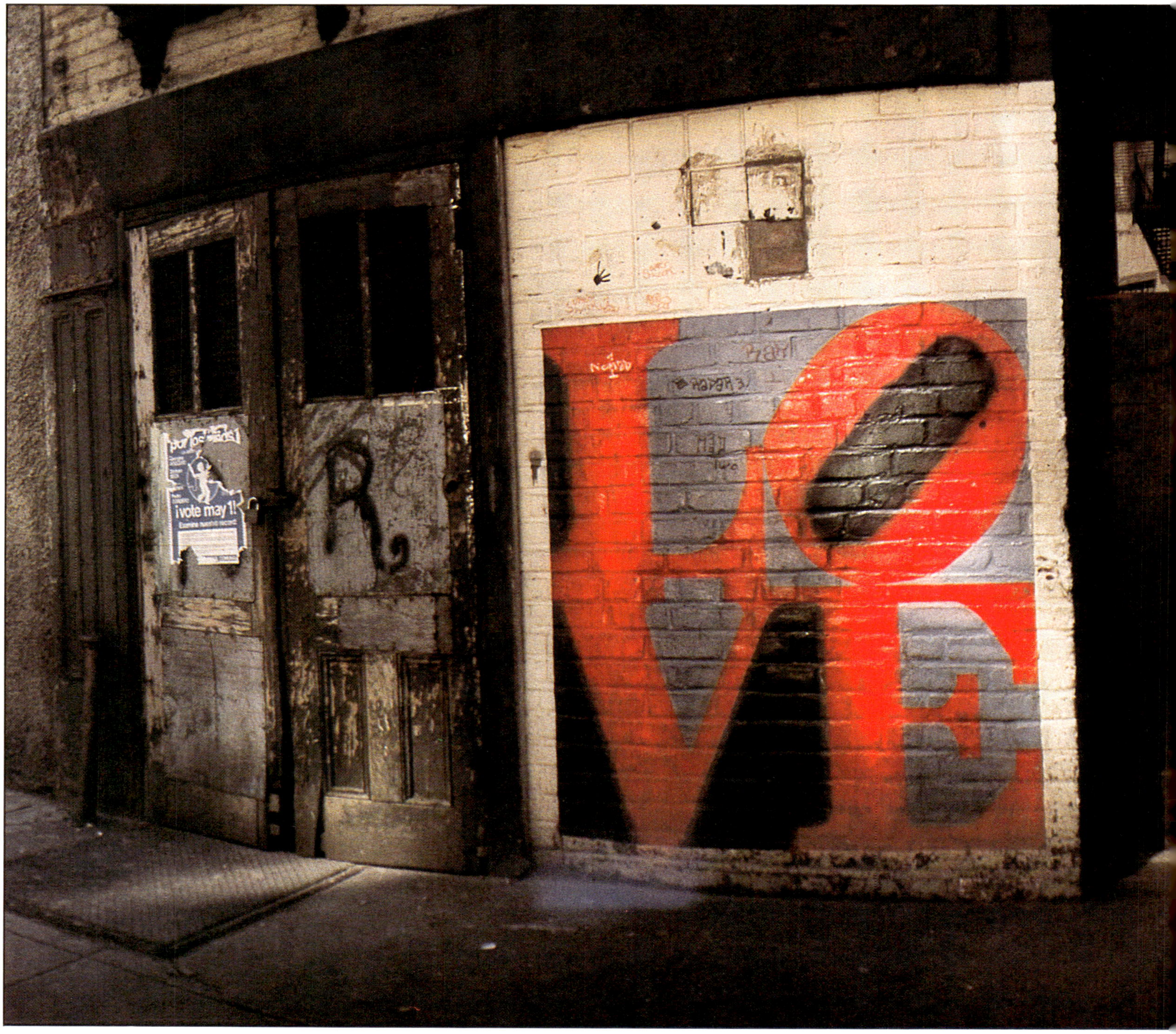

LIKE STRANGE MECHANICAL GROTESQUES,
MAKING FANTASTIC ARABESQUES,
THE SHADOWS RACED ACROSS THE BLIND.
OSCAR WILDE

PALE EVENING STAR, WITH FAR MESSAGE REVEALED,
HOW THY SHINING BROW RENDS THE SUNSET VEILS;

FROM THY AZURE PALACE IN THE HEAVENS' BOSOM,
WHAT WATCHEST THOU BELOW IN THE WEALD?
ALFRED DE MUSSET

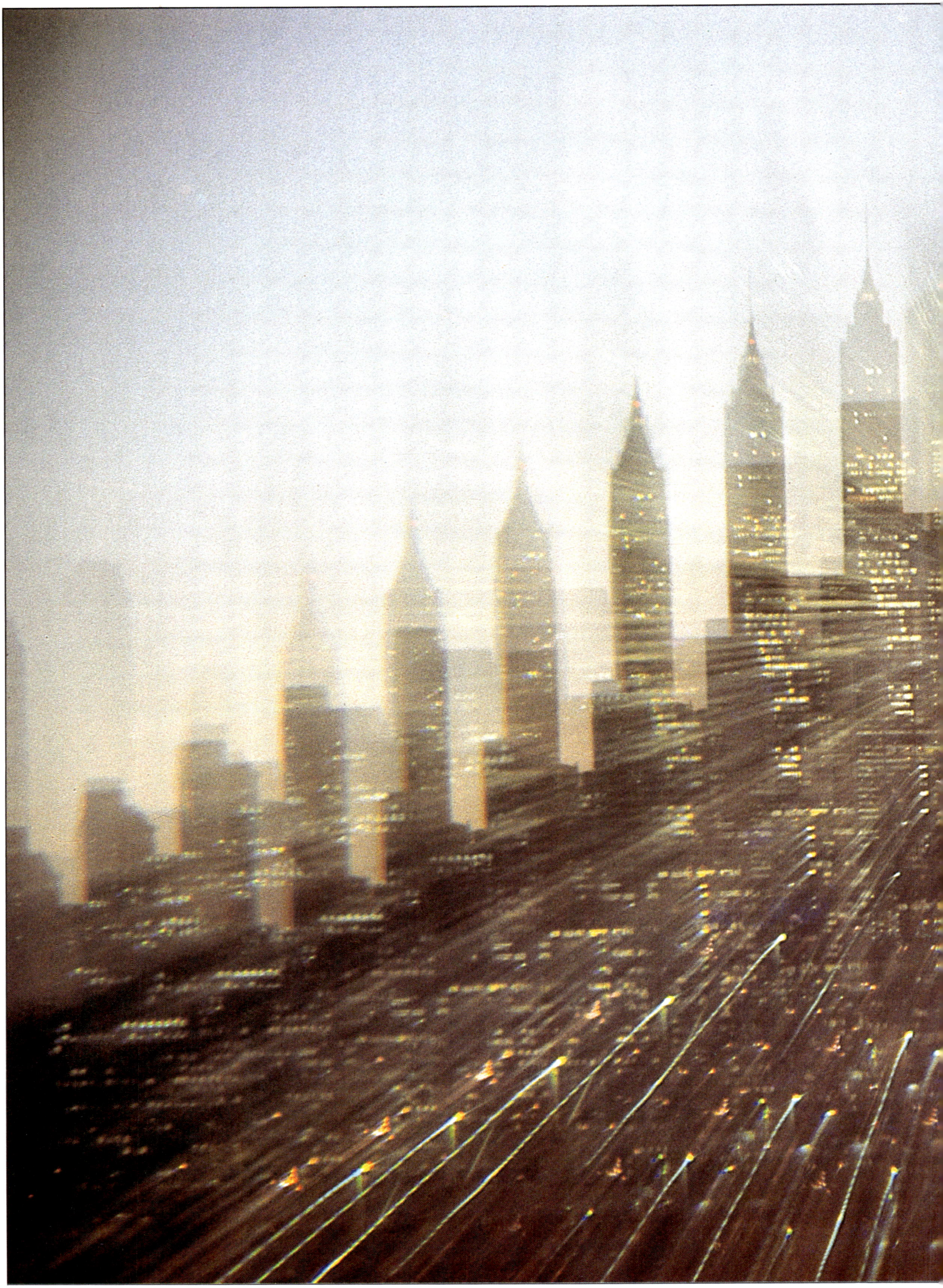

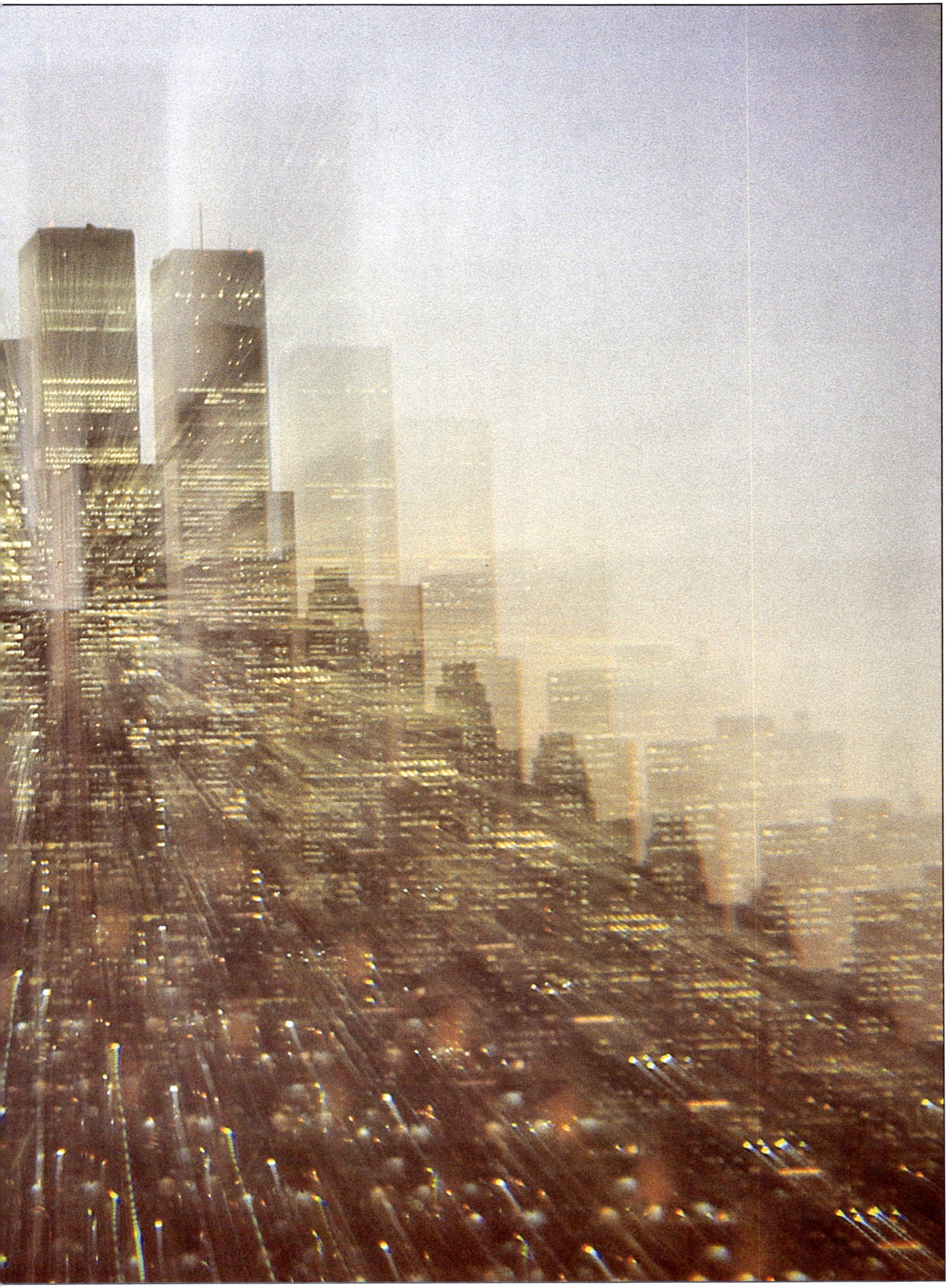

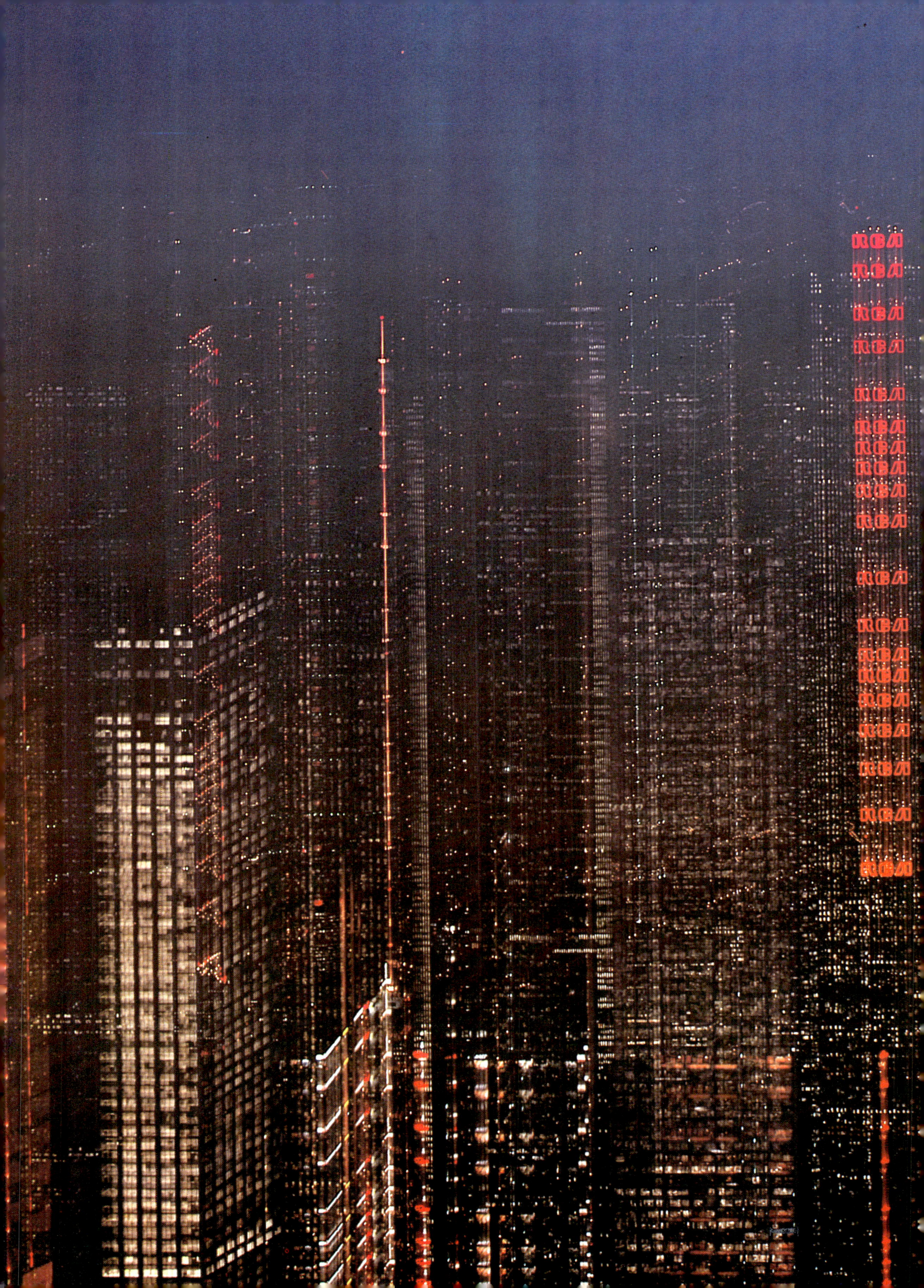
RCA

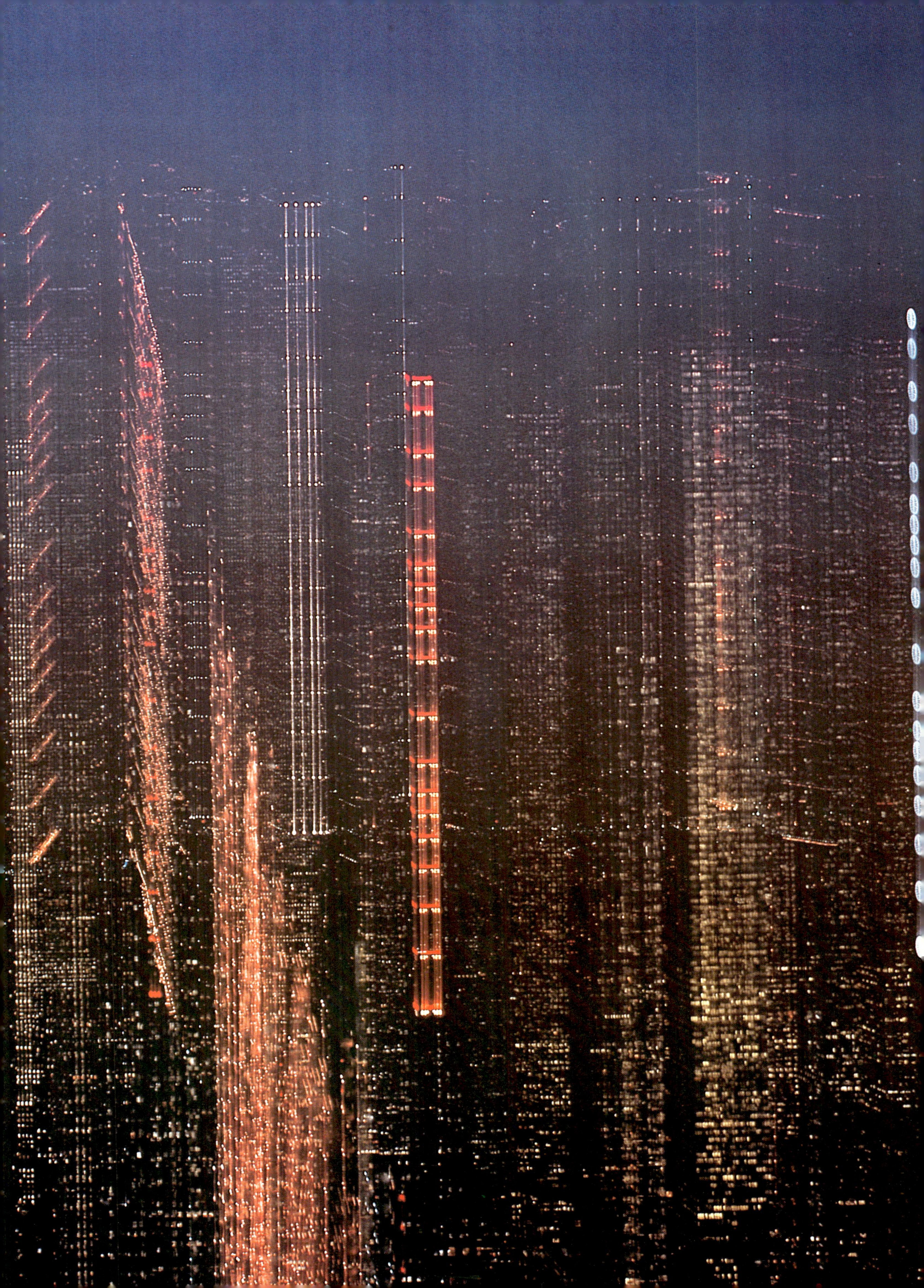

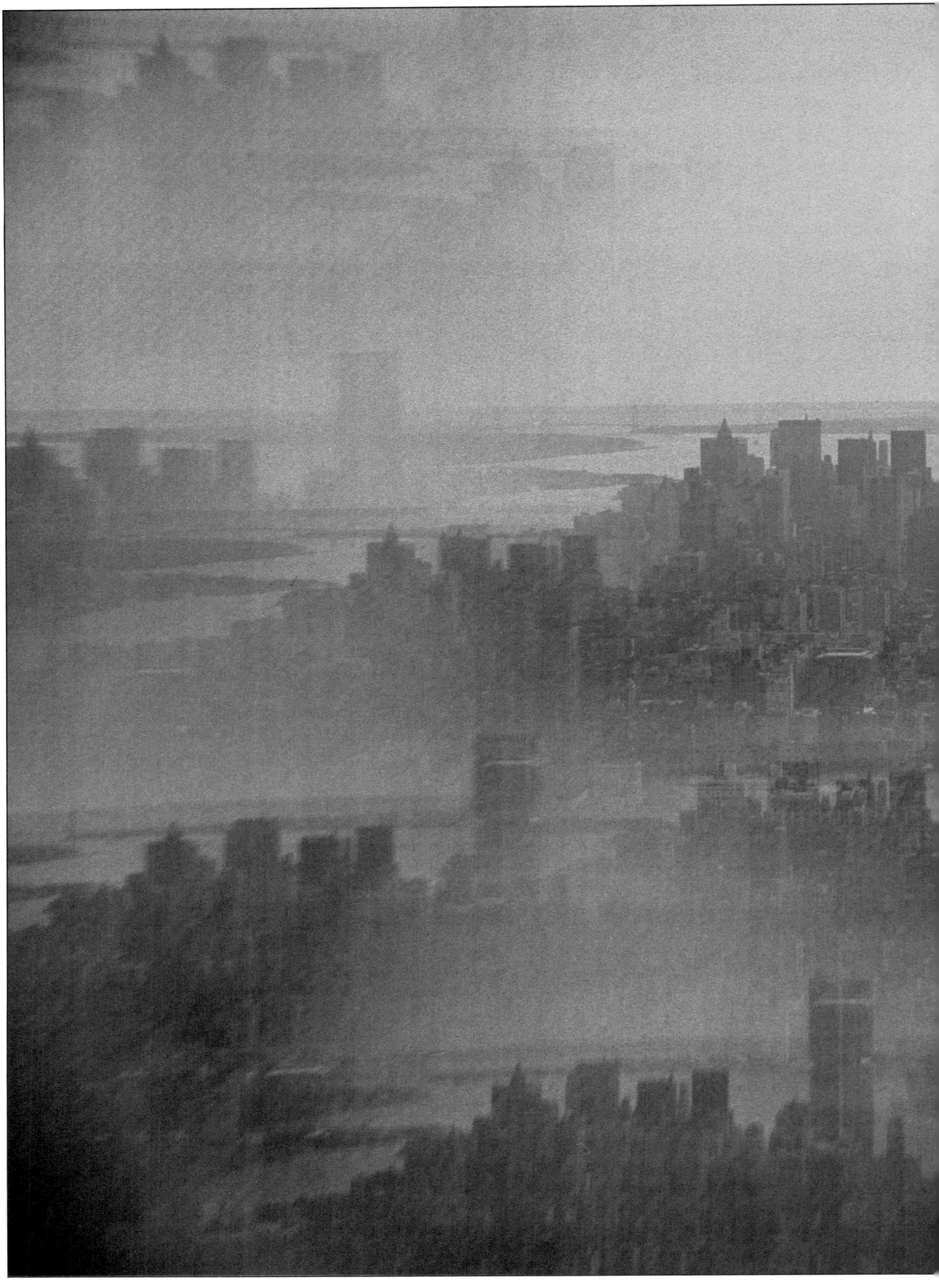

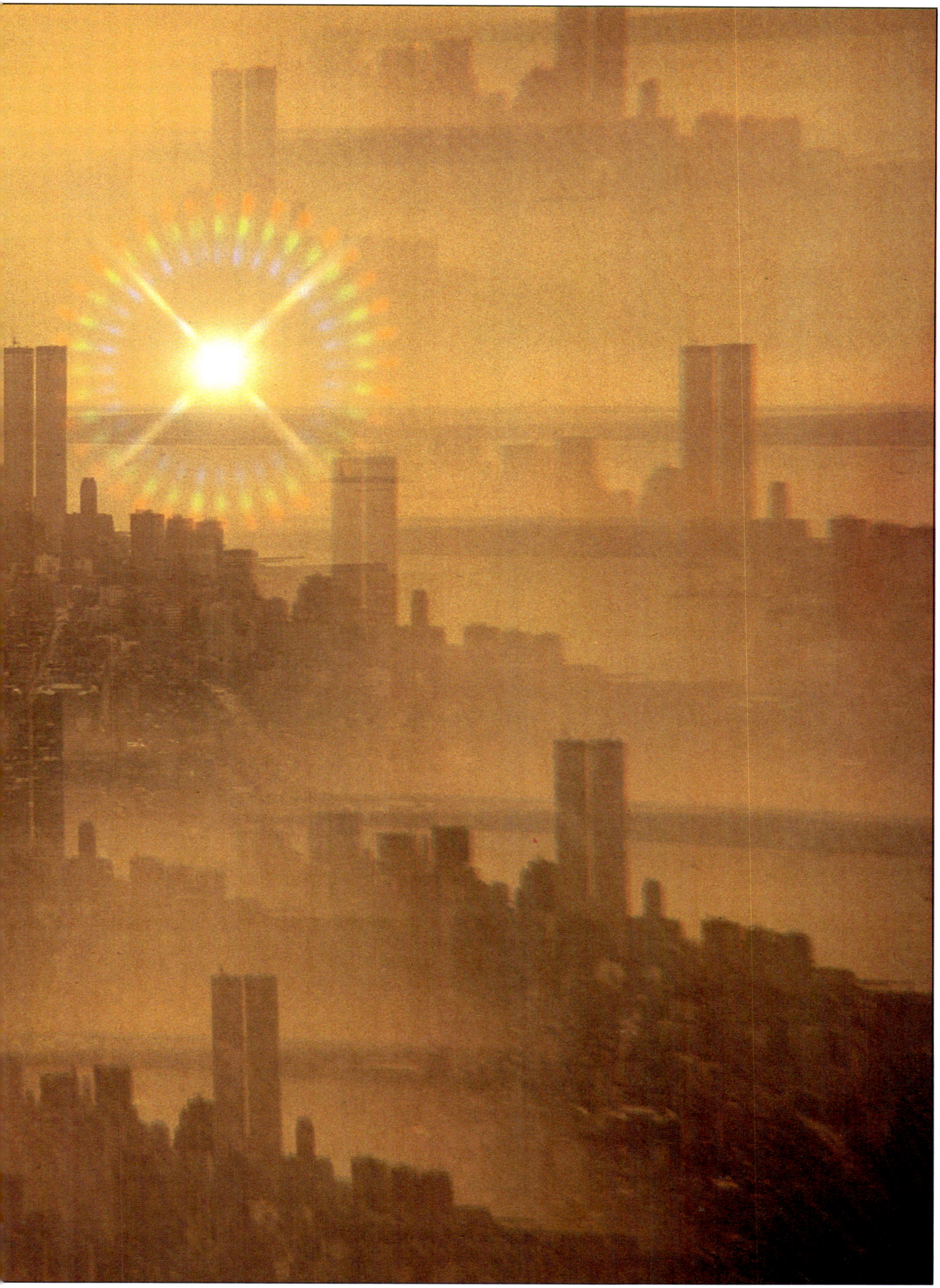

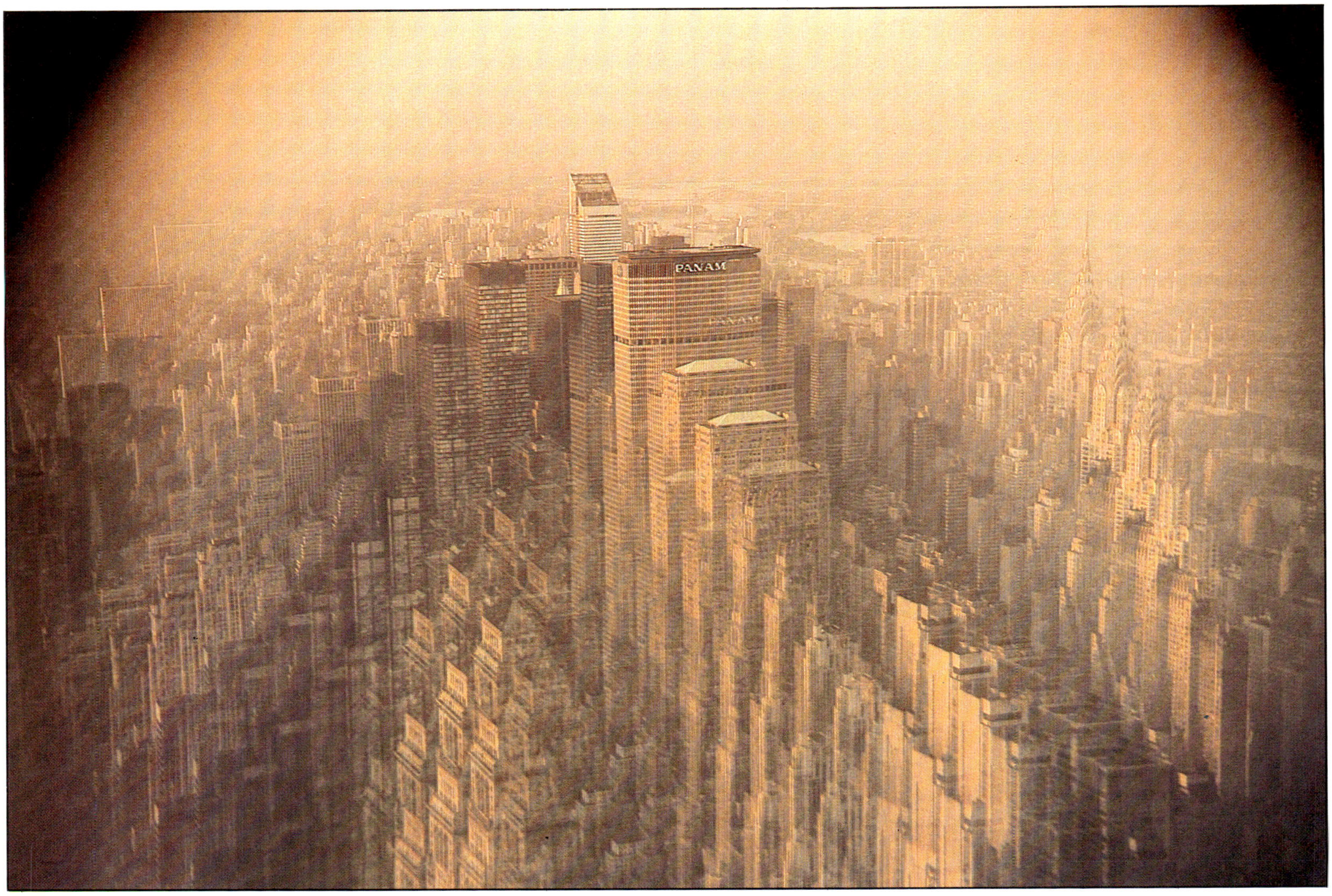
PANAM

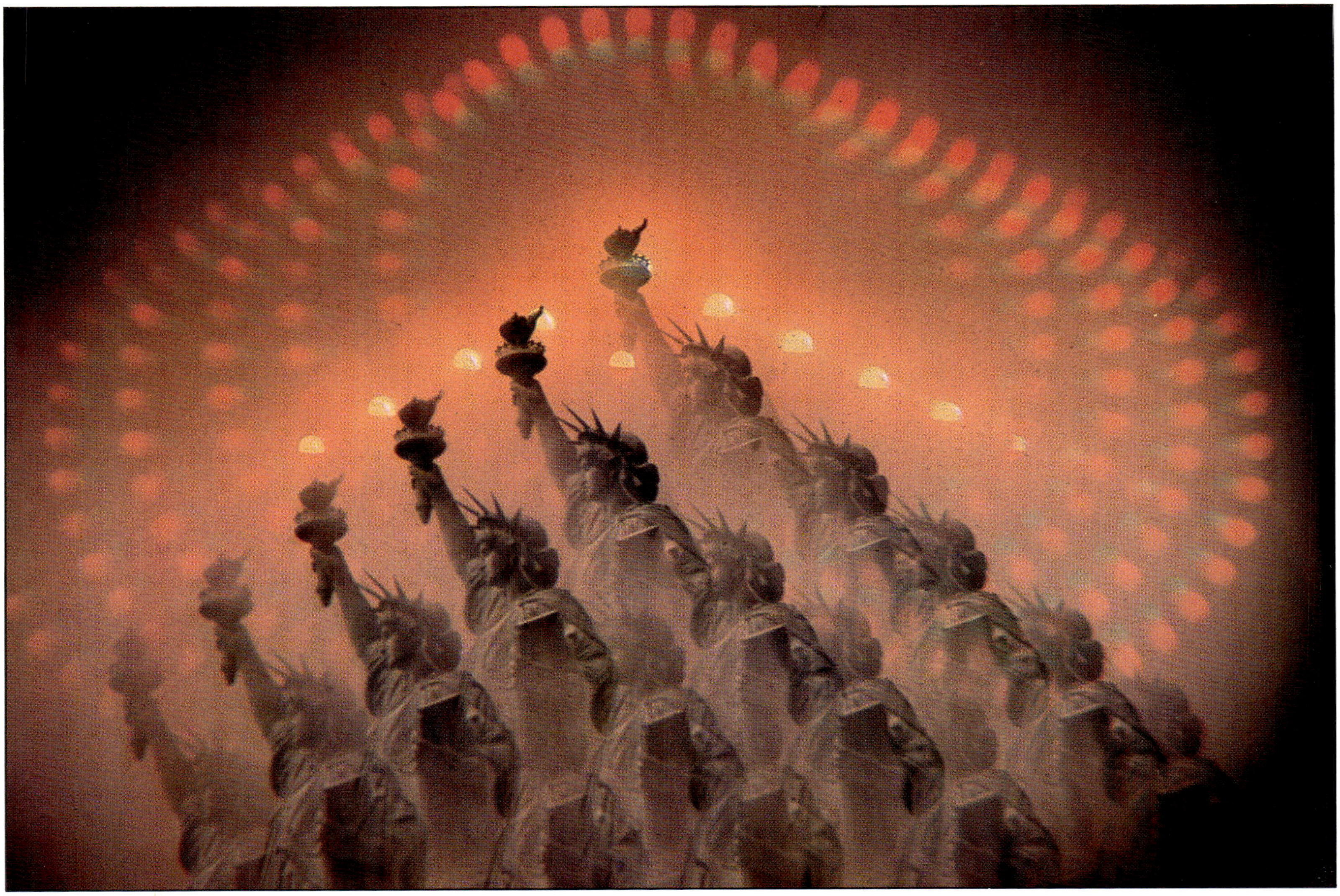

THE WAVES ROLLED HEAVEN'S LIKENESS INFINITE,
AND MERGED IN SOLEMN, MYSTIC SERENADE
THE RICH AND MIGHTY HARMONIES THEY MADE
WITH ALL THE SUNSET COLOURS IN MY SIGHT.
BAUDELAIRE

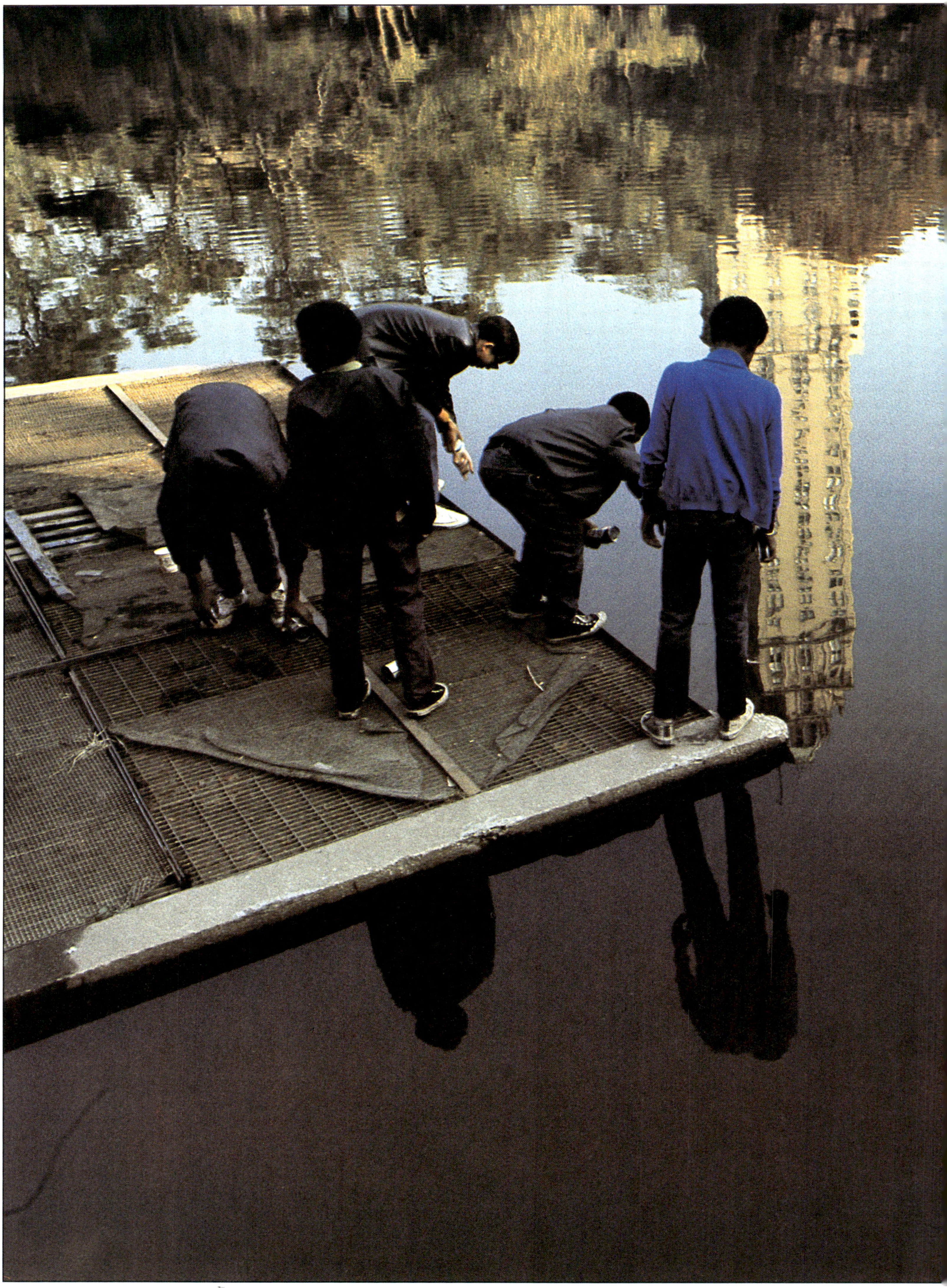

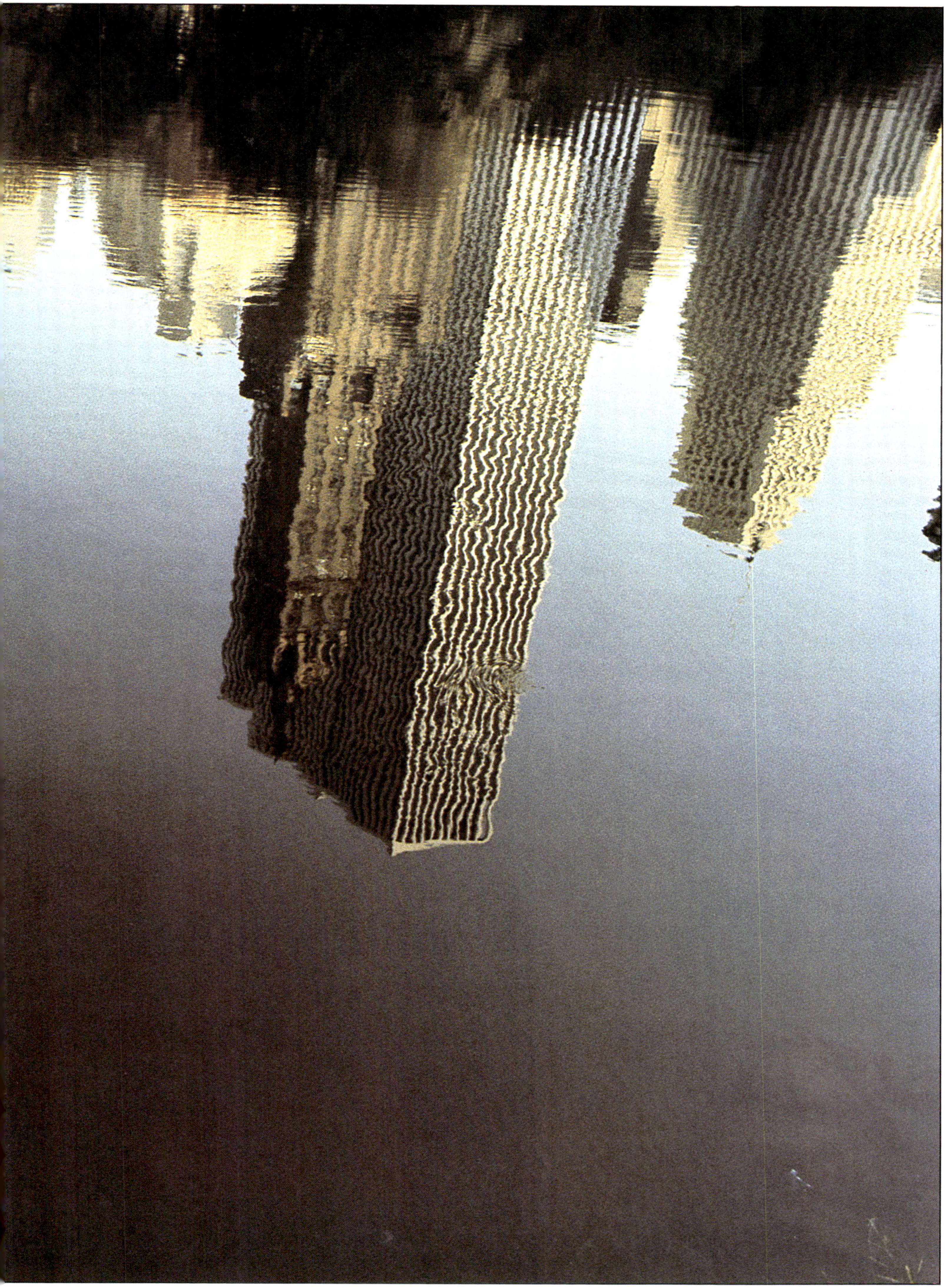

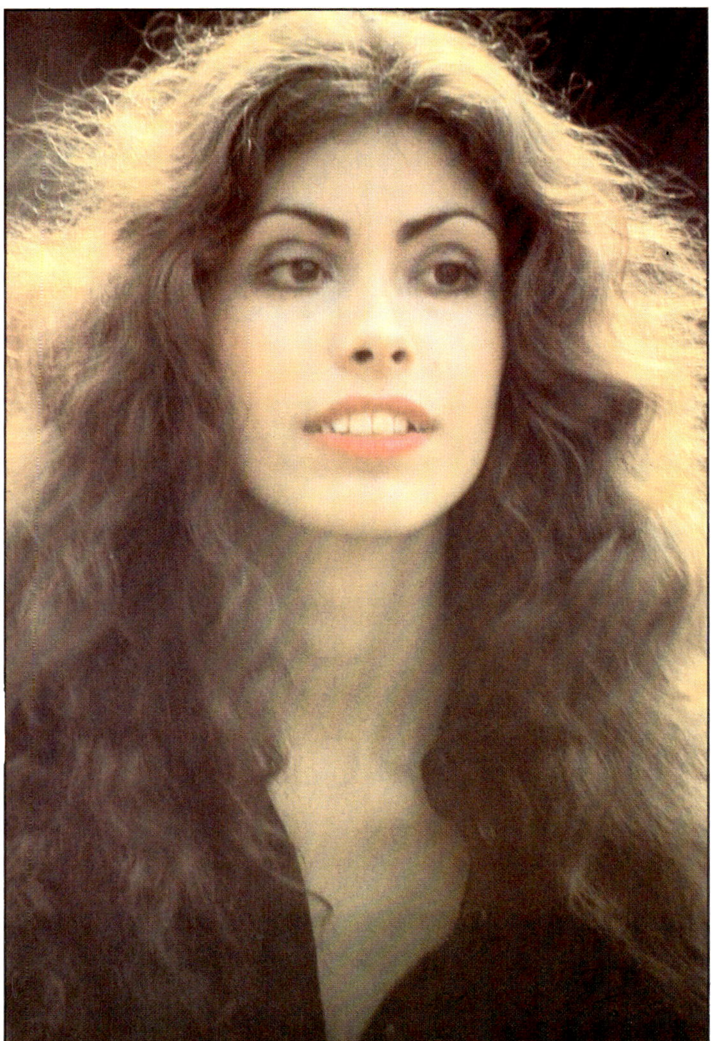
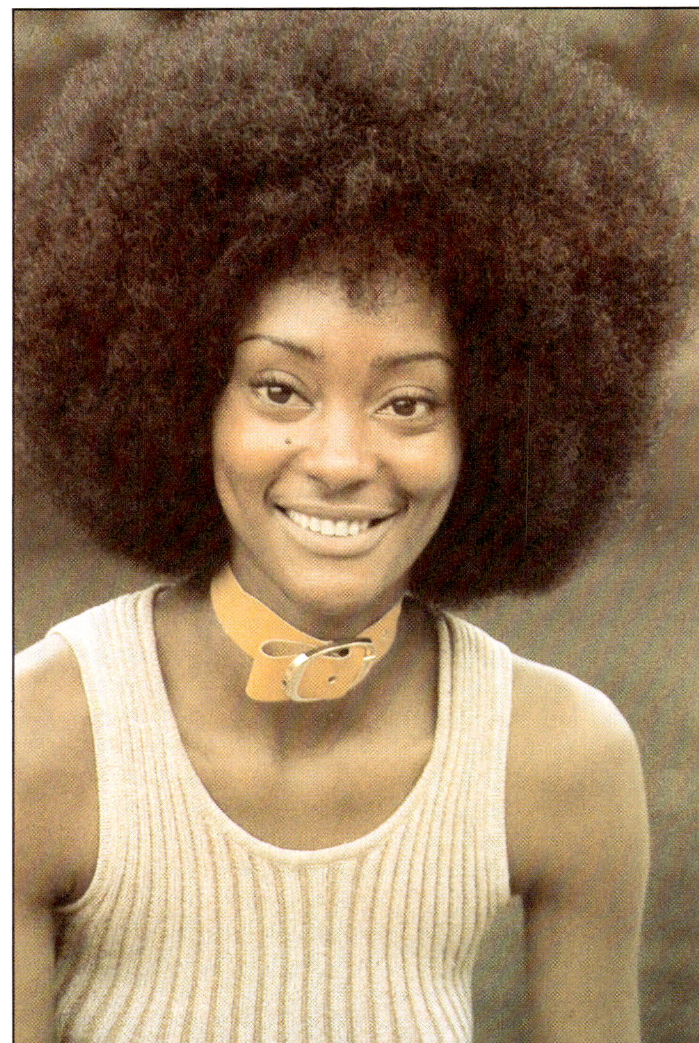

O YET A LITTLE LONGER STAY,
WAIT UNTIL THE DAWN
FOR IN THE JOYOUS LIGHT OF YOUR SMILE
YOUR FESTIVE BODY'S MYSTIC LOVE
IS BY THE SPIRIT MADE FLESH.
OSCAR WILDE

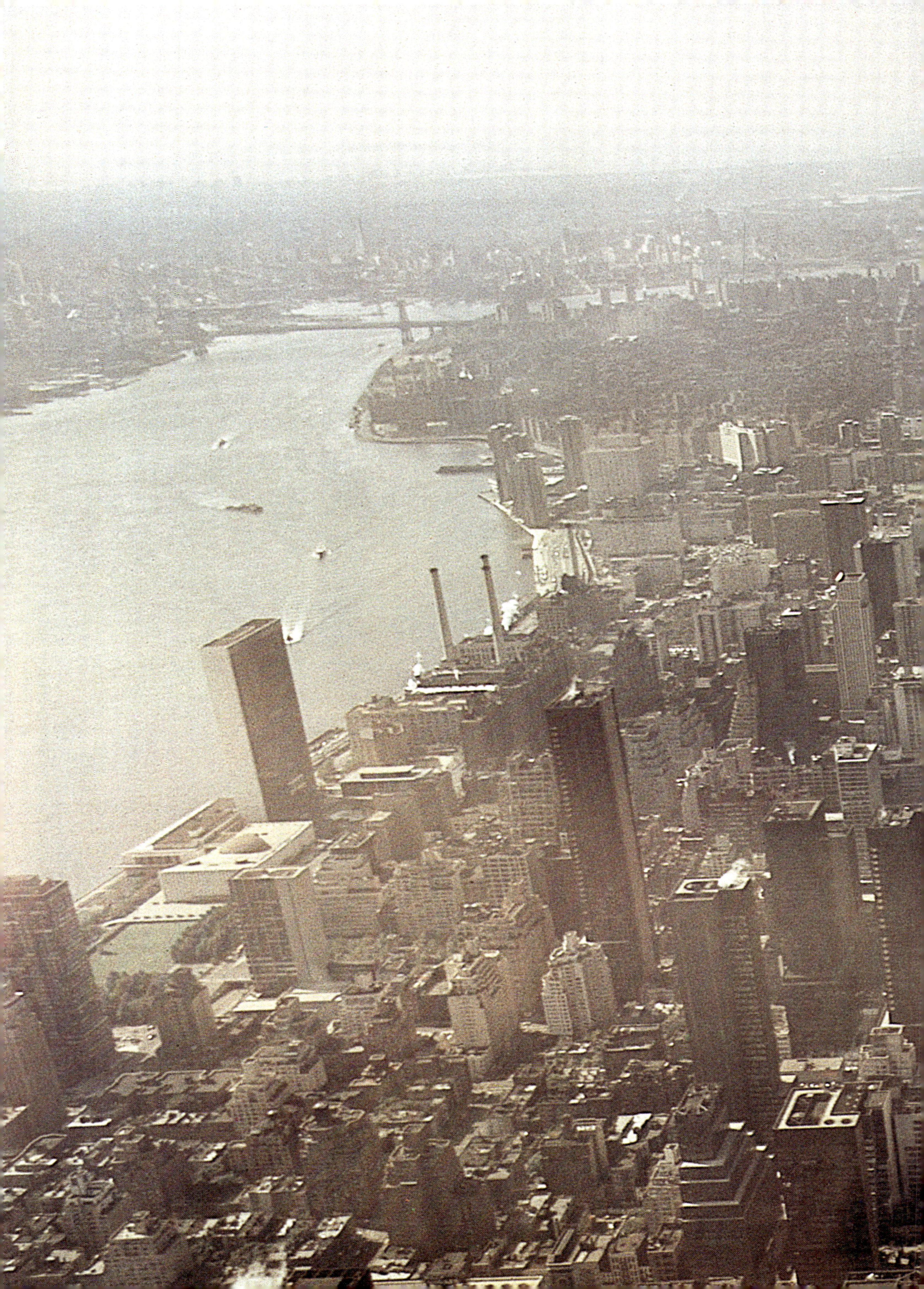

THE LITTLE WHITE CLOUDS ARE RACING OVER THE SKY
AND THE SCENERY IS STREWN WITH THE GOLD OF THE LIGHT OF MARCH.
OSCAR WILDE

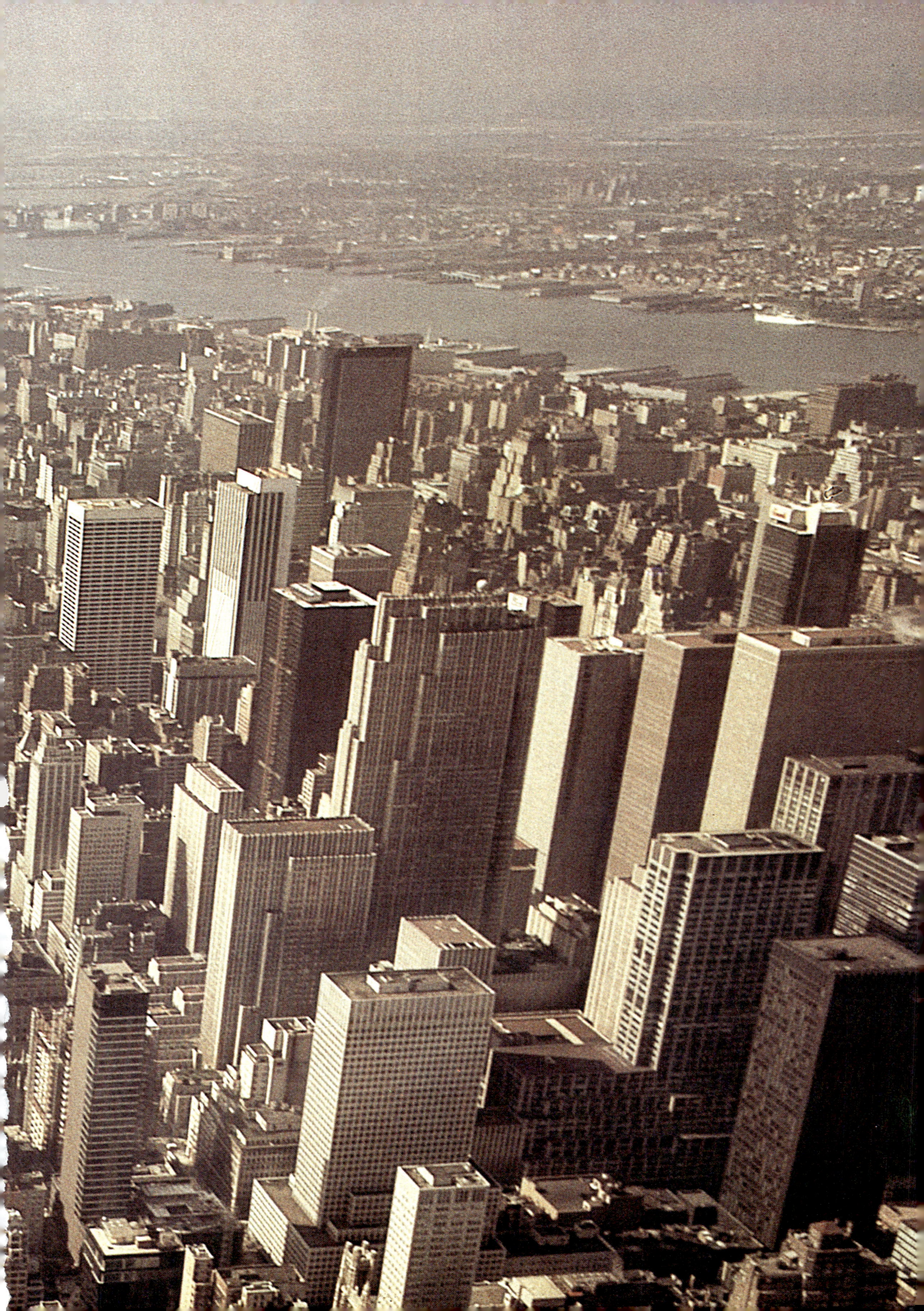

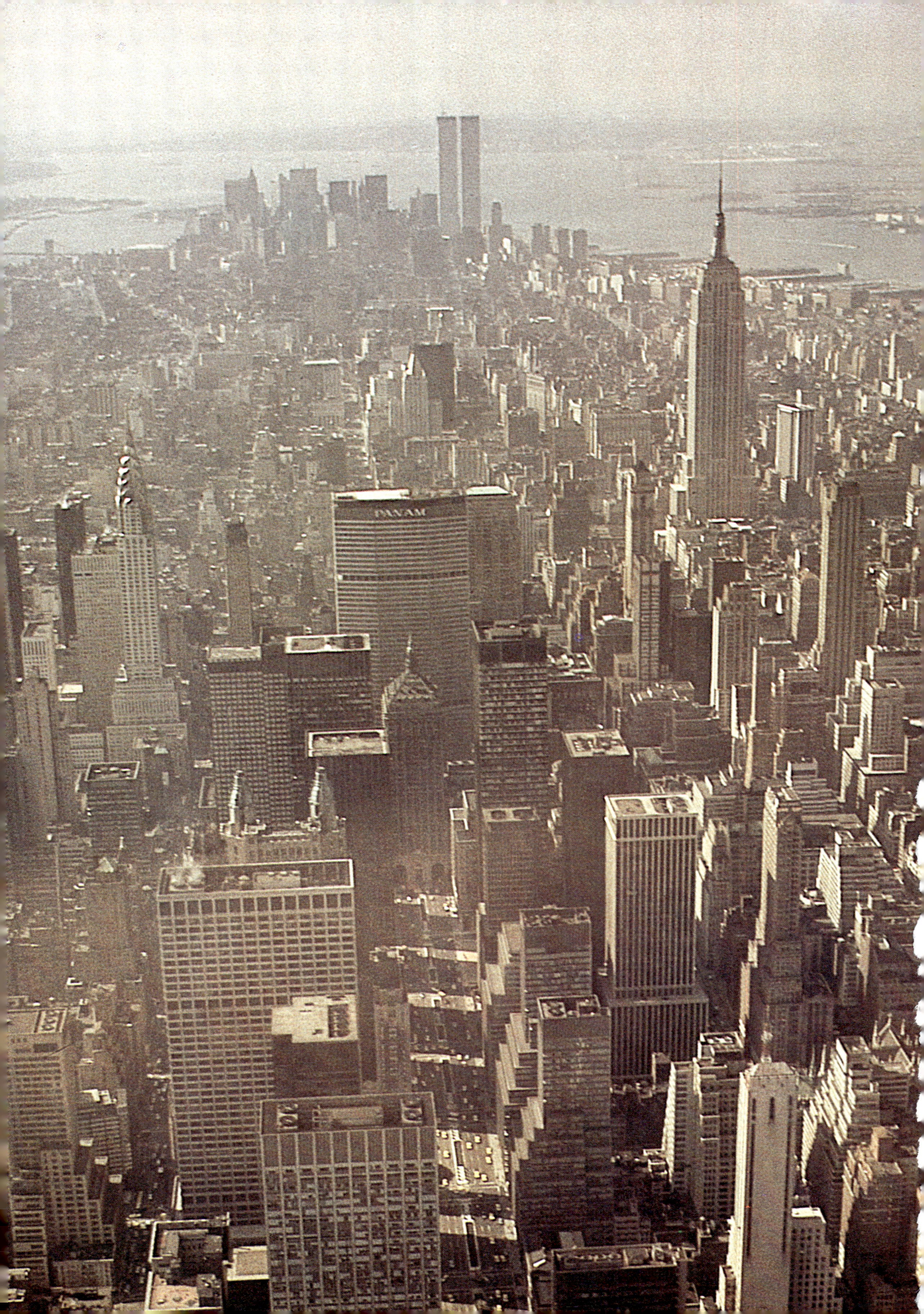
PANAM

ON A BACKDROP OF LIGHT LIKE THE MIDNIGHT SUN,

EMERGE IMAGES OF FURTIVE BEAUTY.
BAUDELAIRE

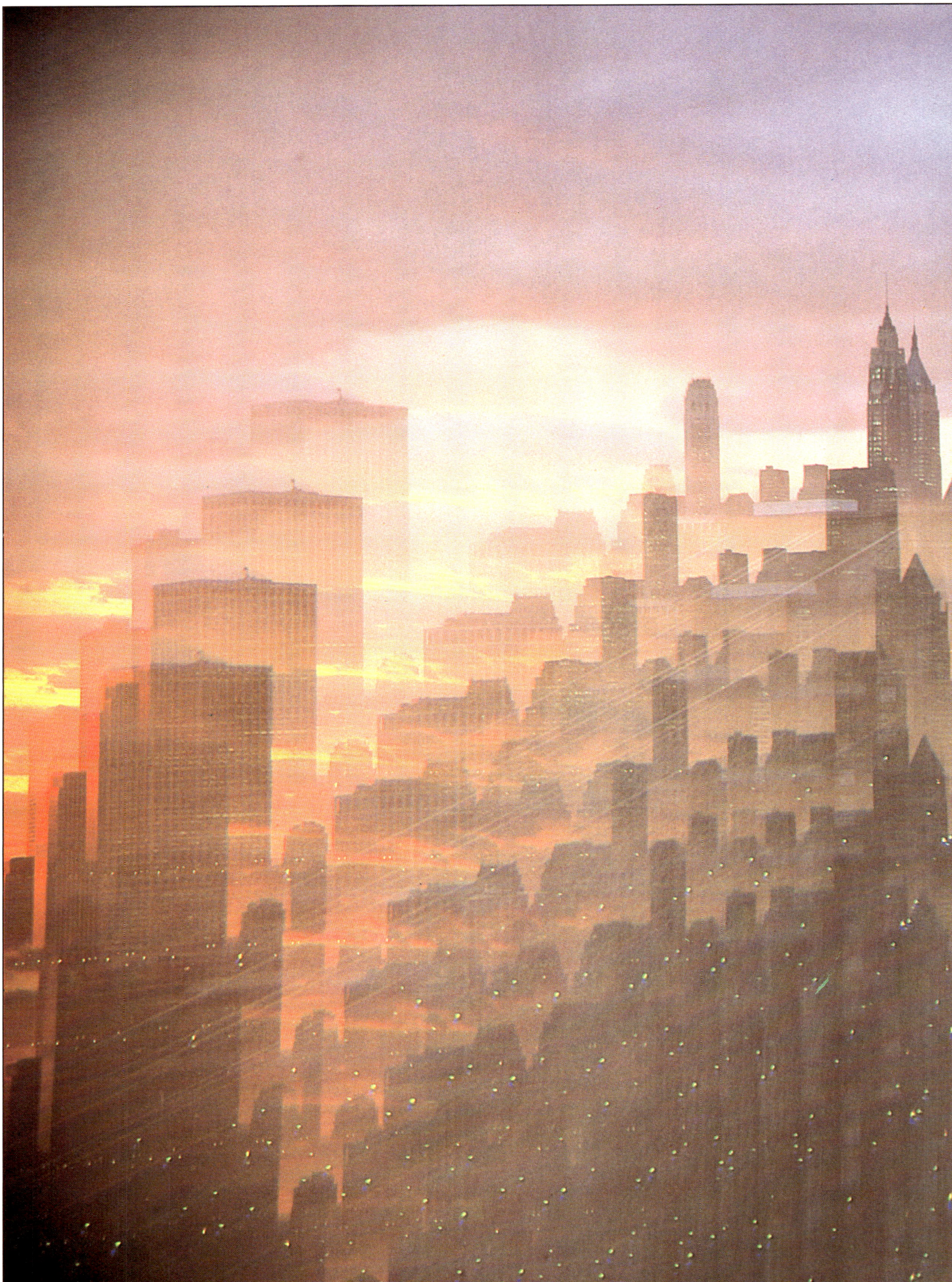

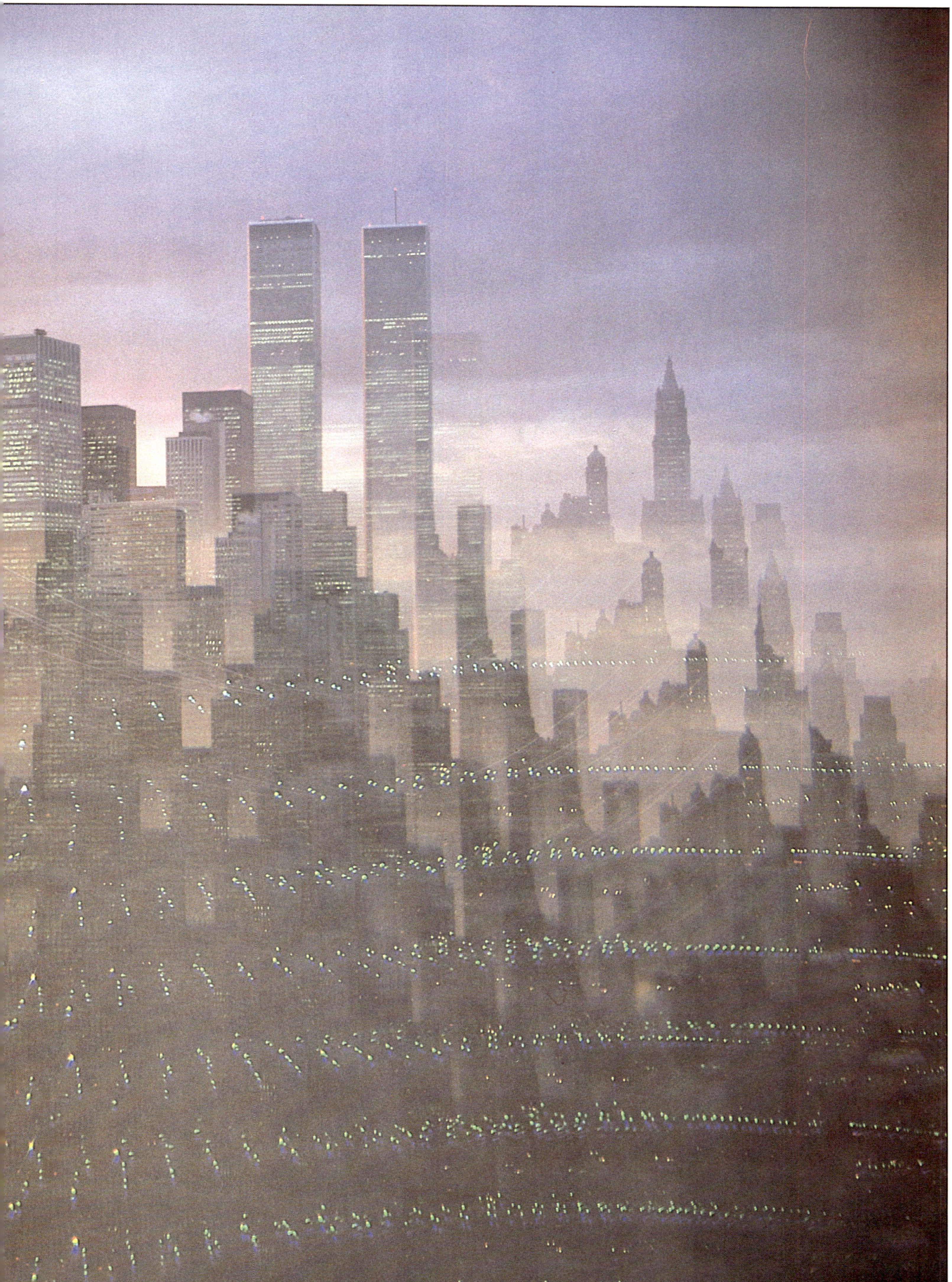

AUTHOR'S COMMENTS

MY FIRST TRIP TO NEW YORK GOES BACK TO 1969. I THOUGHT I ALREADY KNEW THE CITY, BUT OUR FIRST LIVE ENCOUNTER MADE AN INDELIBLE IMPRESSION. THIS ARCHITECTURE CONCEIVED BY MAN ON A WHOLLY NEW SCALE OVERWHELMED ME. THE GLASS-WALLED BUILDINGS FORMED A FANTASTIC KALEIDOSCOPE, REFLECTING IMAGES TO INFINITY. BEAUTY MET THE EYE IN MANY-SPLENDOURED FORMS.

THE FIRST EVENING I TOOK THE STATEN ISLAND FERRY FROM THE TIP OF LOWER MANHATTAN. THE SUN WAS LOW IN THE SKY AND THE SHADOWS OF THE BUILDINGS GREW LONGER BY THE MINUTE, TAKING ON DISTORTED SHAPES. MANHATTAN ISLAND RECEDED SLOWLY OFF TO STARBOARD. THE SUN BATHED THE CITY, PAINTING IT A VIVID RED, LIKE THE EMBERS OF SOME GIGANTIC FIRE. THE WHOLE SCENE WAS REFLECTED IN THE SHIMMERING WATERS OF THE HUDSON RIVER, THE CITY'S SKYLINE FORMING AN IMMENSE BACKDROP TO IT ALL.

THAT NIGHT IN MY HOTEL NEAR TIMES SQUARE I FELL ASLEEP LOOKING OUT THE WINDOW AT THE ILLUMINATED CITY SPARKLING WITH THOUSANDS OF STARS. I COULD STILL HEAR THE NOISES OF THE NEVER-SLEEPING METROPOLIS, LIKE THE CLATTER OF THE OLD EL TRAIN, PASSING THROUGH WROUGHT IRON STATIONS WITH WOODEN PLATFORMS, RUMBLING ITS WAY BETWEEN THE WINDOWED WALLS OF CITY STREETS. THE LAST PASSENGERS DOZED IN CARS DECORATED WITH PSYCHEDELIC GRAFFITI, THEIR DREAMS MINGLING WITH THE NOISE OF THE STEEL RAILS IN THE HEAT OF THE NIGHT. FROM TIME TO TIME THE SIREN OF PATROLLING POLICE CARS SCREAMED INTO A NIGHT ALIGHT WITH BLINKING MULTICOLOURED TUBES. SO THIS, AFTER ALL, WAS NEW YORK, AN ATMOSPHERE UNIQUE IN THE WORLD.

THE NEXT DAY WAS SUNDAY. CENTRAL PARK, 840 ACRES OF GREENERY RIGHT IN THE MIDDLE OF MANHATTAN, THE MEETING PLACE OF THE MOST ECCENTRIC TYPES. AROUND THE FOUNTAIN, PEOPLE RELAXED AND TOOK THE TIME TO TALK AND LOVE AND MAKE MUSIC. HERE A MAN WITH A SHAVEN HEAD, DRESSED ENTIRELY IN LEATHER, WALKED AN OCELOT ON A SILVER LEASH. THERE YOUNG GIRLS OF BREATHTAKING BEAUTY PARADED WITH RAYS OF SUN SHIMMERING IN THEIR GOLDEN HAIR. A ROCK OPERA. ON SUNDAY THIS CORNER OF NEW YORK BECOMES A WORLD APART. TRAFFIC BANNED, PEOPLE WALK OR RIDE BIKES OR HIRE ONE OF THE HORSE-DRAWN HANSOM CABS THAT LOOK LIKE PROPS FROM A 19TH CENTURY PERIOD FILM.

AS A SYMBOL OF EPIC AMERICA, THE STATUE OF LIBERTY HAS ALWAYS FASCINATED ME. I WAS ABLE TO GET PERMISSION TO GO UP TO THE TOP OF THE TORCH, NORMALLY CLOSED TO THE PUBLIC. I CLIMBED UP THE INSIDE OF THE ARM, UP STAIRCASES AS FANTASTICALLY CONVOLUTED AS SOMETHING OUT OF JULES VERNE'S NAUTILUS. ONCE AT THE TOP OF THE TORCH, I FELT I WAS FLOATING IN SPACE. THE STATUE IS LITERALLY A COLOSSUS, THE PEOPLE BELOW LOOK LITERALLY LIKE ANTS. THE PANORAMA WAS ENDLESS, MANHATTAN GLOWING IN THE WARM AND REDDISH GLOW OF THE SUN.

THE FOLLOWING DAY, A NEW ADVENTURE LAY IN STORE FOR ME: A HELICOPTER FLIGHT OVER MANHATTAN. THIS TIME THE SUBDUED LIGHT OF EARLY MORNING ENVELOPED THE CITY, LENDING EXTRAORDINARY BRILLIANCE TO THE CHRYSLER BUILDING AND THE EMPIRE STATE, NOW SURPASSED IN HEIGHT BY THE NEW TWIN TOWERS OF THE WORLD TRADE CENTER, THE TALLEST IN NEW YORK CITY. TO THE RIGHT APPEARED ONCE AGAIN THE STATUE OF LIBERTY. WE HEADED FOR IT, AND CIRCLED ONCE AROUND, PEERING DOWN FROM ALL SIDES. THE LIGHT DANCED ON THE WATER, DISSOLVING INTO TINY FLASHES OF MULTICOLOURED RADIANCE.

IT WAS DURING THAT FIRST TRIP TO NEW YORK THAT MY INTEREST IN PHOTOGRAPHY BEGAN. I DECIDED TO PHOTOGRAPH THE CITY AS I SAW IT, SO DIFFERENT FROM PARIS. IN NEW YORK, EVERYTHING IS IN THE FORMS AND SILHOUETTES, IN THE LIGHTS OF THE CITY. THE LIGHT FILTERS THROUGH THE SKYSCRAPERS LIKE RAYS OF SUN THROUGH THE STAINED GLASS WINDOW OF A CATHEDRAL. IT WAS THIS VISION OF NEW YORK THAT I HAD TO CAPTURE IN MY PHOTOGRAPHS. FROM THE OUTSET I DECIDED TO FORGET THE PHOTOS I HAD ALREADY SEEN AND TO CONCEIVE MY OWN IMAGERY, TRYING TO TRANSLATE EXACTLY WHAT I FELT. THUS BEGAN MY FIRST EXPERIMENTS IN PHOTOGRAPHY, USING ALL THE TECHNIQUES THAT ARE MY OWN. BUT TECHNIQUE IS NOT THE MAIN THING; THE IDEA IS. THE ROLE OF TECHNIQUE IN MY WORK IS TO REINFORCE AN IDEA ALREADY CLEAR IN MY MIND. THE MOST IMPORTANT THING IN ART IS THE CONCEPTION, NOT THE REALIZATION. THE ONLY THING THAT MATTERS IN AN IMAGE IS ITS FEELING. I OFTEN SEE PHOTOS THAT ARE TECHNICALLY PERFECT BUT WHICH EXCITE NO INTEREST IN THE VIEWER. A PHOTOGRAPHER'S WORK SHOULD REFLECT THE SENSIBILITIES OF ITS CREATOR, NOT THE PERFECT PRODUCT OF A MACHINE. ALL THE PHOTOS THAT MAKE UP THIS ALBUM WERE TAKEN DURING MY MANY TRIPS TO AMERICA AND ALWAYS WITH RENEWED PLEASURE. ALL WERE TAKEN WITH 35 MM REFLEX CAMERAS DIRECTLY FROM THE ORIGINAL SHOT. IT IS UNTHINKABLE FOR ME TO TAMPER WITH A PHOTO AFTERWARD. THE FACT, THE TRUE INSPIRATION, LASTS ONLY A FEW INSTANTS. IT IS FOR THIS VERY REASON THAT PHOTOGRAPHY ENABLES ME TO EXPRESS MYSELF IN AN ERA LIKE OURS WHERE EVERYTHING GOES SO FAST. I DISCOUNT THE USUAL CRITERIA APPLIED TO PHOTOGRAPHY. AN IMAGE SHOULD ABOVE ALL TRANSLATE ITS AUTHOR'S IDEA, AND HE HAS TO SUCCEED IN CONVEYING THIS IDEA IN A PERSONAL WAY. IT MAY BE THAT I HAVEN'T SHOWN NEW YORK AS IT REALLY IS. I'VE SHOWN THE NEW YORK I SAW AND LOVED.

FRANCISCO HIDALGO

TABLE OF ILLUSTRATIONS AND TECHNICAL DATA

STATUE OF LIBERTY
ZOOM 200–600 MM

EMPIRE STATE BUILDING
LENS 105 MM

MIDTOWN MANHATTAN
LENS 35 MM

OLYMPIC TOWER. FIFTH AVENUE
LENS P.C. 35 MM

ROCKEFELLER PLAZA
ZOOM 43–86 MM

EMPIRE STATE BUILDING
ZOOM 80–200 MM

PARK AVENUE
LENS P.C. 35 MM

FERRY
LENS 105 MM

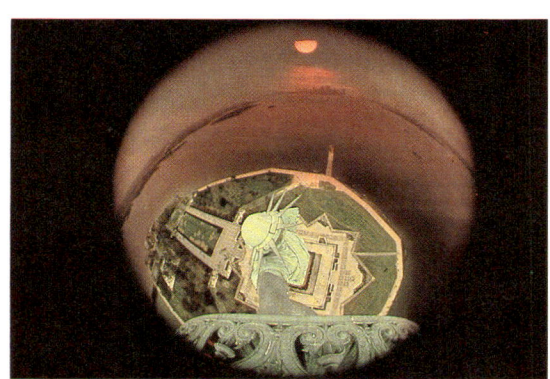

STATUE OF LIBERTY AND LOWER MANHATTAN
FISH-EYE 8 MM

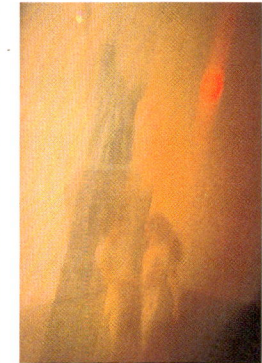

STATUE OF LIBERTY
LENS 28 MM

CHRYSLER BUILDING
ZOOM 80–200 MM

CENTRAL PARK
ZOOM 80–200 MM

CENTRAL PARK
LENS 105 MM

CENTRAL PARK
ZOOM 80–200 MM

LOWER MANHATTAN
ZOOM 43–86 MM

SAINT PATRICK'S CATHEDRAL. FIFTH AVENUE
LENS 15 MM

SAINT PATRICK'S CATHEDRAL. EAST 51ST STREET
LENS 20 MM

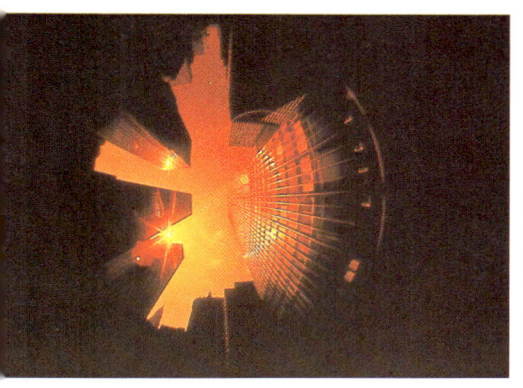

PARK AVENUE
FISH-EYE 8 MM

AVENUE OF THE AMERICAS
LENS 24 MM

STATEN ISLAND, FERRY AND GOVERNORS ISLAND
LENS 85 MM

LOWER MANHATTAN
LENS 85 MM

MIDTOWN MANHATTAN
PANORAMIC CAMERA

CENTRAL PARK
LENS 300 MM

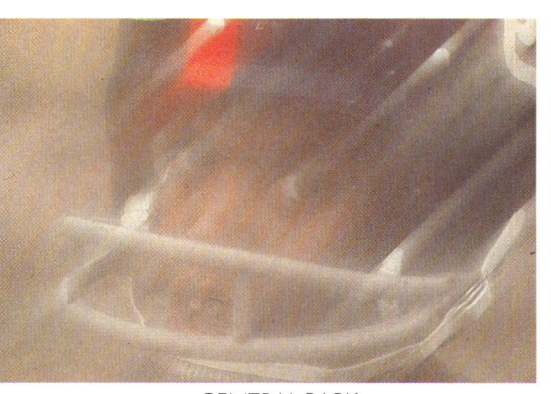

CENTRAL PARK
LENS 105 MM

CENTRAL PARK
LENS 105 MM

CENTRAL PARK
LENS 105 MM

TIMES SQUARE
LENS 105 MM

HARLEM
LENS 200 MM

CENTRAL PARK
MIRROR LENS 250 MM

WALL STREET
FISH-EYE 8 MM

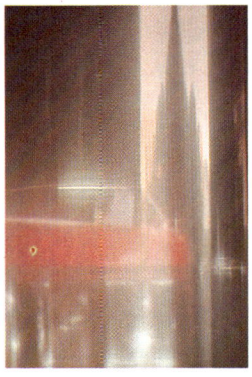

TRINITY CHURCH
LENS 50 MM

WALL STREET. BROADWAY
LENS P.C. 35 MM

WALL STREET.
MAIDEN STREET
LENS P.C. 35 MM

CHINA TOWN
LENS 24 MM

CHINA TOWN
LENS 200 MM

CHINA TOWN
LENS P.C. 35 MM

LOWER MANHATTAN
ZOOM 43–86 MM

BROOKLYN
ZOOM 43–86 MM

BROOKLYN
ZOOM 80–200 MM

CENTRAL PARK LENS 105 MM	**SAINT PATRICK'S CATHEDRAL** FISH-EYE 8 MM	**WALL STREET. NEW YORK STOCK EXCHANGE** LENS 20 MM
WALL STREET ZOOM 43–86 MM	**FIFTH AVENUE** LENS 50 MM	**CHINA TOWN** LENS P.C. 35 MM

CHINA TOWN LENS 105 MM	**CHINA TOWN** LENS 105 MM	**EMPIRE STATE BUILDING** LENS 105 MM	**DOWNTOWN MANHATTAN** ZOOM 43–86 MM

BROOKLYN BRIDGE ZOOM 80–200 MM	**MANHATTAN BRIDGE** ZOOM 80–200 MM	**BROOKLYN BRIDGE** LENS 105 MM

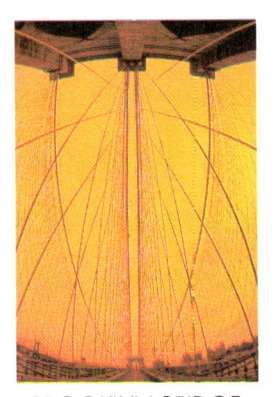

BROOKLYN BRIDGE FISH-EYE 16 MM	VERRAZANO BRIDGE ZOOM 43–86 MM	QUEENSBORO BRIDGE MIRROR LENS 500 MM	MANHATTAN BRIDGE AND EMPIRE STATE BUILDING MIRROR LENS 500 MM	LOWER MANHATTAN LENS 15 MM
WEST SIDE. SAINT PATRICK LENS P.C. 35 MM		MIDTOWN AND DOWNTOWN MANHATTAN FISH-EYE 16 MM		LOWER MANHATTAN LENS P.C. 35 MM
TIMES SQUARE LENS P.C. 35 MM		BROADWAY LENS 50 MM		TIMES SQUARE LENS 50 MM
MUSEUM OF MODERN ART LENS 50 MM	WEST SIDE LENS 50 MM	EAST SIDE LENS 50 MM		WEST 42ND STREET LENS P.C. 35 MM

MIDTOWN MANHATTAN ZOOM 80–200 MM	DOWNTOWN MANHATTAN. EAST SIDE ZOOM 43–86 MM	BROOKLYN BRIDGE. EAST RIVER LENS P.C. 35 MM	STATUE OF LIBERTY ZOOM 200–600 MM
MIDTOWN AND UPTOWN MANHATTAN LENS 15 MM	PARK AVENUE LENS P.C. 35 MM		WEST 42ND STREET ZOOM 43–86 MM
TIMES SQUARE LENS 150 MM	TIMES SQUARE LENS 150 MM	DOWNTOWN AND GOVERNORS ISLAND ZOOM 80–200 MM	GUGGENHEIM MUSEUM FISH-EYE 8 MM
MADISON AVENUE FISH-EYE 8 MM	DRAKE HOTEL LENS 50 MM	TIMES SQUARE ZOOM 43–86 MM	DOWNTOWN LENS 15 MM

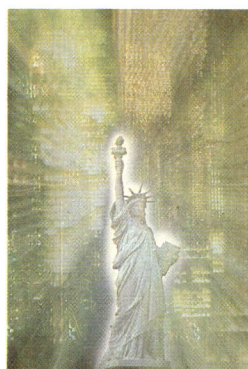

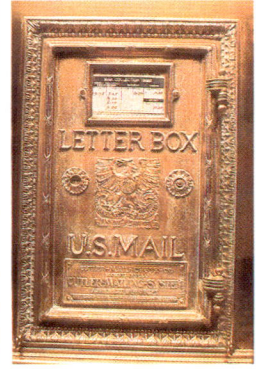

WEST BROADWAY. WORLD TRADE CENTER
LENS 200 MM

AMERICAN ILLUSTRATORS EXHIBITION
LENS 50 MM

GREENWICH VILLAGE
LENS 35 MM

SUNDAY PARADE
ZOOM 43–86 MM

PARADE AT BROADWAY
ZOOM 43–86 MM

THE SALVATION ARMY
LENS 105 MM

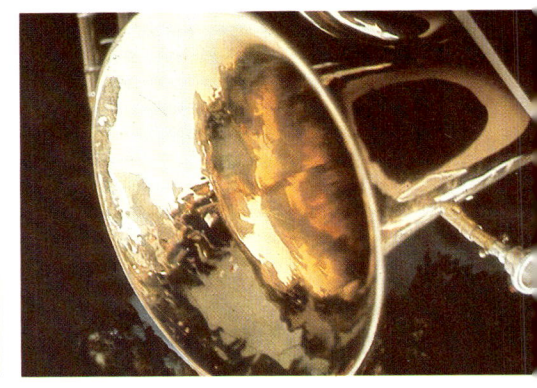

THE SALVATION ARMY, BROADWAY
LENS 105 MM

LOWER MANHATTAN
ZOOM 43–86 MM

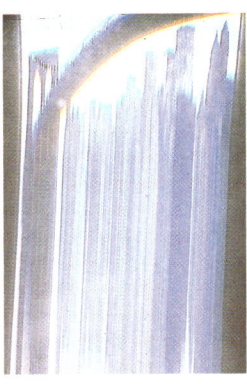

BROOKLYN BRIDGE
ZOOM 43–86 MM

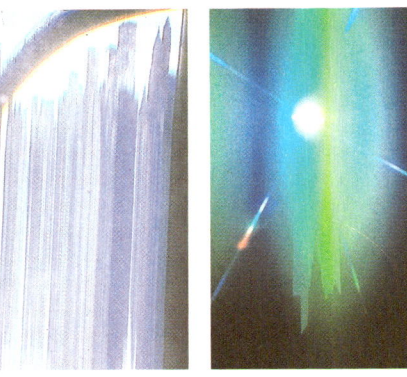

WEST 51ST STREET. SAINT PATRICK
LENS 28 MM

EMPIRE STATE BUILDING
LENS 24 MM

PARK AVENUE
LENS 15 MM

WEST SIDE
MIRROR LENS 500 MM

EAST SIDE
ZOOM 43–86 MM

WEST SIDE
PANORAMIC CAMERA

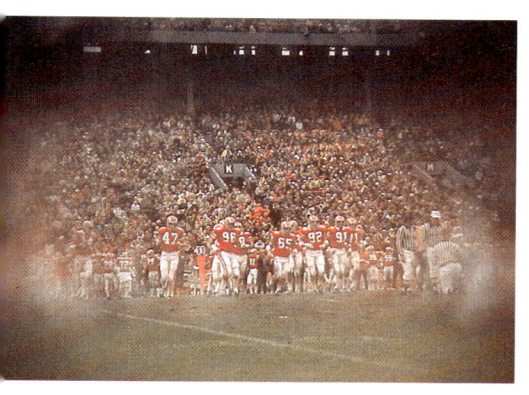

AMERICAN FOOTBALL
ZOOM 43–86 MM

AMERICAN FOOTBALL
ZOOM 43–86 MM

SUNDAY PARADE AT BROADWAY
FISH-EYE 16 MM

FIFTH AVENUE.
CHRISTMAS-TIME
LENS 24 MM

AVENUE
OF THE AMERICAS
LENS 18 MM

SAINT PATRICK AT CHRISTMAS-NIGHT
FISH-EYE 16 MM

MIDTOWN MANHATTAN
LENS P.C. 35 MM

WEST 53RD STREET
LENS 50 MM

PARK AVENUE
LENS 135 MM

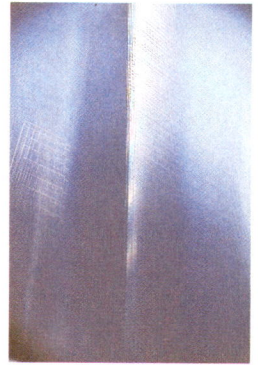

AVENUE
OF THE AMERICAS
LENS 20 MM

FLATIRON BUILDING
LENS P.C. 35 MM

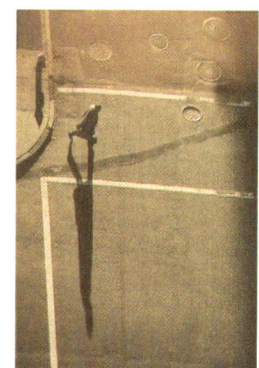

PARK AVENUE
ZOOM 80–200 MM

MIDTOWN MANHATTAN
PANORAMIC CAMERA

LOWER MANHATTAN
ZOOM 43–86 MM

MIDTOWN
LENS P.C. 35 MM

DOWNTOWN
ZOOM 43–86 MM

MIDTOWN MANHATTAN
LENS P.C. 35 MM

STATUE OF LIBERTY
LENS P.C. 35 MM

STATUE OF LIBERTY
AND FERRY BOAT
MIRROR LENS 500 MM

CENTRAL PARK
LENS P.C. 35 MM

CENTRAL PARK
LENS 105 MM

CENTRAL PARK
LENS 105 MM

CENTRAL PARK
LENS 200 MM

DOWNTOWN MANHATTAN
ZOOM 43–86 MM

STATUE OF LIBERTY AND LOWER MANHATTAN
ZOOM 80–200 MM

LOWER MANHATTAN
ZOOM 80–200 MM

DOWNTOWN
LENS P.C. 35 MM

PROTEUS BOOKS IS AN IMPRINT OF THE PROTEUS PUBLISHING GROUP

UNITED STATES, PROTEUS PUBLISHING COMPANY INC. 733 THIRD AVENUE, NEW YORK, NY10017
DISTRIBUTED BY THE SCRIBNER BOOK COMPANIES INC. 597 FIFTH AVENUE, NEW YORK, NY10017
UNITED KINGDOM, PROTEUS (PUBLISHING) LIMITED, BREMAR HOUSE, SALE PLACE, LONDON W2 1PT

ISBN 0 906071 17 8. FIRST PUBLISHED 1981, REPRINTED 1981
© 1981 VERLAG PHOTOGRAPHIE

ALL RIGHTS RESERVED. THIS BOOK OR PARTS THEREOF MAY NOT BE REPRODUCED IN ANY FORM
WITHOUT WRITTEN PERMISSION OF THE PUBLISHER.

CONCEPTION AND DESIGN BY FRANCISCO HIDALGO

PRINTED IN ITALY BY ARNOLDO MONDADORI EDITORE, VERONA